CHILD-CENTRED SOCIAL WORK: THEORY AND PRACTICE

CHILD-CENTRED SOCIAL WORK: THEORY AND PRACTICE

VIVIENNE BARNES

macmillan international HIGHER EDUCATION

palgrave

First published 2018 by
PALGRAVE

Palgrave in the UK is an imprint of Macmillan Publishers Limited, registered in England, company number 785998, of 4 Crinan Street, London N1 9XW.

Palgrave® and Macmillan® are registered trademarks in the United States, the United Kingdom, Europe and other countries.

ISBN 978–1–137–60641–9 paperback

This book is printed on paper suitable for recycling and made from fully managed and sustained forest sources. Logging, pulping and manufacturing processes are expected to conform to the environmental regulations of the country of origin.

A catalogue record for this book is available from the British Library.

A catalog record for this book is available from the Library of Congress.

2\8\19

CONTENTS

List of figures   viii

Acknowledgements   ix

Introduction   x

PART 1 **Background to Child-Centred Practice**   1

1 Child-Centred Practice: The Context   3
Introduction   3
Why child-centred practice?   4
What children and young people say about
   child-centred practice   7
Definitions of child-centred practice in social work   11
A child focus in law and policy   13
Social work principles and standards relating
   to child-centred practice   19
Origins and critiques of child-centred social work   21
Child-centred practice in other professions   24
Conclusion   29
Summary points   30
Further reading   30

2 Perspectives on Children and Childhood   31
Introduction   31
Historical attitudes in the West: are we more
   child-focused now?   32
Theories of childhood   37
The Global child: cultural differences   44
Children, family and environment   46
Children's views of their place in society: what children say about
   adults' attitudes   47
Conclusion   49
Summary points   49
Further reading and resources   50

3 Children's Rights and Child-Centred Practice   51
Introduction   51
The rise of rights   51
Children's rights: theories   53

Children's rights: law and policy   59
Children's rights in Africa and the Global South   62
The growth of children's rights practice and advocacy in the UK   64
What children and young people say about their rights   66
Conclusion   68
Summary points   68
Further reading and resources   69

PART 2   Developing Skills in Child-Centred Practice   71

4 Communicating and Developing Relationships with
   Children and Young People   73
   Introduction   73
   Building relationships   73
   Young people and relationships   75
   Social pedagogy   76
   Building trust   78
   Communication   79
   Observation   85
   Listening   86
   Conclusion   88
   Summary points   89
   Further reading and resources   89

5 Empowerment, Participation and Advocacy Skills   91
   Introduction   91
   Empowerment   91
   Enabling participation   93
   Advocacy   96
   Working with professional advocates   100
   Children and young people's views of advocacy   105
   Conclusion   105
   Summary points   106
   Further reading and resources   106

6 Breaking Down the Barriers?   107
   Introduction   107
   The development of social work services   107
   Organisational barriers to a child focus   109
   Decisions and procedures   113
   Attitudes to children and young people   115
   Barriers to good relationships   116
   Breaking down the barriers?   117
   Conclusion   122
   Summary points   123
   Further reading and resources   123

PART 3 **Specific Fields of Child-Centred Practice** **125**

7 **Child Protection and Safeguarding** **127**
Introduction 127
Findings of public inquiries: two strands: information sharing and
  focus on the child 128
Developments in law and policy 130
Processes of child protection and children's views 135
Initial enquiries and assessments 137
Child protection meetings: case conferences and core groups 141
Specific issues in child protection 144
Older children: child sexual exploitation, cyber-bullying and internet
  abuse 148
Conclusion 152
Summary points 152
Further reading and resources 153

8 **Children and Young People Who are Looked After** **154**
Introduction 154
Law and policy 155
Forms of care 157
Being different in care 161
Processes of care 166
Entering care 167
Being in care 169
Leaving care/After care 175
Conclusion 177
Summary points 178
Further reading and resources 178

Conclusion 180
References 184
Index 202

LIST OF FIGURES

3.1   Ladder of participation   56
4.1   Child's ecomap   83

ACKNOWLEDGEMENTS

I should firstly like to thank the children and young people I have met with through my work as a social worker, an advocate and a researcher. Some of these will be aware of their contribution through generously sharing their experiences with me in research interviews. Many children and young people, however, have contributed to this book without their knowledge, through adding to my understanding as a professional. I pay tribute to their resilience.

Colleagues in practice have also provided inspiration, especially those who took the time to put children first, above the other bureaucratic demands of their work. I thank my many colleagues and students in higher education for their encouragement and ideas. My gratitude goes also to the editorial staff at Palgrave Macmillan and reviewers for their advice and guidance on this publication.

Finally, my thanks for the forbearance and interest of my dear family and friends.

INTRODUCTION

What makes a good social worker? The children and young people quoted in this book have a lot to say about the matter, drawn from their experiences, both good and bad. They want someone who listens, who cares about them and respects them as an individual. Of course, there are many other requirements, but a fundamental one is being 'child-centred'.

Exhortations to social workers to be child-centred have a long history and continue to the present day, to the extent that a 'child focus' in social work practice may be seen as almost a cliché. After all, thirty years ago the public inquiry into the death of 4-year-old Kimberley Carlile reported that professionals involved were unable to '*hold the child in mind*' when the complexity of other factors distracted them (London Borough of Greenwich, 1987). Later, 'The Framework for the Assessment of Children in Need and their Families' (DoH, 2000) situated the *child* in the centre of the '*assessment triangle*', which is still widely used by social workers. More recently, interest in child-centred practice in social work was regenerated by the Munro Review of Child Protection (Munro, 2011) and has continued to be a major feature in 'Working Together to Safeguard Children' (DfE, 2015b). This statutory guidance promotes the principle of:

> *a child-centred approach: for services to be effective they should be based on a clear understanding of the needs and views of children.*
>
> (DfE, 2015b: 9)

This book questions why we still need to be reminded of this and asks whether social workers are still not practising with a 'child-centred approach', and if not why not. Are social workers too busy? Is it easier to communicate with other adults? Do we assume that children will not understand? One of the book's main aims is to consider how social workers can base their practice with children and young people on a child-centred model from the outset: as a student, in practice learning and throughout their careers, despite the difficulties they may face in doing this. It looks at the knowledge base, theory and research, and skills needed for practice. Crucially it draws on children and young people's views and experiences throughout.

The book explores the concept of 'child-centredness'. It looks at how such a model is defined and the benefits it may bring to practice in terms of, for example, children and young people's participation in decision making and having their views and experiences taken seriously. It examines ways that social workers can remain child focused whilst dealing with the other competing demands of their work, since there are constraints on them that can militate against a child-centred approach. For example, current social work practice demands that social workers work inter-professionally, they have to work in partnership with parents and carers and there are increasingly limited resources. Keeping a focus on children and young people can be difficult when other adult professionals, carers and managers have a stronger and more influential voice than the children themselves.

The reader may become aware that this book, with its focus on children and young people, devotes less consideration to working with parents and carers. It is clear that children do not exist in isolation, but are part of family and environmental systems. Social workers have to take account of this and there is plenty of theory and guidance about working with parents and carers elsewhere. However, one main aim of this book is to redress the balance by giving a high profile to children and young people themselves and their concerns.

My interest

My own interest in exploring child-centred practice derives from working as a social worker and manager in children's services for many years. In work with children and young people in the care system and child protection I was concerned that social workers did not always focus on children and young people in the services supposedly designed for them. This was confirmed in research later into child protection procedures, where I found that children and young people were often rendered invisible. I concluded that advocates would be helpful in assisting young people to get their views heard. This led to further research into children's advocacy services and a study of young people's experiences of social work and advocacy in the care system, described briefly below.

Since then, besides teaching social work in higher education, I have also worked as an independent advocate for children and young people. This has given me a different and valuable perspective into what it means to be a child-centred professional. Advocates are present for, and act for, the child only and, unlike social workers, they do not have to take full account of the views of carers and other professionals.

Several of the chapters in the book draw on findings from the author's own original and independent research (summarised in Barnes, 2012). All the names and identifying details of the participants have been changed. The excerpts are used mainly to highlight the views of young people in the care system, but some of the views of social workers and advocates also feature. The study was qualitative, based on in depth interviews with twenty young people, their advocates and their social workers. The study's aims included exploring the young people's and the professionals' experiences of social work and advocacy and their attitudes to, and relationships with, each other.

The young people in the study were between 12 and 20 years old and were living in a range of rural and urban areas in the Midlands of the UK. All but one had been in residential or foster care, with stays varying from six months to fourteen years. They had all received the services of a social worker and a children's advocate. Twenty-one of the professional workers were interviewed. These worked in seven different local authorities.

I tried to ensure that young people were involved in the research process by consulting with an advisory group of young people who were in care or were care leavers and who were also involved with a children's advocacy service. They helped to formulate interview questions and gave their views on the interpretation of findings. Interviews with young people were designed to suit their age and ability. For example, an activity was used with the younger age group to help discussion. The interview questions with all three groups of participants focused on their views and experiences of the work of social workers and advocates and their understanding of social work and advocacy.

A note on terminology

It may have been noticed that I have used variously the terms 'child-centred' and 'child focus', and these terms are used fairly interchangeably throughout the book but Chapter 1 examines these concepts and their meaning in some detail.

It is cumbersome to use the phrase 'children and young people' throughout even though this is generally what is meant, therefore I sometimes use 'children' and sometimes 'young people'. 'Child' usually refers to the younger age group or to the generic usage, while 'young people' generally refers to an older age group.

Strictly speaking, when talking about children and young people who are fostered or in residential care, the terms 'looked after' or 'accommodated' should be used. However, they are rather clumsy phrases and not ones that young people themselves use. Therefore I also use 'in care' and the 'care system', terms that are understood by everyone even if some would say they are outdated.

Structure of the book

Following this Introduction, the first three chapters provide a background to child-centred practice. The first chapter begins with the rationale for this practice and considers definitions and social work principles. It also examines critiques of child-centred practice in social work and how this practice is interpreted in other professions such as health, education and therapy. The chapter includes a section on children and young people's views and a brief overview of the law and policy on child-centred practice. The main focus in this book is on social work in England and Wales. However, I do include some comparisons with law, policy and practice in Scotland and Northern Ireland.

Chapter 2 provides a further context to child-centred practice by considering attitudes to children and young people, firstly from an historical perspective, then going on to look at biological, psychological and sociological viewpoints. The chapter includes a section on cultural differences and the very different experiences and attitudes to childhood in non-Western societies. Discussion of these differences in perspective continues in Chapter 3, which is an examination of the role of children's rights in child-centred practice. The chapter considers children's participation rights in policy and law, including the UNCRC (United Nations Convention on the Rights of the Child, 1989) and its African counterpart, the ACRWC (the African Charter on the Rights and Welfare of the Child, 1990). Finally, the chapter looks at advocacy services for children and young people, their entitlement and what they themselves have to say about their rights.

In Chapters 4, 5 and 6 the book moves on to look at social work skills in child-centred practice, highlighting children's views throughout. Chapter 4 considers relationship building through trust, communication, observation and listening. Chapter 5 discusses the skills of empowerment, promoting participation and advocacy. This chapter highlights the difference between social work and professional advocacy and examines the skills of working with professional advocates. Chapter 6 discusses the barriers to child-centred practice such as lack of resources, organisational cultures and limits to confidentiality. It concludes with a section on how we may begin to break down some of these barriers.

The final two chapters consider specific areas in child-centred practice: child protection and children who are looked after. Unfortunately, the scope of this book precludes the inclusion of other important specialist areas of social work with children and young people, such as youth offending or children's mental health. Chapter 7 is an examination of child-centred practice in child protection and safeguarding, looking first at the messages from inquiries and the Munro Review. The focus is then on children's views about child protection, including being able to tell someone about abuse and being involved in assessments and decisions. The chapter goes on to look at processes in child protection and how children can be involved in these, before looking at some specific issues such as domestic violence, sexual exploitation and internet abuse.

Chapter 8 deals with child-centred practice with children who are looked after, and their experience of difference and discrimination in terms of their status, for example as disabled young people or unaccompanied asylum seekers. There is a brief outline of the law in this area and of forms of care such as residential and foster care. The chapter goes on to look at what children say about entering care, being in care, having to move between placements, contact with their families and being involved in decisions. Finally the chapter looks at young care leavers and their transitions out of care.

The book concludes with a summary of the main points highlighted in the chapters, with a section on possible ways forward.

PART 1
Background to Child-Centred Practice

1

Child-Centred Practice: The Context

Introduction

Social workers in the UK practise in a wide variety of settings with children, young people and their families but children are the unifying centre that all social workers have in common in their work, whether they work in statutory or voluntary agencies such as family support, education units, child protection, fostering and adoption, leaving care or youth offending. In all these agencies they meet and talk with children and young people, their parents and carers and a variety of other workers and professionals, but sometimes, through dealing with the multiple demands of their work and the range of other professionals, the child him or herself may get lost.

For example, a social worker in a fostering agency may have more contact with foster carers than with the children these carers look after, but the welfare of the children must still be their main focus. Similarly, a social worker in a child protection team may spend much of their time assessing parenting, liaising with other professionals and attending and preparing reports for core groups, conferences and court proceedings, but it is the child who must be at the centre of all this activity.

This chapter considers the meaning and origins of child-centred practice for social work and for some of its allied professions. It asks why social workers working with children and young people frequently need to be reminded to keep their focus on the child. It also looks at definitions and critiques of child-centred practice, its possible benefits and some of the barriers. It considers some of the more recent social work professional guidance and standards, as well as the relevant laws and policies that guide social workers. Most importantly and centrally it considers what children and young people themselves have to say.

Why child-centred practice?

Child-centredness or a child focus has become a key principle in social work with children and young people. As such, it can be viewed alongside other elements that are thought to constitute good current social work practice such as effective inter-professional practice, working in partnership and evidence-based practice.

Complaints that social work is not child-centred enough come principally from two main areas of child care practice: These are:

1. Failures in protecting children, especially babies and very young children, from abuse and neglect; and

2. Direct complaints by children and young people looked after in foster and residential care that their voices are not heard.

Protecting children

In relation to the first complaint, it should be acknowledged here that every day social workers diligently work with children and their families to keep them safe, and their many successes are not documented in the media. However, failings in child protection have been very much in the public eye since the 1970s when the inquiry into the death of 7-year-old Maria Colwell hit the headlines (DHSS, 1974). When her mother and stepfather took her to hospital Maria was found to have died from severe bruising and internal injuries, and her stomach was empty. She had suffered prolonged abuse and neglect at their hands. Maria and her family were well known to the authorities and were visited regularly by health and social care agencies. The inquiry highlighted many lessons to be learnt but a major one was that social workers need to communicate with children themselves and see children on their own.

This recommendation has been repeated in subsequent inquiries throughout the following decades and in the more recent well-known inquiries such as those into the deaths of Victoria Climbié (Laming, 2003) and Peter Connelly, known initially as 'Baby P.' (Haringey LSCB, 2009). As noted in the introduction, child death inquiries such as that of Kimberley Carlile (London Borough of Greenwich, 1987) found that social workers and other professionals were able to be distracted from seeing children by their preoccupation with the adult carers, especially where these people were intimidating or plausible. Brandon et al. (2009) found that intimidation was a significant factor in many of the 200 serious case reviews they analysed.

'Serious case reviews' are conducted after a child dies or is seriously injured and abuse or neglect is thought to be involved. They look at lessons that can help prevent similar incidents from happening in the future. Ofsted's (2010a) evaluation of serious case reviews occurring in 2010 found that professionals did not see or speak to children enough in these cases. A subsequent evaluation of serious case reviews from 2011 to 2014 (Sidebotham et al., 2016) also found that children could be 'sidelined' by all adults involved, including the adults who were conducting the reviews. The findings of both these evaluations are examined in more detail in Chapter 7.

Willow (2009) considers the safeguarding process from a child's point of view and emphasises the importance of understanding a child's world. She comments:

> *Finding out children's wishes and feelings, and seeking to understand children's own perceptions of their needs and their life, is still too often viewed by professionals as 'good practice' rather than a 'must do'.*
>
> (Willow, 2009, p. 14)

The Munro Review of Child Protection in 2011 in England and Wales gives some guidance and practical ideas about how social workers can improve their practice in communicating with and listening to children in the child protection process. There is a full discussion of this in Chapter 7, which looks at child-centred child protection practice in detail and considers how social workers can work with children and assess risk in a child-centred way.

The following case example provides an initial reflection on some issues that social workers frequently encounter in engaging with very young children who may be at risk.

Case example: David and Christopher

David is 5 years old and his brother Christopher is age 18 months. They live with mother, Margaret, and father, Peter. The health visitor has been very involved in the care provided for both children, as she has been worried about the conditions and general hygiene of the home. She has been worried that Christopher is not gaining sufficient weight and she has tried to monitor this by weighing him at the clinic. However, Margaret rarely brings him for appointments and usually the family is out, or there is no reply when she calls at the home. She has been concerned that when she does gain access, Peter is usually in the main room drinking with his friends and little Christopher wanders round amongst bottles and ash trays. She describes the home as a health hazard.

There have also been concerns expressed by the school about David. He is a bright, lively boy but none of the other children will sit near him if they can help it

▶

◄

because he is so smelly. The head teacher has spoken to the parents about this in as sensitive a manner as possible and he has sent David home to change his clothes on several occasions, but matters have not improved.

The health visitor has contacted Children's Services to discuss Christopher's welfare again. She saw him for the first time today after two months. Margaret came to the clinic with him and his weight was low. The health visitor is also worried about Margaret since she had a bruised eye and seemed quite wary of talking about the injury. Another woman, a neighbour of the family, who also brings her baby to the clinic, told the health visitor that she has heard screaming and shouting at the house late at night, and she said she has seen Margaret with bad bruises on her face a few times over the past month.

Bearing in mind the findings of inquiries about seeing and talking to children who may be at risk, can you think about how you might be able to engage with these children?

➤ Where would you see them?

➤ How would you talk to David and Christopher?

➤ What difficulties might you face?

Children in care

The second main source of complaint about social work's lack of focus on children comes from the children and young people in the 'care system' themselves. I give more detail of their views in the section below as well as in Chapter 8. Young people who are in the public care suffer discrimination and disadvantage at all stages. Most have left difficult home situations, such as abuse or neglect, before they enter 'care'. Many face problems during their stay in foster or residential care such as losing contact with loved siblings or having several placement moves. Leaving care itself can make young people feel isolated and without financial security. These young people understandably expect social workers to be there for them to help them through these difficult stages and transitions.

Whilst there are many young people who have good relationships with their social workers and talk about them very positively, young people have also reported that their social workers are not child focused and do not see their concerns as central. These young people have complained that social workers may ignore their views, not listen to them and not respect them (Bell, 2002; McLeod, 2008; Barnes, 2012). Young people in care have also protested over many years about their lack of participation in decisions that affect their future, for example in statutory reviews of their care (Thomas, 2000, 2011).

What children and young people say about child-centred practice

Over a period of several years there has been helpful research about children and young people's views of social work, and their views have been notably similar in different research studies over time. The research gives many pointers about what it means to children for social workers to be child-centred.

'Children Speak' (Butler and Williamson, 1994) was one of the first influential pieces of research in the UK that reported the actual words of young people talking about social workers. These were young people who had suffered trauma and abuse. They talked about how they were treated by the social workers who were helping them and what they wanted from them. Some found their social workers *'brilliant'*. A 13 year old girl said, *'I talk to them, they listen. I just want someone to listen and understand what I want to happen'* (p. 97). However, other young people told the researchers that social workers frequently lacked understanding of them, saying *'They don't know nothing about what it's really like for you'* (p. 76). They said that social workers imposed their own views of the situation, which they did not necessarily share. Young people were also concerned about lack of confidentiality. What they did want was for social workers to be trustworthy, honest and good listeners and to be available, not *'always out at lunch, off sick or on a training course'* (p. 88).

McLeod's (2010) research with looked after young people explored the conditions that children and young people felt were optimal in helping them to gain trust in their social worker. She summarised these as their wanting social workers to be *'a friend and an equal'* but emphasised that this 'being a friend' did not conflict with a social worker's professional role or boundaries. In fact, it could be broken down into similar elements to those found by Butler and Williamson (1994) quoted above:

> *...we can gain a composite picture of the ideal social worker; he or she is accessible, trustworthy and reliable; s/he is sociable and listens; s/he offers effective practical and emotional support; perhaps most crucially, good social workers are fair, respect children as autonomous individuals and do not abuse their position of power.*
>
> (McLeod, 2010, p. 779)

Another aspect found in studies with young people in the care system is their desire for a long-term relationship with their social worker and their frustration when social workers moved so that they had to start again with another. In Gaskell's (2010) research one young person reflected on this as follows:

> *As soon as you were beginning to trust them (social workers) they moved on. Just as you were beginning to trust them, if you did put trust in them, they were gone.*

(p. 143)

As described in the Introduction, the author's research explored the views of young people, their social workers and their advocates about their work and relationships. Children and young people talked about the qualities they valued in social workers and the ones they did not appreciate. These qualities were also remarkably similar to those expressed in the much earlier research by Butler and Williamson (1994).

The qualities that young people valued can be categorised as 'professional qualities' and 'caring qualities'.

The professional ones included being:

➤ Reliable

➤ Efficient and giving a quick response

➤ Easily contactable

➤ Fair

➤ Confidential

➤ Honest and trustworthy

The caring qualities included:

➤ Being respectful

➤ Listening

➤ Showing an interest

➤ Being friendly and fun

➤ Not treating them 'like a child'

➤ Showing evidence of valuing them

➤ Taking their side.

Naturally, young people did not appreciate workers who worked in opposite ways from those above, and they highlighted for their particular concern social workers who did not show them respect or did not listen and ones who were impersonal, just *'doing a job'*. They also disliked being patronised and treated as younger than their actual age and not being consulted about decisions. Above all, they wanted workers who cared about them and showed that they cared.

Some young people mentioned social workers who had listened. As one young woman, Laura, who had recently left care said, 'He (social worker) listened to me, didn't lie, told the truth. He didn't try to get me to do things I didn't want to do.' But a more common view was that social workers did not listen. A young woman of 16, Sue, who was moving to a hostel said she blamed her social worker for having to move from her foster home against her wishes and she said of social workers:

> They don't listen to children's views – don't listen to what we want. They just jump in at things like a bull at a gate and think that they've done their best – but sometimes they don't.

The features young people have complained about or appreciated in their social workers seem to have changed little over time. This is despite government initiatives and legislation to try to improve these services for children and young people. For example, the Munro Review (2011) advocated child-centred practice in child protection and the Children and Young Persons Act 2008 aimed to provide higher quality placements in care with better social work support for children.

There has been less specific research about what disadvantaged groups such as disabled and minority ethnic young people think of their social workers in relation to child-centred practice. However, in Turner's (2003) consultation with disabled children and young people in Wales, they shared their views about pitfalls professionals should avoid in their communications and behaviour. In summary, they said the worst professional is someone who:

➤ *doesn't listen and thinks they know what is best for you instead of asking you*

➤ *talks to your parents instead of you, or only talks to your parents because they think that you would not understand but hasn't bothered to find out if you can*

➤ *isn't very friendly or happy and doesn't smile*

➤ *wants you to do things that you know you can't do*

➤ *doesn't explain what they are doing to you*

➤ *is rude and has not got any manners*

➤ *is not caring, helpful or interested in you*

> *doesn't give you the right information*

> *doesn't follow support through*

> *doesn't have enough time and is always too busy*

> *isn't dedicated to their job*

> *talks to you but you can't understand them*

> *is boring or unapproachable.*

(Turner, 2003, p. 19)

Young people from minority ethnic backgrounds have said that they want professionals to try to understand their culture and ethnicity rather than making assumptions. Young people in Barn et al.'s (2005) study of young care leavers talked about the racism they encountered and the support they wanted to deal with this. They found that sometimes efforts to meet their cultural needs were tokenistic.

The following case example illustrates a situation social workers encounter frequently – that of trying to engage with a young person who has had many changes and rejections in her life and many workers. It offers the opportunity to reflect on some of the difficulties in child-centred practice with older children.

Case example: Anna

Anna is 12 and is currently in residential care. She has an older sister, Susan, who is in foster care. Anna has been in and out of care since she was 5 because of her parents' inability to care for her. This was due to a combination of factors including her mother's learning disability and her father's alcohol addiction. Her mother is White British and her father is of Black African heritage. Anna lived briefly with an aunt and uncle but her placement there and in foster homes did not work out because her parents removed her regularly, just as she was beginning to settle. She has now been placed on a Care Order through court proceedings after her latest stay at home resulted in her father violently attacking her.

She has been in the residential home six weeks and seems to be drawn to a group of young people older than her who frequently abscond and go shoplifting.

Anna has had several changes of social worker and doesn't say much to residential staff.

As her new social worker, what do you think you might do to engage Anna, bearing in mind the comments of young people above about their social workers?

Can you think about where you might see her, what you will talk about, and whether there might be ways you could break the ice?

Definitions of child-centred practice in social work

Child-centred practice is a popular concept, but its definition varies and it is often assumed that the reader or listener understands its meaning without definition. The 'Framework for Assessment of Children in Need and their Families' (Department of Health, 2000), discussed further below, explains a child-centred approach in assessment as follows:

> This means that the child is seen and kept in focus throughout the assessment and that account is always taken of the child's perspective.
>
> (p. 10)

The United Nations Convention on the Rights of the Child (UNCRC, 1989) is frequently cited in support of child-centred social work practice since it contains elements central to the welfare of children and young people. (The UNCRC is discussed in more detail later in this chapter and in Chapter 3.) Munro (2011), for example, says:

> The United Nations Convention on the Rights of the Child (CRC) provides a child-centred framework within which services to children are located.
>
> (Munro, 2011, p. 16)

Although Munro does not specifically define 'child-centred' any further here, the following sections of the Munro Review focus on some key aspects that could be said to constitute child-centred practice. These include young people's participation in decisions and the importance of social workers' communications and relationships with children and young people.

Similarly, Rasmusson et al. (2010) relate child-centred practice to the different strands of children's rights in the UNCRC, those of *provision, protection* and *participation*. They say further, '*Child-centred practice includes work* for *as well as* together with *children*' (p. 453). They explain that 'working for' is about providing for and protecting children and meeting their needs, whilst 'working with' is about facilitating their participation rights.

In her book about child-centred foster care, Goodyer (2011) states:

> There is no general agreement of what a child-centred approach is, but the basic principle involves engaging with children and their families, understanding and providing services that reflect their individual needs and taking into account their wishes and feelings, but remaining aware that they may not yet fully understand the risks involved in their choices.
>
> (Goodyer, 2011, p. 17)

This definition does not highlight children's participation rights but rather communication with children to understand them and provide services that take their wishes into account. This could be summarised as taking account of the *best interests* of children, a concept that is central to the Children Act 1989, discussed below. It is interesting that Goodyer includes in her definition the concept of risk. Balancing the risks to children and young people with their wishes is one of the main dilemmas in child-centred practice, as will be seen throughout this book but especially in Chapter 7 about child protection and safeguarding children and young people.

In contrast, Fern (2014) offers a more rights-focused view of child-centred practice, based on her action research with social work practitioners and young people in Iceland. She contends that so-called 'child-centred approaches' do not go far enough in taking account of the inequalities between social work professionals and children. Nor do they take account of children's strengths and their capacity as knowledgeable 'social actors', a concept that we shall return to in Chapter 2. She states her argument thus:

> *Child-centred approaches have not respected children's active role in defining their circumstances and making decisions, because they are not based on a body of theory that takes the power differences between practitioners and children fully into account.*
>
> (Fern, 2014, p. 1111)

Fern advocates a move to '*child-directed practice*', which would mean a shift in the balance of power between social workers and children. This would entail practitioners holding back from making the decisions but providing their resources, knowledge and skills to enable young people *themselves* to make choices and decisions. Fern's study found that social workers were able to develop their practice when given feedback by children and young people, and this helped them to move away from more routine and bureaucratic models where adults made the decisions.

A full discussion of the key concepts mentioned here of *participation*, taking account of *wishes and feelings* as well as *best interests*, continues in later chapters.

However, to conclude this section, I contend that a definition of child-centred social work should include the following:

➢ Ascertaining children's wishes and feelings by communicating appropriately in terms of age, language, ethnicity and ability;

➢ Maximising their participation in discussions about their welfare;

➢ Including them in decision making;

➢ Taking account of their strengths and their unique knowledge of their own situation;

➢ Making sure that any judgements about what is in a child's best interests and any perceived limitations of risk should not be allowed to dominate completely and hinder professionals from taking account of children's agency; and

➢ Facilitating the access to independent advice or advocacy, especially where a social worker's or agency's views conflict with those of a child.

Reflective exercise

What does it mean to *you* to be child-centred?

Think of a recent interaction you have had with a child or young person.

Can you think how this interaction might have been experienced by him or her?

Can you reflect on the power dynamics in the interaction?

A child focus in law and policy

Law and policy in the UK has developed strongly in its child focus since the 1990s. A major landmark in this was the United Nations Convention on the Rights of the Child (UNCRC, 1989), which has promoted children's rights internationally. It contains 54 Articles of children's rights. These can be categorised as rights of provision, protection and participation. Specifically they cover civil, economic, social and cultural rights, including basic rights to life, health, food, shelter and protection as well as education, privacy and freedom of expression.

The rights that the UNCRC enshrines for children and young people are discussed in more detail in Chapter 3. The so-called *best interests* principle (Article 3) and *participation* principle (Article 12) in the UNCRC are particularly relevant to child-centred practice.

Article 3 states: 'in all actions concerning children .... the best interests of the child shall be a primary consideration.'

Discussions and deliberations about the 'best interests' of children and young people are very important in social work. A child-centred approach depends largely on *who decides* what is in a child's best interests, and this question is considered further in later chapters.

Article 12 states: 'parties shall assure to the child who is capable of forming his or her own views the right to express those views freely in all matters affecting the child, the views of the child being given due weight in accordance with the age and understanding of the child.'

General Comment 7 on Article 12 states that children have a right to be consulted about matters that affect them 'from the earliest stage' and 'measures should be taken to ensure that all those with responsibilities towards young children listen to their views and respect their dignity'.

The question of whether a child is capable of *'forming his or her own views'* and how to assess his or her *'age and understanding'* is vital and has been tested out in UK courts in relation to the Children Act 1989, as discussed in the following section.

Despite its force and worldwide influence, the UNCRC does not have legal status in the UK and relies on individual countries to translate its principles into law.

Children Act 1989

The main legal basis of statutory social work with children and young people in England and Wales (with the exception of Adoption and Youth Justice) continues to be the Children Act 1989. Notable amendments and additions include the Children (Leaving Care) Act 2000, the Adoption and Children Act 2002, the Children Act 2004, the Children and Young Persons Act 2008 and the Children and Families Act 2014. Details of these as they have specifically affected children's rights, child protection and looked after children appear in later chapters.

The Children Act 1989 adopted similar 'best interests' and 'participation' principles to those in the UNCRC and was therefore expected to have a transforming influence on social work practice, enabling this to become more *child focused,* with more emphasis on children's rights. Further, these principles were now enshrined in law and therefore enforceable, rather than being merely a Convention, which could be disregarded. However, critics complained that the principles were applied too narrowly, that is to court proceedings (Freeman, 2002). For example, the 'welfare checklist' (s1(3)), a statutory checklist for courts in decision making, included for the first time some element of consultation with children themselves, which is a key factor in child-centred practice. It advised that courts should have regard to the *'ascertainable wishes and feelings of the child concerned'* (considered in the light of his age and understanding). Guardians ad litem (now named 'children's guardians') were to be appointed to ascertain children's wishes and feelings and to present their views in court. Children's guardians also have a duty to balance this presentation of children's views with their own professional opinion of what is in children's best interests.

Besides changes in legal proceedings there was an attempt through the Act to help children and young people become more involved in decisions and to be consulted. For example, in Section 1(3)(a) a duty is placed on local authorities (Sections 22(4) and (5)) to ascertain their wishes and feelings in making decisions about the care of looked after children. Local authorities were also required to ascertain the views of children and young people before statutory reviews of their care and let them know about decisions (Section 26). An amendment to the 1989 Act in the Children Act 2004 extended this consultation about wishes and feelings to children and young people 'in need' (Section 53).

However, many studies over the decades since the Children Act 1989 have continued to report that children and young people are insufficiently involved in decisions and that their views, even where these are expressed, rarely prevail over the views of others (Thomas, 2000; Holland, 2001; Munro, 2001; Boylan and Ing, 2005; Barnes, 2012; Pert et al., 2017). Such studies are considered in further detail later in the book.

Also under the Children Act 1989, children and young people were enabled to make complaints. This applied to looked after children and children in need and was extended to young care leavers under the Children (Leaving Care) Act 2000. Subsequent studies, however, found that children and young people still had difficulty making complaints in practice. For example, Pithouse and Crowley's (2007) extensive study in Wales of children's complaints found that young people did not feel they were listened to by adults when they tried to complain and felt their views were not taken seriously. Other young people in the study were worried about possible repercussions and thought that they would be treated less favourably by carers if they complained.

In other parts of the Children Act 1989 that appeared to favour a child focus, under Sections 38(6) and 43(8) children could refuse medical or psychiatric examinations if they were deemed to be *'of sufficient understanding to make an informed decision'*. Since the Act contained no definition of 'sufficient understanding' the concept has been repeatedly tested out in the court arena, and outcomes have varied. Most famously the *'Gillick competency'* principle had already been established before the Children Act 1989 in a House of Lords decision: *Gillick v West Norfolk and Wisbech Area Health Authority* [1986] AC 112. This case hinged on whether it was lawful for a doctor to prescribe contraceptives to a young person under 16 years of age without parental consent. The ruling by Lord Scarman stated:

> *A minor's capacity to make his or her own decisions depends on the minor having sufficient understanding and intelligence to make the decision and is not determined by reference to any judicially fixed age limit.*

This ruling appeared to improve children's rights to autonomy in decisions about their health and welfare but the failure of the Children Act 1989 to define *'sufficient understanding'* has led to further court rulings overriding children's refusal of treatment. For example, in 1992 a 16-year-old girl's right to refuse treatment for anorexia was overruled (*Re W (A Minor) (Wardship: Medical Treatment)* [1992] 4 All ER 627) and another child's refusal of treatment was overridden in 1993 (*South Glamorgan C.C. v W and B* [1993] 1 FLR 574). Although practice principles were developed from the *Gillick* case by Lord Fraser, ethical dilemmas continue to exist in such decisions. In health care it has been increasingly recognised that children's experience of treatment, as well as their age and ability, can play a vital part in their understanding of their health needs (Carter et al., 2014).

Overall, the Children Act 1989 raised awareness of the importance of children's involvement in decisions, even if this was difficult to deliver in practice.

Similar legal changes were introduced in Scotland and Northern Ireland with the Children (Scotland) Act 1995 and the Children (Northern Ireland) Order 1995. These were based on similar principles to the Children Act 1989 with its increased child focus on participation and consultation, and they employed similar terminology. The Northern Ireland legislation is most similar to the Children Act 1989 but includes some extra provisions about child employment, unmarried parents and guardianship. The Scottish equivalent does differ significantly since it builds on the previous system of Children's Hearings, which unlike the other UK systems uses the more informal 'children's panels' rather than courts for many decisions about children's welfare.

A child-centred assessment framework

In England and Wales, the 'Framework for Assessment of Children in Need and their Families' (Department of Health, 2000) offered for the first time policy guidance in child-centred assessments of children and families. It was a milestone in social work with children and young people, bringing together findings from a range of research and distilling this into guidance about 'holistic' needs assessments. These were to take account of *'safeguarding and promoting welfare'* of the child who was placed in the centre of three other considerations:

➤ his or her *developmental needs*;

➤ *parenting capacity*; and

➤ *family and environmental factors*.

The guidance also attempted to change the balance of children's services from a preoccupation with risk to more emphasis on universal non-stigmatising family support. Sections 1.34 and 1.35 of the guidance were specifically about a 'child-centred' approach:

> ... *the approach must be child centred. This means that the child is seen and kept in focus throughout the assessment and that account is always taken of the child's perspective.*

(p. 10)

The guidance goes on to acknowledge that children can be 'lost' when complex situations and conflicts divert attention from them to the adults involved. It advises that child observation and direct work with children to ascertain their wishes and feelings are vital. A section on communicating with children (p. 43) lists the key ingredients of working with children, summarised here as:

> *Seeing* children whatever their age

> *Observing* their responses and interactions

> *Engaging* them – i.e. developing a relationship with them

> *Talking* to them in a manner that is appropriate to their age, ability and language

> *Doing* activities with children to develop trust.

If these guidelines were followed, such assessments should have provided a more child-focused service with the potential for social workers to build good relationships with children and young people. However, this development was limited by scarce resources and by pressure on workers to assess risk within fixed timescales. These fixed timescales were later changed, and the 'Assessment Framework' has now been incorporated into 'Working Together to Safeguard Children' (DfE, 2015b), which is discussed in detail in Chapter 7. 'Working Together' is the main policy guidance for professionals about safeguarding and protecting children in England and Wales.

Subsequent child-centred changes in law and policy

Further discussion of relevant laws and policies in relation to rights, child protection and looked after children follows in Chapters 3, 7 and 8, but below is a brief overview of child-centred proposals and changes since 2002.

Adoption and Children Act 2002

This Act placed a duty on local authorities to provide advocacy services for looked after young people and those leaving care who want to make a complaint under the Children Act 1989.

Every Child Matters (DfES, 2003)

The Green Paper 'Every Child Matters' (Department for Education and Skills, 2003) defined outcomes for children's well-being, setting the foundations for good practice and shoring up existing safeguarding strategies. The outcomes are to:

> be healthy;

> stay safe;

> enjoy and achieve;

> make a positive contribution; and

> achieve economic well-being.

Children Act 2004

This Act implemented the 'Every Child Matters' programme and made provision for a Children's Commissioner in England (see Chapter 3). It also extended consultation about their wishes and feelings to children and young people '*in need*' under the Children Act 1989.

Children and Young Persons Act 2008

This dealt primarily with the welfare of looked after children and young people and is discussed in detail in Chapter 8. It aimed to offer them better personal and financial support and greater consistency of care.

The Munro Review of Child Protection, 2011

The Review was a comprehensive overview of child protection systems and advocated child-centred safeguarding and protection services overall. It is discussed in detail in Chapter 7.

Children and Families Act 2014

As well as legislation regarding adoption and care proceedings, this Act introduced a measure to enhance young people's experience of 'care' by permitting them to 'stay put' in foster care until age 21. The Act also introduced a statutory time limit on care proceedings of twenty-six weeks to avoid excessive delays to children's future care.

Working Together to Safeguard Children (DfE, 2015b)

This statutory guidance for professionals in child protection has a key principle of 'a child-centred approach'. The guidance is discussed in detail in Chapter 7.

Social work principles and standards relating to child-centred practice

Social work professional standards and guidance are ever changing but basically they have similar core themes over time. These reflect a tension between professional decision making and the individual's right to autonomy. In terms of child-centred practice this may imply a tension between the professional's decision about a child's best interests and the view of the child himself or herself.

A definition of social work is a helpful starting point in considering this. This is the globally agreed definition by the International Federation of Social Workers (IFSW) and the International Association of Schools of Social Work (IASSW):

> *Social work is a practice-based profession and an academic discipline that promotes social change and development, social cohesion, and the empowerment and liberation of people. Principles of social justice, human rights, collective responsibility and respect for diversities are central to social work. Underpinned by theories of social work, social sciences, humanities and indigenous knowledge, social work engages people and structures to address life challenges and enhance wellbeing.*
>
> (IFSW and IASSW, 2014)

This definition stresses the rights-based and emancipatory nature of social work. For children this would imply that their rights and participation should be foregrounded. Similarly, the standards for social work as outlined in the various recent standards and guidance in England and Wales contain this rights-based discourse but also include elements of social control and risk assessment.

The Professional Capabilities Framework (PCF) at qualified social worker level (TCSW 2012) consists of nine domains: Professionalism, Values and Ethics, Diversity, Rights and Justice, Critical Reflection, Intervention and Skills, Contexts and Organisations, and Professional Leadership.

In terms of considering child-centred practice the 'Rights and Justice' domain is most relevant, and rights are mentioned in the PCF ten times. There is also an emphasis on equality, partnership, self determination, advocacy and challenging discrimination. A qualified social worker is expected to:

> *Routinely apply the law to protect and advance people's rights and entitlements, identifying and highlighting situations where interpretations of the law are neither proportionate nor fair to promote autonomy and self-determination.*

> *Where appropriate, set up and/or enable access to effective independent advocacy.*

Also in the 'Values and Ethics' domain social workers are expected to:

> *Ensure practice is underpinned by policy, procedures and codes of conduct to promote individuals' rights to determine their own solutions, promoting problem-solving skills, whilst recognising how and when self-determination may be constrained (by the law).*

The 'Values and Ethics' domain, however, mentions the legal constraints to self determination, which are emphasised in other domains. Other domains highlight safeguarding, the need to balance between rights and risks and the social worker's use of authority (Intervention and Skills domain).

The more recent 'Knowledge and Skills Statement for Approved Child and Family Practitioners' (Department for Education, 2014a) contains ten elements in which social workers should be proficient:

> *Relationships and effective direct work; Communication; Child development; Adult mental ill-health, substance misuse, domestic violence, physical ill-health and disability; Abuse and neglect of children; Child and family assessment; Analysis, decision making planning and review; The law and the family and youth justice systems; Professional ethics; The role of supervision; Organisational context.*

This guidance puts more far more stress on assessment of *risk* than the Professional Capabilities Framework. The word 'risk' is used eleven times and child protection, safeguarding and harm are frequently highlighted. This Knowledge and Skills statement does not mention rights, equality or discrimination at all. The only wording that relates to rights is the mention of children's participation in the 'Relationships and effective direct work' section, saying that a social worker should enable the *'full participation'* of children, families and professionals in *'assessment, planning review and decision making'*.

The Knowledge and Skills Statement for Social Workers in Adult Services (DfE, 2015a), whilst also highlighting risk, places far more emphasis on rights, equality, self determination, empowerment, advocacy and 'person-centred' practice. Even when adults are assessed as lacking capacity under the Mental Capacity Act 2005, social workers are expected to 'empower' service users, be 'person-centred' and encourage choice. This expresses a very different attitude to social work with adults from that to social work with children. It reflects the wider society's attitudes to children and young people as vulnerable and not competent, which is the subject of more discussion in Chapter 2.

Origins and critiques of child-centred social work

Person-centred social work and personalisation

Child-centred social work practice is frequently traced back to 'person-centred' practice, a principle adopted by many professionals working in adult care services such as social work and nursing (Kitson et al., 2013). It is mentioned specifically in the Knowledge and Skills Statement for Social Workers in Adult Services (DfE, 2015a) as noted above.

Person-centred planning for adults with learning disabilities has been developed for many years and has been supported by government policy and legislation such as *Valuing People* (DoH, 2001b). Beresford et al. (2011) track the changes for this group of people from a service-led to a service-*user*-led approach, which promotes choice, potential and autonomy (p. 42). It regards the individual as unique and, instead of fitting people into existing resources, attempts to find out an individual's aims in life and what could be done to achieve them. The government guidance defines person-centred planning as:

> *a process for continual listening and learning, focused on what is important to someone now and in the future, and acting upon this in alliance with family and friends. This listening and learning is used to understand a person's capacities and choices. Person centred planning is a basis for problem solving and negotiation to mobilize*

the resources necessary to pursue the person's aspirations. Those resources may be obtained from a person's personal network, from service agencies or from a range of non-specialist and non-secure services.

(DoH, 2001a, p. 12)

More recently, since the publication of *Putting People First* (HM Government, 2007), a further step has been taken in social care for adults. 'Personalisation' has been supported as an aim for all social work with adults, so that service users may have control over their individual services through their own personal budgets. This initiative has been further supported by the Care Act 2014. Its aims chime with social work values of well-being, social change, social justice and human rights, as expressed in the international definition of social work quoted above (Lymbery, 2012).

Some critics, however, have argued that personalisation could be seen as a cost cutting exercise since there are many barriers to its implementation. Some of the barriers found in the 'Standards we Expect' research (Beresford et al., 2011) included the lack of adequate staffing to give support and information to those trying to manage their own care needs, problems with inflexible bureaucracies and target setting, and paternalism in the organisations they needed to deal with. Nevertheless, in adults' social care there has been a strong move to place the service user at the centre for many years. This is now echoed in children's services. Under Section 49 of the Children and Families Act 2014 personal budgets have been introduced for Education, Health and Social Care Plans for young people who have special educational needs. 'Direct payments' may be made to 'a child's parents or a young person'. However, there are no current plans for children and young people to have control of budgets in other realms, such as the care system.

Reflective exercise

Do you think that children are different from adults in how they want to be treated by professionals who work with them?

Can you think about a contact you had recently with a professional (for example a doctor, optician, solicitor, housing officer)?

What was important for you in your contact with them and the way that they interacted with you?

What other things might be important for a child of 5, or a young person of 14?

Client-centred therapy

The origins of person-centred practice can also be traced back to 'client-centred therapy' as expounded by Carl Rogers (1951, 1957). This approach was founded in humanistic psychology and it expounded a holistic view of humans that placed it in opposition to psychoanalytic theories of unconscious determinism as well as behavioural theories, which it regarded as too narrowly focused (Kondrat, 2014).

Rogers' (1957) client-centred theory and practice applied specifically to counselling and included six conditions for the client to develop in a socially constructive direction. The first three conditions may be most familiar to readers since they feature in many training courses for social work and other 'caring' professions about communicating with service users. They are as follows:

➤ Unconditional positive regard,

➤ Empathy, and

➤ Congruence (or genuineness).

The final three conditions stipulated by Rogers were that there must also be psychological contact between the therapist and client; the client must be in a state of *'incongruence'* and distressed, and there must be communication of the therapist's empathy and unconditional positive regard (Rogers, 1957). 'Incongruence' in Rogers' theory can be defined as the gap that people feel between what they would like to be (their ideal self) and their actual experience in life.

Rogers believed that there was one basic human tendency, which he called the 'actualizing tendency'. He maintained that humans, like other living beings, have an innate tendency to move towards accomplishing their potential, that is to become the best they can. The constraints that they face in this are the circumstances of their environment (Thorne and Sanders, 2013). The task of the counsellor is to provide the right conditions, in terms of those six outlined above, for people to achieve this self actualisation through therapy.

Critiques of person-centred and child-centred practice

Critics of person-centred and child-centred social work argue that these client-centred theories about counselling cannot be simply applied to the practice of social work. Although they would agree that social workers can learn and apply some of the skills of counselling in their work,

Murphy et al. (2013) argue that a 'person-centred approach' in social work is misplaced since social workers are not helping their service users to 'self actualise', rather they are using their relationships with service users instrumentally. Although social workers may need to build a good relationship with their service users to do their job, this is for a different end, for example to make assessments or to minimise risk. In social work with children and families a social worker is unable to allow the child or parents the freedom to reach their potential through the use of a therapeutic relationship when, for example, the parents of a 6-year-old child are unable to care because of drug addiction or severe mental health issues. He or she has to be more directive.

However, some writers argue that there are useful direct applications of a person-centred approach in social work and related professions. Houston (2003), for example, argues that the practice of person-centred planning with adults can be used in working with children and young people in care. He maintains that this would place the child at the centre of inquiry and *'safeguard the human dimension in care planning'* (p. 67), which can be lost through a mechanistic application of the looked after children system. Taylor (2007) argues for its use in working with children who have a multi-sensory impairment in order to maximise their participation in education. She advocates placing these children at the centre of the planning process *'to identify their needs and aspirations with the support of others'* (p. 204) and to generate creative solutions. Her research used principles of person-centred planning to improve communication and consultation with children in the study.

Fern's (2014) critique, cited earlier in this chapter, is of a very different nature as she contends that child-centred practice does not go far enough since it does not permit children and young people the power to direct the practice of social workers.

Child-centred practice in other professions

In considering child-centred practice in social work it is instructive to see how other professions have interpreted this concept. Social work owes particularly to education and to therapy for some of its ideas about child-centred practice. I shall look at the concept in terms of therapy, health and education, ending with children's advocacy, which can have a role with children in all these spheres.

Child-centred play therapy

Kottman (2014) traces the origins of child-centred play therapy back to Carl Rogers' (1951) client-centred therapy discussed above. This was combined by Virginia Axline (1964) with 'relationship play therapy' to create her 'non-directive child-centred play therapy', which has provided an important foundation for the theory and practice of subsequent play therapists. Her methods depend on the belief that, given the right therapeutic environment, children, like adults, can move through therapy to self actualisation and constructive growth. Her main principles can be summarised as follows:

> The therapeutic relationship must be warm and friendly to create rapport.

> The child must be unconditionally accepted by the therapist.

> The therapeutic environment must be non-judgemental in order for the child to feel free to express emotions, feelings, and behaviour.

> The therapist relies on the child's ability to find solutions to his or her own problems and understands that the responsibility to make choices and to institute change is the child's.

> The therapist must be attentive to the child's feelings and behaviour in order to reflect this back to the child so that he or she may develop self-awareness.

> The therapist allows the child to lead and does not attempt to direct the child's actions or conversations in any manner.

> The therapist recognises that therapy should progress at its own pace, not a pace set by the therapist. It is a gradual process.

> The only limitations and boundaries set are ones that ensure the therapeutic process stays in the realm of reality, and the child is aware of his or her purpose and role in the therapy.

These principles position children as able to benefit from a non-directive approach, on the assumption that they will move through this to more positive and better selves. Issues such as past or present risk and best interests are not considered here, although clearly, therapists may sometimes have to address these in their work with children. In this respect, such therapy is unlike social work, which has to take full account of a child's relationships with those providing care and his or her environment. Furthermore, as noted above, social workers will usually need to be more directive in their approach, since their interactions with children are for specific purposes such as assessment. However, many of the principles contained in this model of play therapy, such as building rapport with children and going at their pace, are useful for social workers in their practice with children and young people.

Child-centred education

In education child-centredness has different connotations from those in social work but has been similarly influenced by social and political pressures. The concept has a long history in education, and the tensions between child-centred education and a more authoritarian approach continue to exist. Focus on the 'whole child' in the present rather than on what the child should *become* as an adult lies at the heart of the debate.

Doddington and Hilton (2007) trace the origins of the concept back to Jean-Jacques Rousseau's ideas about education in *Emile* in 1762. Rousseau advocated an appreciation of the natural child in *his* own right and maintained that good education should be based on an understanding of each child's developing nature. (Rousseau has been criticised in modern times since he did not apply his ideas to the education of female children.)

Later, the Kindergarten movement carried these child-centred ideas forward into practice in the education of very young children. A pioneer of this movement, the Prussian educationist, Froebel (1826), expounded his ideas about the natural instincts and play of young children, and he maintained that active play helped children's development. Talking of the 3-to-5-year-old child he says: '*In the period of childhood (the child) is placed in the centre of all things*' (Translation by Hailmann, 1887, p. 97).

The Kindergarten movement spread across Europe to Britain and to the United States later in the nineteenth century. In England in the twentieth century the Hadow reports (1926, 1931 and 1933) confirmed the importance of a child-centred approach for primary school children age 5–11 years, but this approach was soon undermined by the pressure for grammar school places at age 11 and the 'eleven-plus' test. The competition for places governed by intelligence testing meant that children were often tutored to pass the test and the curriculum was narrowed. Following changes to secondary education, the Plowden report (1967) continued and extended a version of this child-centred education. It also took account of the effects of disadvantage on children and established Educational Priority Areas in areas of deprivation. Plowden said: '*At the heart of the educational process lies the child*' (1967, Chapter 2: 9).

From the 1970s onward, however, there were concerns, especially from right wing sources, about anarchy in schools. Entwistle (2012) argued that critics saw child-centred education as 'the source of all society's ills' (p. 12). They disputed the value of this form of education and considered it dangerous to begin with the child, enabling them to learn through exploration, rather than with a preset idea of what a child needs to learn. Child-centredness in education is still a contested concept and debate continues about aspects such as 'attainment targets' and a national curriculum, which was introduced by the 1988 Education Reform Act.

Chung and Walsh (2000) have identified three major different meanings of child-centred practice in education that have developed over time. These are described as follows:

> *Froebels' putting the child at the centre, smack dab in the middle of her world, the developmentalist notion that the child is the centre of schooling and finally the progressive notion that children should direct their activities.*

> (p. 229)

Given these diverse interpretations, they question how meaningful a concept 'child-centred' is, but nevertheless conclude that it has at least the benefit of giving educationists with similar ideas a common language.

For social work, ideas about child-centred practice in education encourage us to consider the whole child, rather than seeing children primarily in terms of their problems that need to be solved. This is also a feature of social pedagogy, often seen as a synthesis of care and education (Cameron and Moss, 2011). The approach of social pedagogy to children and young people has been current in parts of Europe for many years. Social pedagogues are highly trained to work holistically with children and young people, adopting a relational approach that also builds on an understanding of young people's rights (Petrie et al., 2009). They have a distinct role with more direct contact with children and young people than social workers but provide child-centred practice when social workers cannot (Boddy and Statham, 2009). There is more detail about the practice of social pedagogy in Chapter 4's discussion about communicating with children and young people.

Child-centred health care

The concept of child-centred health care has developed gradually since the latter part of the twentieth century. One of the most disputed aspects of this was about parental visits to children in hospital. Open visiting is now universal in the UK but until around the 1950s parents were allowed to visit their sick children only once per week and sometimes not at all. Bradley (2001) cites the case of a mother's experience taken from *The Lancet* as late as 1965. Her 3-year-old daughter died after a tonsillectomy operation. She was not allowed to see her daughter on the day of the operation or on the following day when the child was critically ill, dying and in need of comfort.

Similarly strict regimes operated in Australia. Street (1992, p. 11) quotes the visiting rules from the Royal Children's Hospital in Australia in 1947:

> *Patients are not allowed visitors unless they have been in the hospital for a period of four weeks, after which time only the parents or guardians (no friends or relatives are allowed) are permitted to visit on each alternate Sunday in each month, between the hours of 2pm and 3.30pm.*

These strict regimes were supposed to safeguard children's health but they also served to ease the functioning of the institution. Relatives were seen as getting in the way of the hospitals' routines and children were sometimes upset when their parents arrived and departed. The idea that children and their families' interests should be central was slow to develop but was influenced by the recognition that children experience psychological trauma from separation (Carter et al., 2014). The work of John Bowlby (1969) on attachment and loss, and the heart rending films made by James and Joyce Robertson (1952) showing the distress of children separated from their parents, helped to effect change. The Platt Report (Ministry of Health, 1959) encouraged parents to visit whenever possible and help with children's care.

Child-centred health care generally has similar concerns to that of social work about risk and best interests. The focus here is on respecting children and young people's health choices whilst also balancing this with parents' and carers' views, as well as with the views of health professionals. Carter et al. (2014) express a tension in this between 'family-centred care' and 'child-centred care'. Whilst appreciating that *'children and their interests need to be at the centre of our thinking and our practice'* (p. 25), and that health professionals need to understand that children may have different views from those of their parents and of their health carers, they emphasise that children need to be in active partnership in respect of their care and participate in decision making. They need to be listened to and kept informed. Nevertheless they say:

> *Child-centred practice still recognises the central role of parents and families in relationships and interactions with health care professionals.*

Much of the debate in health care centres on children's competence to make decisions, as discussed earlier in this chapter in terms of the *Gillick competency principle*. One of the important factors taken into account is the age of the child and some believe this is the most important. However, research has found that children can be involved in decisions at a very young age. For example, Alderson's (2007) research into children's consent in health care has found that age is not necessarily a determinant of competence in decision making and that even very young children, who may have extensive experience of their own illness and treatment, can become well informed (p. 81). They become experts in their own care and treatment through living with illness and therefore have a vital role in planning and decisions.

Social work can profit from the detailed discussion and research in the health sphere about the understanding and competence of very young children. This can inform social work practice with young children who are the subject of child protection enquiries or children who have to be accommodated away from their birth parents. It is important to understand that even very young children will have a view and that they need to be consulted and properly informed.

Children's advocates

Child-centred practice is clearly vital to children's advocacy. Children and young people themselves are the focus of advocacy, and children's advocates are not hampered by some of the limitations that social workers may experience in this respect. Whilst social workers can also advocate for children and young people to a certain extent, they may be restricted through organisational pressures, resource shortages and the demands made by carers and by other professionals. A professional advocate works for the child or young person only, in whatever situation children find themselves, in family matters or in their education and health.

It is the role of advocates to enable children and young people's views to be heard by other professionals rather than to consider their best interests. However, safeguarding is everyone's business and advocates are bound by concerns about risk and child protection. They also need to share information with other professionals when there are suspected risks to children and young people.

Social workers can learn from advocacy practice to focus more fully on children and young people in their work and to uphold their rights. The advocate's role and working with advocates are considered in detail in Chapter 3.

Conclusion

Placing service users at the centre of professional practice has its origins in person-centred therapy with its focus on client self determination. As such it may not be fully achievable in social work, which is constrained by principles of social control and risk avoidance. Nevertheless, the concept of child-centred practice in social work has ongoing support from law, policy and research. All these, including children themselves, have added weight to a call for social workers to practise in a way that gives more attention to children's concerns and their viewpoint.

Summary points

➤ Complaints that social work is not child-centred enough have arisen from inquiries into child deaths from abuse and from young people themselves, especially in the care system.

➤ Children and young people want their social workers to be there for them, to listen and to care.

➤ Child-centred practice is variously defined but is centrally about good communication with children and including them in decisions.

➤ Law, policy and social work standards in the UK support child-centred practice.

➤ The concept of child-centred practice can be traced back to person-centred therapy and practice.

➤ Some critics argue that social work cannot be fully child-centred since social workers have other agendas about, for example, risk assessment.

➤ Social work can draw on elements of child-centred practice in other professions such as education and health.

Further reading

Brammer, A. (2015) *Social Work Law,* 4th edition. Harlow: Pearson Longman.
Helpful for further detail of the law relating to social work with children.

Carter, B., Bray, L., Dickinson, A., Edwards, M. and Ford, K. (2014) *Child-Centred Nursing: Promoting Critical Thinking.* London: Sage.
For an overview of child-centred practice in health care.

Doddington, C. and Hilton, M. (2007) *Child-Centred Education: Reviving the Creative Tradition.* London: Sage.
For an overview of child-centred practice in education.

Munro, E. (2011) *The Munro Review of Child Protection: Final Report – A Child-Centred Approach,* Vol. 8062. London: The Stationery Office.
For discussion and guidance about child-centred practice in child protection.

Murphy, D., Duggan, M. and Joseph, S. (2013) Relationship-Based Social Work and Its Compatibility with the Person-Centred Approach: Principled Versus Instrumental Perspectives, *British Journal of Social Work,* 43 (4), 703–719.
Argues the limitations of person-centred practice in social work.

2

Perspectives on Children and Childhood

Introduction

Attitudes to working with children and young people in social work and in other professions do not exist in a vacuum. The views of society – its politics, cultures, values and norms – influence all members of society. This chapter explores whether we have a child-centred society and, if so, whether that is something new.

In the late twentieth century the renowned German sociologist, Ulrich Beck (1992), argued that children are 'overloved' in late modernity and that the Western focus on children is a result of the instability of our other primary relationships. He claimed that we see children as an alternative to loneliness:

> *The child is the source of the last remaining, irrevocable, unexchangeable primary relationship. Partners come and go. The child stays. Everything that is desired, but not realizable in the relationship, is directed to the child.*
>
> (Beck, 1992, p. 118)

This is an argument that such attitudes are *too* child-centred and border on being pathological.

Other commentators such as Cregan and Cuthbert (2014) have argued that Western society (which they term the 'Global North') holds a particular construction of childhood not shared by other societies and one that did not exist in the developed West until relatively recently. This latter view was shared by the social historian Ariès and is one we shall consider in more detail below.

This chapter aims to provide a context by considering how children and young people are regarded in Western society and how this may affect child-centred practice. The status of children and young people is traced back briefly in time to see what, if any, the changes have been. It examines societal values and cultural and geographical differences in the treatment of children, as well as adults' perceptions of children and young people at their different ages. The chapter also includes children's views about their place in society.

The debate looks at the contribution of other disciplines, especially those of psychology and sociology. Child psychology has mainly focused on the development of children's cognitive and emotional development whereas the sociology of childhood has considered society more from the perspective of children themselves. It has questioned whether children and young people should be considered 'social actors' in their own right and how their agency may be promoted. It foregrounds children's lived experiences in terms of their class, gender, disability and culture.

Historical attitudes in the West: are we more child-focused now?

The rise in popularity of Childhood Studies in higher education in the UK provides support for the notion that we currently have a strong interest in children in their own right in the Western world. Seventy-two Childhood Studies courses were advertised in the UK in 2016. We study children, not just as a route to a profession such as child nursing, social work with children or child psychology, but because the concept of childhood has an innate appeal and provokes academic curiosity.

However, this intellectual interest is not entirely new. The Greek philosopher, Plato, born in the fourth century BC, was interested in the concept of childhood and discussed the enduring nature of the impressions made on us from our early infancy. Much later, the seventeenth-century English philosopher John Locke had a strong influence on thinking about childhood. In his 1689 work '*An Essay Concerning Human Understanding*', he asserted that an infant at birth could be regarded as being like a *tabula rasa,* a blank slate waiting for experiences to be written there, although he did consider that children are born with innate dispositions. His writings also discussed children's development in their powers of reasoning and their education into moral citizenship.

The influence of Ariès

In more modern times the French social historian Phillipe Ariès has had an important influence on thinking about childhood in the Western world, especially in the spheres of sociology and children's rights (Lee, 2001; Kehily, 2015). His theories support the view that our world has become increasingly child focused over recent times. Even though there are many criticisms of his views, these still serve as central points of reference for studies of childhood. His book *Centuries of Childhood* (English Translation) (1962) charts the changes in the meaning of childhood in Western society from mediaeval times.

Ariès' central thesis was that the *concept* of childhood itself did not fully emerge until between the fifteenth and seventeenth centuries. He suggested that before this time children over the age of about 7 years old were not seen as separate from adults. Although infants under 7 years old were recognised as more fragile and vulnerable, older children were absorbed into the adult world, helping, for example, with adult work such farming or other family business. They also played similar games and wore clothes of the same style as adults, albeit smaller ones. Ariès claimed that a change in attitudes began from the fifteenth century onwards when adults began to see children as requiring special and different treatment from adults. They needed, for example, to be 'coddled', that is for adults to make allowances for their age and to celebrate their incompetence in the realms of their physical, mental and emotional development. Children were then later regarded as immature beings who required discipline and training, and gradually education was extended to a wider age range and to all classes. School became, like today, the proper sphere of children.

Ariès argued that former views of children contrast with modern day expectations that society should have separate places and activities for the young. They now have separate areas such as schools and playgrounds, they wear different clothing styles from adults and they play with toys, designed specifically for a variety of age groups.

Reflective exercise

Can you think of other places where children and adults are separated?

In what other ways are children treated as separate from adults?

What effects do you think these separations have on adults and children?

Critics of Ariès complain that his thesis relied on a narrow interpretation of children as portrayed in Western art and that this might not have reflected wider thinking of the time (Gittins, 2015). In paintings before the fifteenth century there were few portraits of contemporary children. In fact the majority of art works had religious themes. Those portraits that did exist showed children as miniature adults, whereas later paintings in the eighteenth century differentiated them from adults, showing them in specifically 'childish' clothing and playing with toys or pets. A further criticism is that Ariès judged previous eras by the standards of the present day. These specific portrayals of children did not necessarily denote an absence of the concept of childhood in mediaeval times but may have meant that they just had a *different* concept of childhood from our current one (Archard, 2015).

Nevertheless Ariès' influence has persisted. It does not take a global view of childhoods throughout the world, but it has laid the groundwork for the academic exploration of childhood and theories about its socially constructed nature, as discussed further below.

Development in attitudes and legislation from the eighteenth century to modern day: protection and control?

In the developed West the separation of childhood and adulthood into distinct worlds continued over the eighteenth and nineteenth centuries and was strengthened in the UK by a plethora of legislation (Hendrick, 2015). Some of the laws concerned the education of children. The Forster Act 1870 and the Education Act 1880 introduced compulsory schooling for 5–10 year olds. This had a far reaching effect since it meant that children no longer shared in the family labour for the majority of their time.

As noted in the previous chapter, the French philosopher Jean-Jacques Rousseau had emphasised the importance of protecting the goodness of the 'natural child' and he promoted an education that respected this. This theme of natural goodness and innocence was taken up in Britain and expressed by the Romantic poets such as Coleridge and Wordsworth. Wordsworth's poetry expresses this view very clearly. Experience here is seen as corrupting:

> *Heaven lies about us in our infancy!*
> *Shades of the prison-house begin to close*
> *Upon the growing Boy.*

> From *'Ode: Intimations of Immortality*
> *from Recollections of Early Childhood' (1804)*

Since children were newly regarded as innocent and vulnerable they were also seen as needing special protection. As James and James (2004) comment,

> *The later 19th century and early 20th century positively bristled with all kinds of reforms designed to protect children.*

> (James and James, 2004, p. 21)

Many labour laws were introduced. For example, The Factory Act 1833 aimed to protect children from long hours and dangerous and unhealthy conditions in mills and factories. Also typically, we think of little boys used as chimney sweeps in that era. The Chimney Sweepers Act 1834 raised the minimum age for this work to 14 years and this minimum age was raised again six years later.

The Prevention of Cruelty to, and Protection of, Children Act 1889 was the first legislation to try to protect children from abuse and neglect in the home and workplace, and at this time the National Society for the Prevention of Cruelty to Children (NSPCC) was also set up.

Children were protected more from the rigours of the law by means of The Youthful Offenders Act 1854, which was enacted to protect children from being as harshly treated as adults in the courts. Nevertheless, very young children could be sent to prison for hard labour and to harsh reformatories or even transported to the colonies for petty theft. There is interesting documentation for this from the National Archives Collection where the cases of individual young children include their age, disposal and length of sentence. Eleven-year-old John Greening, for example, was sentenced to one month's hard labour and five years' reformatory for stealing a 'quarter' of growing gooseberries. There was therefore also a strong element of control and discipline in this treatment of young people, in line with the Christian concept of 'original sin', a view that children are naturally evil and need to have this evil controlled (Jenks, 1996).

This mix of attitudes to children as innocent and evil, in need of protection and control persists in modern day UK society, in relation to safeguarding young children and in our youth justice systems. For example, when a child like 'Baby P.' or Victoria Climbié is abused and killed by parents or carers, there is outrage. An angry public wants to know why we are not protecting innocent and vulnerable infants and who we should blame. The accompanying public and media uproar calls for better laws, better procedures and better social workers (Jones, 2014).

This concept of children's vulnerability can also be seen to lead to adult controlling behaviour since it is used to exclude them from a variety of public spaces such as pubs and restaurants. Parents increasingly restrict children's movements to a narrow area near the home when they are not at officially sanctioned venues such as schools or clubs (Jack, 2008). For example, in a survey by The Children's Society (2007), nearly half the adults consulted expressed the view that children under 14 years should not be allowed to go outside with their friends without adult supervision.

With older children we take a more punitive stance. The English Youth Offending system aims to control and discipline children from the age of 10, the age of criminal responsibility. Incarceration of teenagers is routine and their movements, until recently, have been controlled through Anti-Social

Behaviour Orders (ASBOs). What constitutes anti-social behaviour was not clearly defined, and ASBOs were seen as contributing to the criminalisation of young people and their use of public space through curfews and exclusion from public areas (Bradford, 2012). ASBOs have now been replaced by IPNAs (Injunctions to Prevent Nuisance and Annoyance), which are arguably more likely to criminalise young people since they widen the parameters to include *threatening* to cause nuisance and annoyance.

Teenagers are frequently portrayed in the media as out of control through binge drinking, drug taking and under-age sex. This so-called 'deviant' behaviour of challenging the social norms is a common feature of adolescence, and neurologists have argued that young people may be 'hard-wired' to behave in this way (Bessant, 2008). Nevertheless, as writers about deviance have argued, adolescents have often become the focus for moral panics (Cohen, 1972) and scapegoated as 'folk-devils'. Some social groups or subcultures of young people have been portrayed in this way, especially in the media. 'Teddy boys' in the 1950s, 'mods' and 'rockers' in the 1960s and more recently young people wearing 'hoodies' give rise to social anxiety and become the subject of legislation to control their behaviour. However, as Bradford (2012) points out, deviance is not synonymous with criminality although it can include criminal behaviour. On the contrary, deviant behaviour in youth can be a positive and creative force,

> Deviance in youth can include colourful expressive behaviour, creative musical and theatrical work, body manipulation and art and other practices that make positive contributions to cultural life.
>
> (Bradford, 2012, p. 132)

In social work teenagers are often seen as difficult to deal with by practitioners. In Barnes' (2013) study of inter-professional practice with education, social work and health professionals, social workers and teachers talked about their difficulties in handling teenagers' behaviour and in communicating with them. One social worker said:

> I find working with the teenagers more challenging – they can be very difficult to work with. I've got one teenager at the moment that it's just such a nightmare trying to sort out the situation because he's had so many professionals come in and out of his life that he doesn't see the point of talking to us any more because, as far as he's concerned, nothing changes.

Having to deal with so many professionals is a frequent complaint from young people and is one of the reasons why relationships with social workers can break down. Chapters 4 and 5 look at positive ways of communicating with young people and some of the pitfalls.

Reflective exercise

Can you think of other examples of adults treating children as:

➤ Innocent and in need of protection?

➤ 'Bad' and in need of control or discipline?

Theories of childhood

In this next section I shall outline two different perspectives on childhood, both of which could be described as being child focused or child centred in different ways. The first concerns children's development in the physical and emotional sense, and is governed largely by the disciplines of biology and psychology. These disciplines consider children's growth and maturation against a perceived norm and are widely used by health and social care professions as an evidence base. Some critics term such theories as 'developmentalist', arguing that they treat children as objects of physical observation and surveillance (Foucault, 1975; Cregan and Cuthbert, 2014; Wyness, 2015).

In contrast, the second perspective looks at children's place and relationships in society and belongs mainly to the discipline of sociology. Increasingly, sociologists of childhood argue that children are active participants in the world with their own views, and they try to foreground these views.

'Developmentalist' theories: biology and psychology

Children are often simply seen as immature adults and the biological foundation for this could be regarded as obvious. Childhood is a time of fast physical and mental growth:

> The human brain grows most rapidly during the prenatal period and the first few years of life, reaching 50 per cent mature weight by six months and 90 percent by the age of eight. Children's physical growth is also very rapid during the early years.
>
> (Woodhead, 2006, p. 9)

Historically, the Child Study Movement in the nineteenth century was a pioneering group of scientists who studied children's 'natural' biological development. Charles Darwin studied his own son's development and published his observations in *Biographical Sketch of the Infant* in 1877. His focus was on cognition, motor skills and communication, and he related the development of humans to that of other animals. His work provided a foundation for later psychological theorising such as that of Sigmund Freud.

We can see the continued use of theories of 'normal' physical development in health and social care practice. For example, health visitors and medical clinics refer to child development charts to check whether an infant's development is within the 'normal' parameters. The paediatrician Mary Sheridan's charts include norms for infants at various intervals such as at 6 months, *'Lying on back, lifts and grasps foot'* and at 12 months, *'Walks around furniture lifting one foot and stepping sideways'* (Sheridan, 1997).

Critics of this biological focus have argued that there is a wide variation in so-called normal development. Archard (2015) points out that, for example, the onset of puberty in Western cultures has taken place increasingly earlier over the last century. Other critics argue that development is affected by children's unique experiences within their particular culture since it may be affected by variables such as diet and activity (James and James, 2004).

Psychological theories

Psychological theories such as those of Freud, Piaget and Bowlby have had a major influence on the study of childhood since the nineteenth century. These have also been central to professional practice with children and young people in health, education and social work.

Piaget's (1955) work portrayed childhood as a series of stages in cognitive development that children achieve at different ages on their road to reach adulthood. He observed and questioned children in experiments designed to understand how they make sense of the world and learn to conceptualise. The stages he charted began with children's experiences through their senses and movement. He described a 'Sensorimotor' stage between birth and 2 years where children begin to learn 'object permanence', the understanding that toys, for example, do not cease to exist when we no longer see or feel them. As they grow, children then learn more advanced motor skills and logical thinking about number and weight and develop the capacity for abstract thought. Piaget's theories are still used, particularly in education, to chart 'normal' cognitive development, for example in tests for children with a learning disability and in testing children's ability to apply mathematical concepts (Colle et al., 2006; Shayer et al., 2007).

Critics of Piaget have pointed out that children do not all reach the developmental stages he describes at the same rate, and some may not reach them at all. Furthermore, some of these so-called stages depend on social and cultural experiences, and the cognitive competence that Piaget describes is a specifically Western model that cannot be universally applied (Archard, 2015). For example, the concepts of specific weight and number feature far less in societies where technology and trade are not developed.

Sigmund Freud's contribution to our understanding of childhood was based on his theories of psycho-sexual development. These still influence practice in child psychology and psychotherapy and have been developed specifically in relation to children by his successors such as Anna Freud and Melanie Klein. Like Piaget, Freud saw childhood as a series of developmental stages but his focus was on emotional rather than cognitive development. He asserted that children needed to successfully negotiate each stage to attain an equilibrium in adulthood. For example, if a child did not successfully come through the 'oral' stage in feeding as an infant he or she would develop an 'oral' personality and be predisposed to a preoccupation with eating and drinking or addiction to alcohol or smoking. Many of Freud's theories have been disputed. For example, his theories about Oedipus and Elektra complexes have been challenged by subsequent theorists, since there is little evidence for the existence of these supposedly unconscious sexual desires of a young child for the parent of the opposite sex. Like Freud, Erikson (1950) posited a series of stages that children and adults needed to resolve at different ages such as 'basic trust versus mistrust' (birth to 18 months approximately) and 'autonomy versus shame and doubt' (18 months to 3 years approximately). His work on adolescent identity is still influential in theory and practice.

John Bowlby's (1969 and 1973) theories of attachment have most currency and application in modern day social work. They contain a similar theme to those of Freud and Erikson with respect to negotiating early developmental stages but the focus here is on the quality of interaction between the infant and his or her primary carer. Originally, this primary carer was assumed to be the mother but his theories have been developed since Bowlby's claim in 1951:

Mother love in infancy and childhood is as important for mental health as are vitamins and proteins for physical health.

(1951)

Now, it is recognised that attachment is not just between mother and child but is important also in relationships with fathers, siblings and other carers. The relevance of attachment styles has also been applied to people's ongoing relationships with a range of others from childhood and throughout adulthood (Howe, 2011).

Mary Ainsworth's research found different patterns of 'secure' and 'insecure' attachment to carers and argued that children's emotional development could be endangered through unresponsive or abusive care (Ainsworth et al., 1978). Social workers and other professionals still use these measures of attachment, for example to assess parent–child relationships and to consider appropriate fostering and adoption placements in terms of the attachment styles of carers and children.

Recent discoveries in neuroscience have added weight to attachment theory through the exploration of infant brain development (Gerhardt, 2004; Stewart-Brown, 2008; Cozolino, 2014). Researchers in this field have argued that the pathways or 'neural networks' of the brain are definitively affected by attachment, and irreparable damage may be done to the infant brain in the first few critical years through neglect or abuse. This critical period, however, is still debated. Critics such as Wastell and White (2012) dispute some of these assertions and maintain that the critical period of three years for a baby for satisfactory brain development is at best exaggerated since flexibility and recovery are possible. They assert that dogma about irreparable damage has been used in policy making to remove children from their families and to push for their adoption without trying to offer proper support to the birth family.

Reflective exercise

How do the psychological theories discussed above apply to social work?

Think about these in relation to:

➤ Assessing adopters and placing children for adoption

➤ Assessing the possible neglect of children by their carers

Like Piaget's theories, psychodynamic and attachment theories have also been criticised for their cultural specificity, and it can be argued that they apply largely to Western societies. In many non-Western societies young children may be brought up by a larger community network of adults and older children in a rural village, for example, so that biological parents or one main attachment figure is not of the same vital importance.

Biological and psychological developmental theories generally focus on children's immaturity and lack of competence and are criticised for these negative associations for children. Some argue further that it is a false assumption that adulthood is a complete and ideal state, and that children are incomplete beings until they arrive there (Lee, 2001; Prout, 2005; Cregan and Cuthbert, 2014; Archard, 2015). These ideas are discussed further in the next section below.

As noted above, however, developmental theories are very influential in professional, legal and political attitudes to children, and these determine the structure of our society. Western educational structures and health and welfare systems are founded on developmental theories that lead professionals to chart progress in an individual child's growth and their emotional and cognitive development (Cregan and Cuthbert, 2014). In social work, developmental theories are used in assessing children's care and in determining 'good enough' parenting. For example, the Framework for Assessment of Children in Need and their Families (DoH, 2000) (now incorporated into Working Together (DfE, 2015b)) and its accompanying guidance is based on psychological theory even though it also includes an 'ecological' context. Guidance on the 'Assessment Framework' says the following about assessments of children: *'the criteria for defining their needs is clearly developmental, grounded in psychological literature'* (Seden, 2001, p. 58).

Sociological theories

Sociological theories as they have developed since the end of the twentieth century are arguably more 'child-centred' than psychological theories. Although the latter focus on children and childhood, they are more likely to see children as objects of study or concern (Foucault, 1975). Sociologists have challenged this approach to children and place more emphasis on the child as an active participant in society.

The first socialisation theories from earlier in the twentieth century fit more into a developmental model, however. As typified by Talcott Parsons (Parsons, 1956) they considered the ways in which children become imbued with the attitudes, morals and norms of their culture in interaction with the adults in their world. This is also a form of seeing children as *developing* beings and has been criticised for being preoccupied with families rather than children themselves. In this respect, Jenks (2004, p. 88) argued that socialisation theories *'have little or no time for children'*.

Later sociologists have emphasised the active role of children in society. They built on the work of Ariès as discussed above and developed theories about the social construction of childhood, arguing that childhood is not a natural *given* but that society's separation of childhood from adulthood according to age is largely arbitrary (Jenks, 1982; James and Prout, 1997). This can be demonstrated in, for example, the age in England at which one can marry (16), vote (18) or be convicted of a crime (10). These age boundaries are not self evident and they differ from society to society. For example even in European societies the legal age of sexual consent varies. In the UK it is 16 whilst in Germany and Italy it is 14 and in Ireland 17.

Prout and James (1997) developed a 'paradigm' to challenge accepted views about childhood. It emphasised the diverse experiences of children, rather than seeing childhood as a universal state.

Some of the 'key features' of the paradigm can be summarised as follows:

> *Childhood is understood as a social construction.*

> *Childhood is a variable of social analysis (along with other variables such as gender, class or ethnicity).*

> *Children's cultures and relationships are worthy of study in their own right.*

> *Children are and must be seen as active in the construction and determination of their own social lives.*

(Prout and James, 1997, p. 8)

They also advocated that using ethnographic research rather than experiment or survey is important in giving children a direct 'voice' about their lives, as well as seeing them in an active role as 'social actors'. Wyness (2015) debates the prevalent notion of children's *agency* in childhood studies. He notes that whilst children are by definition actors in society, their agency is mediated by the powers of adults who, as carers or educators, for example, may oppose or support children and young people in their wishes and aims.

Sociologists have also used ideas from poststructuralist theory to analyse the concept of childhood (Jenks, 1996; James and Prout, 1997; Lee, 2001). These assert that the words 'child' and 'childhood' are not fixed in meaning but are socially produced. They take their meaning from prevailing social and political discourses and these are constantly changing. Jenks (1996) explains this in relation to the way that professional practice and institutions play a part in defining childhood:

The archetype of the child is sustained in language and in the discourses of the professions, the institutions and the specialisms which serve to patrol the boundaries marked out around childhood as a social status.

(Jenks, 1996, p. 12)

Some proponents of these theories also argue that adults may use the concept of childhood to exercise their power over children and young people (Wyness, 2006). They explain how the binary concepts such as *child* and *adult, mature* and *immature* may be used by adults to exclude children and young people from certain spheres of activity. This is an argument used by proponents of children's rights as we discuss in the next chapter.

Reflective exercise

Can you think of other binary or opposite terms used to describe children in relation to adults?

As remarked above, developmental theories generally have been criticised for their assumption that adulthood is a complete and ideal state and that children are incomplete beings until they arrive there (Lee, 2001; Cregan and Cuthbert, 2014; Archard, 2015). In relation to this, there has been a debate about children as *beings* or *becomings* (Lee, 2001; Walkerdine, 2004; Prout, 2005). Lee's argument is that this supposed distinction between childhood (*becoming*) and adulthood (*being*) is false or at least blurred since it is difficult to maintain in the modern world that even adults attain an ultimate completeness. In a society where rapid change is the norm, adults must often adapt to changes in their employment and may need to retrain to meet requirements for new skills and in new technologies. In their personal life they are also more likely to change partners and change their place of residence:

> As adulthood is led into flexibility by socio-economic and cultural change across the globe, it is clear that stable, complete standard adulthood can no longer be presumed to exist.
>
> (Lee, 2001, p. 19)

On the other hand, children have increased economic power previously afforded to adults since they are now important consumers, exposed to goods and services through television and the internet and able to influence adults' purchases through 'pester power' (Lee, op. cit., p. 75). As is discussed in more detail in Chapter 7 they are also party to adult knowledge including sexual content through these media and are no longer the 'innocents' of old (Buckingham, 2000).

Lee (op. cit.) argues further that no human being is complete and we could all be best described as being in a state of 'unlimited becoming' since we all depend on the assistance of tools, animals and other people to extend our powers.

Reflective exercise

What are the implications for social work practice of adopting some of the above sociological views about children and childhood?

Recently, there has been a move to combine the insights and understandings of children and childhood from the different disciplines of biology, psychology and sociology to reach a more sophisticated and complex theoretical model (Smith, 2010). Wyness (2015) questions whether such a fully interdisciplinary approach, integrating different disciplines, is possible but accepts that different perspectives can provide *'broader and richer analyses of childhood'* (p. 6).

The Global child: cultural differences

The emphasis on children's experiences and the diversity of their lives in James and Prout's (1997) social constructionist paradigm has continued to be a key feature in childhood studies. In the late twentieth century, studies by a variety of researchers in Northern Europe and Scandinavia explored children's lived experiences about, for example, the way their lives were structured by adults who dictate where they should be in terms of place and time such as school, playgrounds and bedtimes (Ennew, 1994; Qvortrup, 1997; Solberg, 1997).

As noted earlier in the chapter, many writers on the subject of childhood now argue that the construction of childhood discussed above from Ariès to the modern day in Western society (or the 'Global North') is based narrowly in time and place (Smith, 2010; Cregan and Cuthbert, 2014; Wyness, 2015). Cregan and Cuthbert (2014) argue that the concept of childhood in the Global North is a relatively recent phenomenon and geographically limited:

From the 1920s onwards children and childhood came to be understood and approached in developed modern societies in ways that were utterly foreign prior to, and for the majority of the world's population at, that time.

(Cregan and Cuthbert, 2014, p. 4)

The day to day realities for children who do not live in the Global North are very different from the ones referred to in many studies of 'Western Childhood'. Current concerns about children also differ significantly. In the developing world (or 'Global South') many predominant concerns are associated with poverty, such as lack of access to education, the need for children to work and forced marriages. In the Global North some of the recent concerns for children arise from increased affluence and centre on the dangers of technology, including online grooming, early sexualisation and lack of activity both in and outside the home.

Cregan and Cuthbert (op. cit.) consider the lives of children for whom childhood remains different from the Western ideals, ideals that have been enshrined in global policies and conventions such as the United Nations Convention on the Rights of the Child. Examples include those of child labour in societies where children are needed to contribute to the economics of their family and the experiences of child soldiers and child 'orphans'.

Wyness (2015) explains how such children's experiences differ from 'standard childhoods', as defined by the Western model of childhood. In the Western model children are regarded as being exploited if they are in paid labour and miss their schooling. Definitions of child labour by the International Labour Organisation (ILO, 1999, 2011) do not take into account the real dilemmas that children face in the Global South, nor their wishes to contribute materially to the welfare of their households. Whilst these children have no wish to be exploited and want to have safe conditions of work, they may see more value in working than in education for the survival of themselves and their families. Kjørholt (2013) interviewed children who attended children's parliaments in Ethiopia and found that, in this fragile economy, children recognised that their parents should be sending them to school but also that their own contribution was necessary to keep their family out of extreme poverty. One young boy in the study asked, *'who is going to do my part of the work?'* if he went to school (Kjørholt, 2013, p. 250).

Nieuwenhuys (2009) reports on an international meeting of working children in Kundapur who objected to the International Labour Organisation's pressures. They objected, for example, to a boycott on products made by children. They wanted to work but also wanted security from exploitation and to have their hours at work adjusted to enable them to attend education as well. They also wanted the ILO to tackle their fundamental problems of poverty and poor health care.

There are similar dilemmas for children in so-called child-headed households, children who are left caring for their families after their parents or guardians have died. Payne (2012) interviewed young people in Zambia who became the head of their household after the death or serious illness of the adults in their family. She found that these young people had difficulty not just in maintaining their households but in coping with the interventions of social workers and aid agencies. Whilst the children wanted their admittedly precarious situations to be legitimised, these agencies often considered them to be 'at risk' and did not help to support them in their role. This has been seen as an issue for children in a range of African countries such as Rwanda and Zimbabwe. Tsegaye (2009) has argued that children in these circumstances often do feel they are capable of caring for younger siblings and they do not want to be separated from each other by being taken into institutional care. They wish to stay in their communities and keep their parents' property, which they might lose if this were entrusted to extended family members. There is more debate in the next chapter about some of these issues in the Global South in relation to children's rights.

It is instructive to note that young carers in the UK face a similarly ambiguous situation. Their relationships with professional workers are often like those experienced by children in child-headed households in Africa. These young carers are involved in caring for parents or other relatives who, for example, have a disability or who have mental health issues. They may do nursing tasks such as giving medication and bathing as well as basic domestic work (Aldridge and Becker, 2002). These young people often wish to continue with these responsibilities, but would like to receive support with this rather than being regarded by professionals as victims at risk who need protection or care themselves.

Children, family and environment

It is not within the scope of this book to consider in detail the many theories about the family, but it is important to take account of children's relationships with their family, friends and neighbourhoods and the wider environment. Social workers need to take a holistic view of children to conduct assessments of children in need and their families in accordance with the assessment guidance outlined in Chapters 1 and 7. This guidance, whilst placing children centrally, also requires social workers to consider child development, parenting and environmental factors.

Proponents of relational theory suggest that individuals cannot be understood without an understanding of context. Thus, Smart (2007) argues that an understanding of individuals will need to take account of all people's meaningful connections with relatives and friends, living or dead, and with animals, possessions and so on. In thinking about children in their families and about parenting, attachment theory, discussed above, is one of importance to social work practice as are socialisation theories such as that of Talcott Parsons.

Bronfenbrenner's (1979) ecological model considers the impact of systems on the individual child, some near, such as immediate family, friends and school (the 'microsystem'), and those whose influence is further removed such as community and wider family networks and institutions (the 'exosystem'). The 'macrosystem' consists of more widespread cultural, social and economic context. Thus the influence of environment on an individual child, for example poverty, can be tracked through the various systems in which the child lives.

The Good Childhood Report (The Children's Society, 2016) adds to our understanding of the context of children's lives through its multiple surveys about the well-being of more than 60,000 children over a period of eleven years. Many of these surveys were based in England but some have included other countries. The 2016 report confirmed earlier findings that children's direct experiences of, for example, positive family relationships and a good local environment were stronger indicators of their well-being than structural factors such as poverty, which affected adults more than children. A significant trend over time has been an increasing gender gap, with girls becoming more unhappy with their lives in the UK than boys.

> Girls are less happy than they used to be, with 1 in 7 (14%) 10 to 15 year old girls unhappy with their lives as a whole – up from 11% over a five year period. By contrast, the proportion of boys of the same age who are unhappy with their lives as a whole has remained stable at 11%...The difference is even starker when it comes to how children feel about the way they look. More than one third (34%) of girls are unhappy with their appearance – up from 30% over five years. By contrast, the proportion of boys of the same age who are unhappy with their appearance has remained stable at around 20%.
>
> (The Children's Society, 2016, p. 3)

The report recommends governmental monitoring of children's well-being, better access to mental health services and a 'voice' for children in decisions about local provision of services.

Children's views of their place in society: what children say about adults' attitudes

The main focus of this book is on children and young people's views about their treatment by professionals, especially social workers. However, young people who are not involved with social work can provide a broader picture of their experience of adults' attitudes. Studies have researched young people's views about their worlds and about how they are treated generally by adults. This gives an idea of children's everyday lives and how they experience the impact of adults' attitudes.

Mayall's (2002) studies with children from as young as 4 years old attempted to understand their worlds from their point of view, how they experienced their daily life in the home and school and their relationships with adults. Mayall (op. cit.) found that children saw themselves as defined by their relationships with parents and how their parents behaved:

> *Parental definitions constitute them as children. While, according to young people, these definitions vary somewhat between families, it is through their parents' behaviour that people learn to do childhoods.*

> (Mayall, 2002, p. 45)

Young people talked about their negotiations with adults for free time, about tasks in the house and their control of their own use of time and space. By virtue of their age and authority, parents had the upper hand in such negotiations. However, young people used strategies such as refusing to comply, bargaining and delaying to help their cause.

Corsaro (2009) conducted a variety of ethnographic studies of pre-school and primary school children. He spent time with them in nurseries, schools and playgrounds, playing the role of an incompetent adult to try and be accepted as part of their group in order to observe their worlds. In relation to adults he found that children as young as 2 years made persistent efforts to gain control of their lives and used strategies for challenging the rules laid down by adult authority. Some of the examples he found used by pre-school children to thwart authority were:

➤ Lining chairs across the room to walk on

➤ Children smuggling forbidden 'mini toys' in their pockets

➤ Avoiding 'clean up time' by e.g. pretending not to hear, feigning injury, going round hugging other children.

He found that the older children aged 7–12 he studied were still challenging adults' rules, and their desire for autonomy increased as they got older.

Butler et al.'s (2005) study of the relationship between children and parental authority found that children said they largely accepted the decisions that parents made on their behalf, although not without question. Where they did assert their own views this tended to be in relation to aspects of their personal identity such as choosing what clothes to wear or organising their bedrooms. Other studies such as those of Morrow (1999) with school-aged children reported that these often felt they were not sufficiently heard by the adults in their life at home and school or their views regarded with respect. As one young participant age 15 memorably said:

> *we are people too and shouldn't be treated like low-lifes just because we are younger. I think kids deserve the same sort of respect that we are expected to give to so-called adults.*

> (Morrow, 1999, p. 167).

This view is very similar to the reports of young people throughout this book about their dealings with social workers.

Conclusion

This overview of perspectives on children and childhood has demonstrated ways that children's lives have changed over time and differ according to geography and culture. In the developed West, children's lives are separated from those of adults by the times when, and places where, they are allowed to be. Western society continues to be particularly concerned about the protection of babies and young children from abuse and the control of older young people's behaviour. Professionals in health, education and social care use theoretical perspectives from biology and psychology in their work with children and young people, while insights from sociology that are arguably more child-centred have less influence. The question remains whether as a society we are child-centred.

Summary points

➢ The separation of children's and adults' spheres of activity in the 'West' has developed over the last few centuries.

➢ Modern day attitudes to children and young people vary between protection and control.

➢ Theories about childhood from biology, psychology and sociology give differing perspectives on children's lives, the former two stressing the developing child and the latter children's active participation in society.

➤ Children's lives in the 'Global South' mean that their concerns and those of adults differ from the 'Global North', and are more affected by issues relating to poverty.

➤ Children's direct experiences in their families and their environment have an important impact on their well-being.

➤ Children themselves have found their lives defined by adults, sometimes to their dissatisfaction.

Further reading and resources

Cregan, K. and Cuthbert, D. (2014) *Global Childhoods: Issues and Debates*. London: Sage.
This highlights the differing lives of children in the Global North and South.

James, A. and Prout, A. (eds) (2015) *Constructing and Reconstructing Childhood*, Classic edition. London: Falmer.
This classic text outlines research and theoretical perspectives on childhood.

Smith, R. (2010) *A Universal Child?* Basingstoke: Palgrave Macmillan.
Considers childhood and the various contexts in which children find themselves.

Wyness, M. (2015) *Childhood*. Cambridge: Polity Press.
Considers children's agency from many perspectives.

The Children's Society (2016) *The Good Childhood Report*. London: The Children's Society.
Provides interesting insights into children's experiences and the factors that influence their feelings of well-being.

The *Child of our Time* BBC Series by Professor Robert Winston charted the development of 25 children born in 2000 and gives their perspectives and those of other family members on their lives at annual intervals. Some of these are available at: http://www.bbc.co.uk/programmes.

3
Children's Rights and Child-Centred Practice

Introduction

How does the championing of children's rights contribute to child-centred practice in social work? This chapter considers the rise of children's rights awareness in Britain and the West and its impact globally. It examines the laws and policies that have been drawn up to support the development of children's rights and looks at children's views about their rights. It also considers the impact of children's rights on professional practice, in particular on social work practice. Included in the discussion is the role and rise of advocacy, although the practice of advocacy and working with advocates will be featured in a following chapter.

The rise of rights

To understand children's rights in theory and practice it is helpful to look back briefly at the development of human rights generally in modern Western society. In former times, 'human rights' alluded to the rights of able-bodied white men. One of the most quoted assertions about human rights regarded such rights as natural and self-evident. The 1776 Declaration of Independence of the United States stated:

> We hold these truths to be self-evident, that all men are created equal, that they are endowed by their Creator with certain inalienable Rights, that among these are Life, Liberty and the pursuit of happiness.

However, rights theorists such as Dworkin (1978) and MacIntyre (1984) have disputed this self evidence and have seen rights as value laden despite their moral force. Dworkin (1978, p. 165) spoke of rights as 'moral trump cards' because the declaration that 'this is my right' has often been used to stop all counter argument. They argue that asserting people's rights does not free society from moral dilemmas about decision making and whose rights should prevail.

Reflective exercise: *Conflicting rights*

What are your rights as a citizen, worker or student?

You may think of the right to vote, the right to be treated equally as an employee.

Can you think how asserting these rights may conflict with the rights of others?

Who should have rights and what these consist of have changed over time, and their assertion has been used to exclude certain categories of people who are least powerful in society, such as women, children, disabled people and minority ethnic groups (Brown, 1995; Taylor, 1996). Critics have argued that a society based on rights leads to selfishness and a lack of social cohesion since it implies that each individual should pursue their own wants and needs rather than a collective goal. These arguments are not new. Karl Marx (cited in McLellan, 1971) expressed this negative viewpoint:

> *None of the so-called rights of man goes beyond egoistic man, man as he is in civil society, namely an individual withdrawn behind his private interests and whims and separated from the community.*

(McLellan, 1971, p. 104)

Whether selfish or not, certainly Western society has become increasingly rights aware and litigious over the past decades. This is evident from the large funds needed to pay for legal claims in the National Health Service in the UK and from the numbers of lawyers who cold call for business, asking if you want to claim compensation for an accident you might not have had.

Feminist critics of rights discourse have argued that morality based solely on rights ignores the fact that we are not all independent, autonomous beings, but that we need to take account of our relationships and our dependence on each other (Gilligan, 1982; Tronto, 1993; Sevenhuijsen, 1998). They have advocated instead that an *'ethic of care'* should be more central to thinking about morality. This ethical model emphasises the importance of care in our networks of relationships and our commitments to one another and society.

This model applies well to children since, like other groups in society, they are dependent on their relationships with carers. However, the importance of care does not suggest that the notion of rights should be abandoned since, as Cockburn (2005) has argued, a rights discourse can be a useful strategy to further children's interests. I have argued elsewhere that an ethic of care alongside rights provides a good practice model for work with children and young people (Barnes, 2012).

Children's rights: theories

Children's rights have also been promoted in Western society since the 1990s and, like human rights generally, there are complexities in children's rights discourse. Whereas some authors have assumed the self evidence of children's rights (Lansdown, 2001; Franklin, 2002), others have argued against this, especially where children's autonomy is concerned, since they see children as naturally part of their family network rather than as individuals with separate rights (Cooper, 1998).

Protectionists, best interests and liberationists

The rights of children are usually divided into the categories of *Provision*, *Protection* and *Participation*, which are categories in the United Nations Convention on the Rights of the Child (1989) discussed in detail below. In the Western world the main debates and contentions are not around the first two of provision and protection, but participation rights, often termed autonomy or *citizenship* rights, are the subject of more dispute. Most adults would agree with the need to provide care for children, such as food and shelter, and to protect them from harms such as abuse and exploitation. Even these, however, are obviously more difficult to achieve in societies where poverty and war exist.

Until the late twentieth century the concept of children's rights was mainly a *protectionist* one, conforming to views considered in the previous chapter that children are immature and vulnerable (James and Prout, 1997). This is a model that regards children as not yet rational or capable of making decisions for themselves, a model that justifies the control of adults (Archard, 2015). Children were long regarded as the property of their parents, who should make decisions for them, acting responsibly in their *best interests* and on their behalf. If a child disagreed with any decision at the time, it was expected that they would recognise, once mature, that their parents had been right (Archard, 2015). An example that is often given is that of a child's education. The argument is that children would quite often choose not to attend school if left to make this choice for themselves. However, as adults they would thank their parents for making sure they had a good education, which enabled them to have a satisfying career and so on. The negative side of this model, however, is that children would play no active part and have no voice in their life decisions.

A *best interests* model remains problematic since there is no objective way of determining this. Even if we decide in good faith something that we think, as a parent or as a professional, will be in a child's best interests, there are so many options and variables that we cannot know the future outcome of our decisions (Archard, 2015). It can also be argued that these decisions vary over societies and cultures. For example, in many cultures the physical punishment of children is still regarded as being in their best interests, helping them to be disciplined and respectful to adults. It should also be noted that, whilst the majority of adults act in children's best interests, it is very clear from the instances of abuse and neglect in society that this is not universally the case. Many rights proponents argue that children should therefore have more say in determining their own best interests (Boylan and Dalrymple, 2009).

A *liberationist* perspective of children's rights advances an extreme opposite position to that of protectionists. It sees children as an oppressed group in a similar way that women or minority ethnic groups are often seen as marginalised by the more powerful in society. This was a view taken in the 1970s by child liberationists such as Farson (1974) and Holt (1975), who maintained that children should be afforded the same rights and privileges as adults, if they wished. Included in this should be the right to vote, to live where they wished and to decide about their own education. They did believe, however, that children should be nurtured and protected by adults if they so wished. This radical view is not one that receives much credence in our society currently, and extreme autonomy rights such as children deciding to live away from home have not been supported by later children's rights proponents. However, these commentators still argued that there is an oppressive segregation of children (Ennew, 1994; Qvortrup, 1994). Social constructionist theories discussed in the previous chapter also see the distinction between childhood and adulthood as arbitrary but do not support full *liberation* (Jenks, 1982; Prout and James, 1997). They argue instead that children should be afforded the opportunity to express their views and participate in decisions as competent 'social actors'.

Reflective exercise

Where would you place social work in the scale of protectionist and liberationist views of children's rights?

Citizenship rights and participation

Children are not regarded as full 'citizens' in society, even in the liberal West. They can best be described as being *potential* citizens since government policies see them as future workers rather than current participants in the state (Lister, 2003). Their lack of economic independence also prevents them being taken seriously as equal citizens (Qvortrup, 1994; Alderson, 2008), although, as Lee (2001) has argued, children's access to the media has increased their participation as consumers even though this is normally mediated through adults.

There have been recent moves to lower the age of voting in the UK but most commentators have not seen this as necessary or desirable for children younger than 16 (Roche, 1999; Archard, 2015). The creation of a Commissioner for Children in England in 2005 (following the appointment of a Commissioner in Wales) aimed to increase children's participation in the state. The Commissioner's remit was to represent and report on the interests of children through their direct involvement but this was mainly through consultation.

At the time of writing, a group named 'Amplify' is involved in advising the Children's Commissioner in England and her team. In 2017 this was a group of around 20–30 young people from ages 11 to 18 who met together 'to share views and experiences' three times a year and who met in smaller groups more frequently. The website says:

> They are at the heart of the Children's Commissioner's work and make sure the voice of children and young people is listened to and taken seriously.
>
> (Children's Commissioner's Office, 2017)

Initially, the Commissioner's office had very limited powers to investigate and access information or enter establishments, since such activity was subject to the Secretary of State's approval, but these powers were increased in the Children and Families Act 2014 and the success of this has been under review.

I discuss the detailed practice skills of promoting participation in social work with children and young people in a later chapter since this is a key feature of child-centred practice. Briefly here I look at some theories of participation. Hart's (1992) 'ladder of participation', adapted from Arnstein (1969), is well known. It charts the various degrees or 'rungs' of children's participation starting with the very minimal level (1) at which adults may manipulate children for their own ends, through a level where children are consulted and then up to the highest level (8), where children share their decision making with adults (Figure 3.1).

The Ladder of Participation

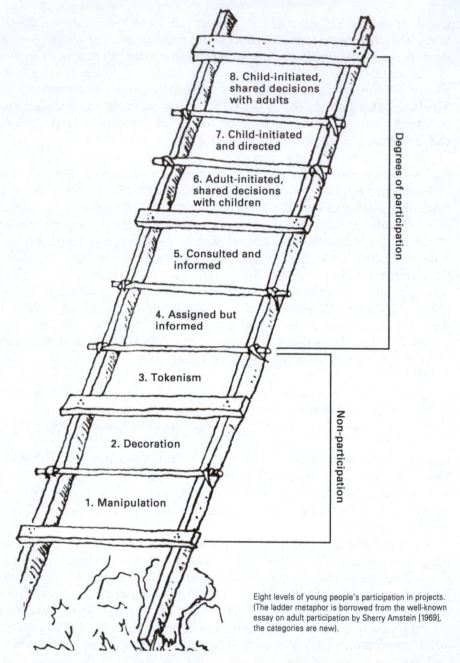

8. Child-initiated, shared decisions with adults

7. Child-initiated and directed

6. Adult-initiated, shared decisions with children

5. Consulted and informed

4. Assigned but informed

3. Tokenism

2. Decoration

1. Manipulation

Degrees of participation

Non-participation

Eight levels of young people's participation in projects. (The ladder metaphor is borrowed from the well-known essay on adult participation by Sherry Arnstein [1969], the categories are new).

Figure 3.1   Ladder of participation

Source: Adapted from Hart (1992) with kind permission from UNICEF

A major issue in the participation and autonomy debate is whether individual children have the competence or capacity to be able to participate meaningfully. This is something that we explored in Chapter 1 in relation to children and young people's decisions about their health care and the *'Gillick competency'* principle. As discussed there, because there is no definition of what is 'sufficient understanding' in law to make these decisions they have to be tested out in court on a case-by-case basis.

The Fraser guidelines developed from the *Gillick* case base a young person's competency to make decisions (in this case regarding contraception) on a professional's assessment of their understanding of the advice given and on their best interests but also on whether the young person can be persuaded to inform their parents. This element of *persuasion* is contentious since it involves an unequal balance of power between the professional and the young person. Guidance to social workers in work with looked after children (DfE, 2015d) can be applied to work with children and young people in other areas of social care.

> *Can the child understand the question being asked of them?*

> *Do they appreciate the options open to them?*

> *Can they weigh up the pros and cons of each option?*

> *Can they express a clear personal view on the matter, as distinct from repeating what someone else thinks they should do?*

> *Can they be reasonably consistent in their view on the matter, or are they constantly changing their mind?*

(p. 94)

People question whether judgements about children's competence can be correlated at all with their age. Clearly there is a difference between the competence of an average 2 year old and that of a 16 year old. Archard (2015) argues that because of such differences it does not make sense to 'lump' all children together with regard to assessment of their competence. He suggests that older children should be assessed in terms of their rationality, maturity and independence. There is a drawback to this view since such assessments can be quite subjective. Children and young people, even those of the same age, vary considerably. Nevertheless, other writers have argued that young people are unfairly excluded from participation since many adults could also be judged incompetent (Lee, 2001; James and Prout, 2015). Not all adults are wise and capable but they are still afforded rights denied to children and young people.

Another way of looking at the issue, suggested by Woodhead (2006) and Cockburn (2007), is to consider what adults need to do to enable young people's participation by making public and political spaces more child friendly. In Chapter 8 there is a good practice example of this – of a social work manager who made efforts to completely alter the ambience of statutory review meetings for looked after children to make them more child friendly.

Children's rights in families

To afford children rights does not necessarily deny adults their rights. For example, if 16 year olds had the vote this would not deny the vote to adults. However, some people express concerns that the promotion of children's rights may sometimes infringe the rights of adults. This has been of particular concern with regard to the rights of parents and carers. Wardle (1996), for example, has argued that family relationships can be undermined by insistence on children's rights. Similarly, Cooper (1998) has maintained that the lives of family members are so interdependent that asserting rights can lead to unhelpfully polarised views and that what is really needed are negotiation and flexibility. This anxiety is also held by some foster carers and residential workers in respect of caring for children. An advocate in the author's research expressed her view that it could sometimes be counterproductive for young people to assert their rights in these situations:

> We have had occasion when they've marched back in the children's home or foster care and said, 'I know my rights – you can't do this and you can't do that'. I think sometimes they take it a bit literally.

This indicates one of the difficulties for young people in upholding their rights, especially if they are in the care system, since they risk jeopardising their relationships with carers if they complain and may also risk rejection and having to move to another placement. This also indicates the relatively powerless situation of children in relation to the adults in their lives, an issue that is explored further in Chapter 5.

Since parents and carers are responsible for providing for and protecting children in their care, they may wish to restrict their children's right to self-determination and choice if they think this poses a risk. For example, a young teenager may wish to use her mobile phone to 'chat' to strangers but her parents, becoming aware that she may be putting herself at risk of grooming, decide to limit her use of the mobile. This is a dilemma illustrated by the following case example.

Case example: Sani: Rights and risks

Sani is 13 and she has been in foster care for six months. Her family came from Pakistan and settled in England in the 1970s. She has a younger brother and sister still at home. Her father was quite strict and did not want her to have any boyfriends, but Sani, who is very mature for her age, became involved with a boy of 15, Ronnie, whom she met at school. Her parents, especially her father, were very angry about this relationship and told her to stop seeing Ronnie but she kept on seeing him and coming home late. Sani's father then found on her mobile phone some naked images of herself, which she had sent to Ronnie, and explicit texts that made it apparent they had a sexual relationship. He refused to let her stay at home, saying to children's services that she was out of control.

The police have become involved and have interviewed Ronnie about his relationship with Sani. She is now not allowed to see him or communicate with him at all, and she is not allowed to have her mobile phone.

Do you think this is this an infringement of Sani's rights?

How would you balance rights and risks in this situation?

Lee (2005) has argued that one reason for many adults' ambivalence about children's rights is that they have difficulty in seeing their children as separate individuals in their own right and retain some of the old notions of children as possessions. He has presented a concept of 'separability' defined as the *'possibility of children's temporary and partial separation'* (Lee, op. cit.: 37). He maintains that this view could lead to adults valuing children more and seeing children's rights as less threatening, since it poses less threat to adult–child relations.

Children's rights: law and policy

United Nations Convention on the Rights of the Child

In Chapter 1 we discussed briefly the United Nations Convention on the Rights of the Child (UNCRC), which is a major landmark in the history of children's rights internationally. Following the Second World War there were movements to promote rights generally in response to the horrors of that war, in particular the Holocaust and the nuclear bombing of Hiroshima and Nagasaki. The Universal Declaration of Human Rights was drafted in 1948 and the European Convention on Human Rights in 1950. The UNCRC was based on the earlier UN Declaration of the Rights of the

Child, 1959 and was adopted by the UN General Assembly in 1989. It was ratified by the UK government in 1991 and has, to date, been ratified by all governments apart from the United States, where it has had vocal opponents. Some factions in the US have seen it as an attempt at state control of the family home and a dangerous attack on parents' rights (Kilbourne, 1998).

As noted in Chapter 1, the UNCRC contains 54 articles, which include basic rights such as those to life, health, food, shelter and protection, as well as rights to education, privacy and freedom of expression. It also encompasses a 'best interests' principle (Article 3) and 'participation principle' (Article 12), which are particularly relevant to child-centred practice. However, it is worth highlighting other very important articles:

> Article 1 crucially defines what is meant by 'a child': *'every human being below the age of eighteen'*, although this is qualified, *'unless under the law applicable to the child, majority is attained earlier'*. This leaves states signed up to the Convention leeway to set their own upper age limits.

> Article 2 asserts that children's rights in the Convention should be ensured without discrimination on any grounds of *'race, colour, sex, language, religion, political or other opinion, national, ethnic or social origin, property, disability, birth or other status'*.

> As we have seen in Chapter 1, the primary best interests principle is contained in Article 3, but Article 18 also asserts the responsibility of parents and legal guardians to act in the best interests of children.

Other 'participation' rights besides Article 12, discussed in Chapter 1, which is a right to express views and be heard are encompassed in:

> Article 13: right to freedom of expression

> Article 14: right to freedom of thought, conscience and religion

> Article 15: freedom of association

> Article 16: right to privacy

> Article 17: right to information.

There are also numerous Articles to ensure protection and provision for children, such as Article 19: the right to protection from violence, abuse and neglect; and Article 35: the right to protection from trafficking. Other articles cover rights of children separated from parents, refugee children and disabled children and adoption rights. There are also articles regarding health and education rights and rights in relation to penal law.

Since the Convention does not have legal force in the UK, progress in implementing its articles has been slow and patchy. Freeman (2002), protesting about this lack of progress ten years after ratification in the UK, called for it to be incorporated into law. It has been embedded in Norwegian law since 1989. Also, as commented in Chapter 1, the Children Act 1989 and similar legislation in Scotland and Northern Ireland did not transform the children's rights agenda to the degree expected in the UK. This was despite some new participation principles for young people who are the subject of court proceedings and for looked after children.

Human Rights Act

Initially, it was hoped that further emphasis on rights via the Human Rights Act 1998 (HRA 1998) might strengthen children's rights also, because it incorporated the European Convention on Human Rights (ECHR). Until the introduction of the HRA 1998 in the UK, the European Convention was the only access to ruling on individual cases, but it involved a lengthy and expensive application procedure via the European court in Strasbourg and was therefore very difficult for children to access. The introduction of the HRA 1998 in 2000 gave rise to fears of mass applications but as Brammer (2015) reports, *'fear that courts would be swamped by applications does not appear to have materialised'* (p. 116). The main exception to this has been in respect of immigration and asylum.

There have been rulings under several sections of the Human Rights Act for children. For example, under Article 3: *'No one shall be subjected to torture or to inhuman or degrading treatment'*, a local authority was found in breach of its duty to protect children (*E v United Kingdom* [2003] 1 FLR 348). The authority failed to monitor the behaviour of a known offender living in the family, and it was found that if they had done so, damage to the children could have been minimised or avoided.

Some commentators argued that the combination of the Human Rights Act and the UNCRC might bring great benefits in policy and practice with young people (Fortin, 2002) but there has been little recourse in legal and governmental systems to promote children's rights (Fortin, 2006; Lyon, 2007; Williams, 2007). Lyon (2007) questioned whether there has been any real commitment to children's rights in the UK since the government has emphasised the unenforceable rights under the UNCRC rather than the enforceable ones of the ECHR.

At the time of writing there are debates about plans to repeal the Human Rights Act 1998 and introduce a 'Bill of Rights'. This development has been commented on by the review of the UK's progress on UNCRC as noted below.

Progress of children's rights in the UK

The UN Committee reviews all governments' progress in implementing the UNCRC. A report of the Children's Commissioner on implementation was published in the UK in 2015 (Children's Commissioner's Office, 2015). This drew particular attention to austerity measures resulting in child poverty, reductions in recourse to legal advice for children and their carers, the government's intention to repeal the Human Rights Act 1998 (thus breaking the link with the ECHR and individual recourse to law) and the need for proper funding of children's mental health services. It also reiterated matters previously highlighted in the 2008 report such as the low age of criminal responsibility. Many of the recommendations are UK wide but the review also includes specific recommendations for changes in Scotland, Northern Ireland and Wales. For example, it recommends a fully integrated education system in Northern Ireland for Catholic and Protestant children.

Reflective exercise

Do you think that children in the UK have enough rights?

What rights do you think are most important for them?

Children's rights in Africa and the Global South

As briefly noted in Chapter 2, not all nations are equally comfortable with the tenets of the UNCRC. They challenge the notion that childhoods can be seen as universal and object to the individualistic principles imposed by the Global North (Cregan and Cuthbert, 2014). This challenge echoes the complaints of feminist writers about the individualism of rights, as explored earlier. For the 'Global South', the UNCRC's emphasis on rights rather than on family responsibilities for children as well as adults does not fit with their lives and experiences. The African Charter on the Rights and Welfare of the Child (ACRWC) was prepared by the African Committee of Experts on the Rights and Welfare of the Child (1990) as a specifically African alternative to the UNCRC. Whilst it adopts principles in its articles that are contained in the UNCRC such as best interests, non-discrimination and the rights to health and education and to protection from harm, in Section 31 it also contains a set of children's responsibilities to parents, elders, their community and their nation:

Every child shall have responsibilities towards his family and society, the State and other legally recognized communities and the international community. The child, subject to his age and ability, and such limitations as may be contained in the present Charter, shall have the duty:

(a) *to work for the cohesion of the family, to respect his parents, superiors and elders at all times and to assist them in case of need;*

(b) *to serve his national community by placing his physical and intellectual abilities at its service;*

(c) *to preserve and strengthen social and national solidarity;*

(d) *to preserve and strengthen African cultural values in his relations with other members of the society, in the spirit of tolerance, dialogue and consultation and to contribute to the moral well-being of society;*

(e) *to preserve and strengthen the independence and the integrity of his country;*

(f) *to contribute to the best of his abilities, at all times and at all levels, to the promotion and achievement of African Unity.*

(ACRWC, 1990)

As seen in the previous chapter, a child's right to education can clash with their feeling of responsibility to their family and their wish to contribute to its economic survival. Working children's groups have been set up for children working on the streets of Bangalore (Reddy, 2007), and the International Child Movement of Working Children was set up in 1996 with child representatives from Africa, Asia and Latin America. These groups want their work to be respected by adults and they want to be protected from exploitation, as well as having the right to education alongside their work (Liebel, 2003).

The Millennial development goals (United Nations, 2000) have been seen by some as a retreat from rights to an emphasis on child well-being (Jones, 2005; Mekonen, 2010). This is thought to be in recognition that the rights it set to achieve in the UNCRC could not be effected in conditions of poverty and war. The goals are to:

➤ Eradicate extreme hunger

➤ Achieve universal primary education

➤ Promote gender equality and empower women

➤ Reduce child mortality

➤ Improve maternal health

➤ Combat HIV/AIDS, malaria and other diseases

➤ Ensure environmental sustainability

➤ Develop a global partnership for development.

(UN, 2000)

Thus a rights-based agenda is not necessarily agreed by all in the West or elsewhere. However, attempts to put rights into practice for children continue in the UK both by social workers and by children's advocates. A brief consideration of the development of this movement follows, while the practice skills of advocacy in social work and elsewhere follow in Chapter 5.

The growth of children's rights practice and advocacy in the UK

The development of children's rights in practice in the UK has been promoted by a range of campaigning and lobbying groups but it has not been central to social work itself. Organisations such as the Children's Legal Centre, the Children's Rights Alliance for England and Children 1st in Scotland have an advisory capacity and have promoted awareness of children's rights generally and the case for reform. Other organisations have promoted children's rights in the care system. 'Become', formerly known as the 'Who Cares? Trust', was established in 1977. It continues to advise young people in care and young care leavers and encourages their participation in achieving positive change.

Other organisations promote children and young people's participation in decision making. The Youth Parliament, for example, is more of a campaigning group than a decision-making forum akin to an adult parliament. Children's Commissioner's Offices in all four parts of the UK also promote children's consultation and participation. Apart from the Children's Commissioner's Office in England, there is the Children's Commissioner for Wales, the Northern Ireland Commissioner for Children and Young People (NICCY) and the Children and Young People's Commissioner Scotland (CYCPS).

Local children's advocacy services

The first local children's advocacy service in the UK was established by Leicestershire Social Services in 1987 following funding for such services under the Quality Protects initiative (DoH, 1998). The Utting Report (1997) had exposed the large-scale abuse and poor treatment of children living away from home and had made a recommendation '*to provide more effective avenues of complaint and access to independent advocates*'. This led to a dramatic increase in the number of these advocacy services from around forty in 1999 to over a hundred by the end of 2000. Nearly all local authorities now provide advocacy services for children.

In a survey in 2011 a report for the Children's Commissioner's Office noted that children and young people are only entitled to professional advocacy in limited circumstances based on their care status, mental health or situation in the youth justice system (Brady, 2011).

Children's entitlement to advocacy

The following is a summary of children and young people's entitlements to advocacy in legislation, statutory guidance, minimum standards and rules:

> **Statutory entitlement in child care legislation**: for looked after children, care leavers and children in need in making complaints and representations (Children Act 1989, Children (Leaving Care) Act 2000, Adoption and Children Act 2002)

> **Statutory entitlement in mental health legislation**: for young people age 16 or over for representation if they are judged to lack capacity (Mental Capacity Act 2005); for those sectioned or in other circumstances under mental health legislation (Mental Health Act 1983, amended 2007)

> **Statutory guidance**: for looked after children in care planning and reviews and for care leavers and children in residential care (DCSF, 2010a; DfE, 2015c)

> **Under National Minimum Standards**: for looked after children in foster and residential care (DfE, 2011)

> **Under the Rules for Secure Training Centres (STCs)**: for young people detained in an STC to have access to support and representation from an 'independent person' (STC Rules, 1998)

Adapted from Brady (2011, p. 21) and updated.

Details of the major developments in law and policy regarding advocacy and rights are further discussed in this and other chapters. At the time of writing, although nearly all local authorities provided access to children's advocacy services, the nature of this was still patchy. A report for the Children's Commissioner's Office found that there was a wide variation across England in the numbers of advocates available and groups of children served, with the amount individual local authorities spent on these services also varying considerably (Thomas et al., 2016). The Report 'No Good Options' (All Party Parliamentary Group for Children, 2017), an inquiry into children's social care in England, recommended that advocacy services should be protected to improve children's participation in decisions.

Some of the local advocacy services have been entirely managed and funded by local authorities themselves but most are contracted out to voluntary sector organisations including Barnardo's, The Children's Society, Coram Voice and the National Youth Advocacy Service. Even here local authorities provide much of the funding, and this lack of independence may lead to a lack of power to challenge on behalf of children and young people (Dalrymple, 2005; Oliver et al., 2006).

Other issues in practice concerning local authority children's services and children's advocates are discussed in Chapter 5 when looking at social workers working with advocates. There, I also outline the principles of advocacy since it is important for social workers to understand these in order to work with advocates for the benefit of children and young people. National Advocacy Standards were published in 2002 (DoH, 2002) to outline the responsibilities of advocates when working with children.

What children and young people say about their rights

It is clear from a range of studies that children and young people appreciate advocacy services (Oliver et al., 2006; Barnes, 2007; Thomas et al., 2016). This is for a variety of reasons, which are explored in detail in the next chapters about practice issues. But what do they know and say about their rights?

Article 42 of the UNCRC states that parties to the Convention should *'make the principles and provisions of the Convention widely known, by appropriate and active means, to adults and children alike'*.

The most recent report on the progress in the UK towards achieving the realisation of Article 42 found no evidence that any of the governments in the UK (England, Wales, Scotland or Northern Ireland) had taken a systematic approach to raising awareness, knowledge or understanding of the UNCRC amongst children or amongst professionals working with children (Children's Commissioner's Office, 2015). They recommended that this awareness should be included in the schools' curricula.

When asked about their rights, therefore, it is not surprising that young people in the UK are not always well informed. In Norway a survey found that children were very aware of their rights and the UNCRC since schools were active in promoting this awareness (Sandbaek and Einarsson, 2008). A survey in the UK in the same year found that children knew little about the UNCRC and had not received information about it from their school (Children's Rights Alliance for England, 2008). Goodyer's study (2011) found that the foster children she interviewed about their experiences of foster care were also not aware of their rights:

> ...children and young people formed individual understandings of their situation with little apparent awareness of their legal status or their rights or entitlements.
>
> (Goodyer, 2011, p. 118)

In the research conducted by the author outlined in the Introduction, young people who had advocates and social workers were asked about children's rights and said, '*I don't really know what it's about*' and '*Hard to know what children's rights are*'. Some of them, like this 16-year-old girl, gave a more elaborate but still vague answer:

> It's about your rights and stuff and what you've got a chance to be involved and you've got every right to do something – find out your rights basically – what you can and can't do.

This was despite the fact that many of them had attended group meetings with advocates and other children specifically about their rights. However, I did not conclude that rights were not important to these young people; rather, they talked about rights in different language. For example, they were able to talk about elements of rights in practice such as being treated as an equal and being involved in decisions and, very importantly to them, being listened to and treated with respect.

In an investigation into school children's views about rights both before and after the ratification of the UNCRC in the UK, Morrow (1999) found that they felt denied the opportunities and rights that adults take for granted. As noted in the previous chapter, they wanted to be included in decisions that affect their lives, especially as they became teenagers. They wanted to '*have a say*', and, as one young woman expressed it, '*not be treated as low-lifes just because we are younger*' (Morrow, 1999, p. 167).

When children are informed about their rights, however, they are able to understand and find these meaningful. Ofsted (2010b) engaged with 1,834 children and young people between the ages of 4 and 24 about their rights in a variety of contexts, such as a web survey, a national conference, residential schools, and other services. The children were asked to vote on the principles of the UNCRC and the Human Rights Act as well as some extra principles that had emerged for them as important, and this shows more the language that they found meaningful. The five principles they found most important can be summarised as follows:

> To be protected from abuse

> To have an education

> To be helped to keep alive and well

> Not to be discriminated against because of my race, colour, sex, disability, language or beliefs

> Not to be treated or punished in a way that is cruel or meant to make me feel bad about myself.

Other principles they found important that are not in the Human Rights Act or the UN Convention included not being bullied, being able to keep in touch with family members such as grandparents and siblings and being able to 'enjoy myself' (Ofsted, 2010b, p. 15).

Conclusion

This summary of the development of children's rights is important for an understanding of the debates about child-centred practice, since children's rights are now fundamental in national and international law and policy. There is still a debate about the extent of children's rights and whether our society is too protectionist or liberationist. For social work, there is a tension between upholding children's rights and considering risks, which will be seen more starkly in relation to child protection practice discussed in Chapter 7.

Summary points

> The movement for rights, including children's rights, has grown since the late twentieth century and this is echoed in the growth of local children's advocacy services.

> Debates still exist about protectionist and more liberal views of children's rights.

> Children's participation is seen to depend on their age and competence.

> Children's rights are framed by the UNCRC, the Human Rights Act and national law.

➤ In Africa a different set of rights for children emphasises their family responsibilities.

➤ Many children and young people in the UK are not conversant with their actual rights under the UNCRC but can express what is important to them in terms of rights.

Further reading and resources

Archard, D. (2015) *Children, Rights and Childhood*, 3rd edition. London: Routledge.
Contains an informative discussion of children's rights theory and practice.

Brady, L. (2011) *Where is my Advocate? A Scoping Report on Advocacy Services for Children and Young People in England*. London: Office of the Children's Commissioner.
Useful overview of the availability and progress of children's advocacy in England.

Jones, P. and Walker, G. (eds) (2011) *Children's Rights in Practice*. London: Sage.
An accessible overview of children's rights in different practice settings.

UNCRC (1989) *The Convention on the Rights of the Child*. United Nations.
Central to the debate.

Websites for Children's Commissioner's offices in the UK providing advice and consultation for children about their rights:

England: https://www.childrenscommissioner.gov.uk/
Northern Ireland: http://www.niccy.org/
Scotland: https://www.cypcs.org.uk/
Wales: https://www.childcomwales.org.uk/

PART 2
Developing Skills in Child-Centred Practice

4

Communicating and Developing Relationships with Children and Young People

Introduction

What skills do social workers need to become more child-centred in their practice? There is a wealth of literature giving helpful guidance in social work skills, and this chapter examines and summarises some key areas in this, such as building trusting relationships and good communication with children and young people. It also highlights the views of children and young people themselves with illustrations from the author's research and from other studies.

Chapter 1 reports findings on the views of young people about the qualities they appreciated in their social workers. These indicate some skills that social workers can usefully develop. For example, children and young people talked about the importance of social workers building a relationship of trust and listening and respecting them.

Building relationships

It has long been recognised that relationships between professionals and service users are fundamental to social work practice and there is good advice to be found in textbooks such as that by Trevithick (2012) and Davies and Jones (2016) about building relationships with a range of service users.

> **Reflective exercise**
>
> What are the key elements in building good relationships?
>
> Think of a good relationship you have, professional or personal. What are the elements that contribute to this?
>
> What can you learn from this about building relationships with children and young people?

The 'casework relationship' was seen as central in early texts about social work in the 1960s when social work was based on a psycho-analytic model (Biestek, 1961; Hollis, 1964). This earlier model was based on several premises that led to an in-depth exploration of the individual and their personal and interpersonal world:

> That past, particularly early, experience affects our current behaviour and attitudes.

> That we are not always consciously aware of this.

> That our professional relationships and the feelings these evoke may be related to our own earlier experiences, even though we may not be conscious of this.

A shift from this professional model in the 1970s and 1980s came about in part because this individualist approach appeared to ignore the environmental and social factors that impact on people's lives. Structural factors such as poverty, class, gender and race were understood to have significant influences as well as personal psychological states. Social workers became more aware of the importance of anti-discriminatory practice and of understanding the experience of minority and oppressed groups (Dalrymple and Burke, 2006). Focus on the relationship between professional and service user was relegated to a less prominent role. The old model was also criticised for its tendency to pathologise service users and to put the professional in an inappropriately powerful role as 'expert'. Over the last few decades commentators have complained that social work has become impersonal, bureaucratic and mechanistic, driven by managerialist demands about outcomes and meeting targets (Harris, 2003; Parton, 2003). Social work had followed a business model that treated service users as though they were 'consumers' of welfare services. However, the 'marketisation' of welfare that was supposed to promote choice through a consumer culture arguably led to a resource driven service where the needs of the more marginalised were not met (Ruch et al., 2010).

Ruch et al. (2010) have advocated a return to the principles of 'relationship-based' social work to counteract this impersonal approach to service users. Ruch (2010) argues that a lack of focus on relationships may be blamed for promoting superficial assessments in circumstances like that of young Victoria Climbié's death where social workers did not engage with Victoria. Ruch proposes a model for this new species of relationship-based social work that improves on the old casework relationship model of the 1960s. It aims to counteract the imbalance of power between service user and professional in the old model by including collaboration and empowerment of service users. The proposed new principles take account of people's individuality, their conscious and unconscious behaviours and their internal and external worlds.

The model also draws on elements of the previous psycho-analytic model. Ruch (2010) argues that practitioners need to understand the 'use of self' in relationships with service users and to do this they need to be aware of such psycho-analytic principles as 'transference' and 'counter-transference', 'mirroring' and 'defence mechanisms'. The concept of transference, for example, draws on the theory that our current behaviour and relationships are influenced sometimes unconsciously by our early experiences. The theory holds that in dealing with people in authority we may unconsciously react as we did to our parents in our childhood, or act like a punitive parent ourselves with young service users. Ruch (op. cit.) argues that this understanding of our own reactions and emotions and those of our service users is vital to effectiveness in professional relationships. She provides further detail and discussion of the psycho-analytic principles mentioned here.

Trevithick (2012) also stresses that being able to build good relationships with service users is a central social work skill. She acknowledges that such relationships should not be idealised since social workers sometimes have to make 'tough' and unpopular decisions. Yet she regards the relationship as a vehicle:

> *a thread that can open up the possibility for defences to be lowered, for the truth to be faced, for doubts and fears to be worked through, and change to be integrated and embraced in ways that are not possible without this connection to another trustworthy and reliable human being.*

(Trevithick, 2012, p. 13)

Young people and relationships

The law and policy frameworks that govern child-centred practice in the UK are considered in Chapter 1. There has been a range of statutory guidance that emphasises the importance of social workers' relationships with children and young people. For example, guidance about safeguarding children has stressed that these relationships should be based on seeing and speaking to children, listening to what they say and taking their views seriously (DfE, 2015b). Guidance about assessments of children in need (DoH, 2000) highlights that such relationships should involve seeing and talking to children, observing and engaging them and doing activities to develop trust. With children who are looked after a relationship should involve engaging with them to develop their strengths and resilience (DCSF, 2010a).

In Scotland, 'Getting it Right for Every Child' (GIRFEC) (Scottish Government, 2012) guidance for professionals places a similar emphasis on relationships with children. In Northern Ireland, 'Understanding the Needs of Children in Northern Ireland' (UNOCINI) (DHSSPSNI, 2011) emphasises a child focus, the child's perspective and working in a partnership.

For children and young people, for example those looked after and those at risk, relationships with professional workers may be able to compensate to some extent for poor relationships with parents and carers. Bell (2002) conducted research interviews with twenty-seven young people between 8 and 16 years old who were involved in child protection processes. She found that a positive, honest and trusting relationship with their social worker led to good outcomes for them. She drew on two models of attachment behaviour as described by Heard and Lake (1997) to theorise about relationships between social workers and children. These were supportive–companionable patterns of relationships and dominant–submissive patterns. The former were seen as helpful and led to greater participation and choice. The latter were experienced as controlling, an additional abuse of power for young people who already felt powerless in relation to the abuse they had experienced. Similarly, McLeod's (2010) study with social workers and looked after young people found that they wanted their social workers to be like a friend and to treat them as an equal in their relationships.

In the following sections of this chapter we examine these relationships in more detail and explore the elements that constitute them. We consider what children and young people say they want from these relationships and the skills that social workers need to bring, but first an overall, holistic approach to working with young people is outlined, that of social pedagogy.

Social pedagogy

As noted in Chapter 1, approaches to communicating with children and young people can draw on the approaches used by social pedagogy. This is a holistic approach described by Cameron and Moss (2011) as *'where education and care meet'* (p. 8). However, its practice across different countries in Europe is quite diverse so it is difficult to generalise. Some of the emphasis of social pedagogy is on the care of children in, for example, residential and foster care. However, it can be seen as a fundamental approach for all those who work with children and young people, involving generic training. Cameron and Moss (2011) list the principles that are common to the approach, which I summarise as follows:

> There is a focus on the child as a whole person and support for the child's overall development.

> The practitioner sees himself or herself in relationship with the child or young person. This relationship is central and the importance of listening and communicating are stressed.

> Children and staff are seen as inhabiting the same lifespace; not as existing in separate hierarchical domains.

> Pedagogues are encouraged to reflect on their practice and apply both theoretical understandings and self-knowledge.

> Pedagogues are practical, so their training prepares them to share in many aspects of the children's daily life and activities.

> Children's lives in groups are seen as an important resource; workers should make use of the group.

> Pedagogy builds on an understanding of children's rights, not just legal requirements.

> There is an emphasis on teamwork in bringing up children, including other professionals, the community and especially parents.

This emphasis on the child as a whole person with rights, on communication and on practical skills can be helpful in day to day practice for social workers. Ruch et al. (2016) analysed data from a study called the 'TLC Project' (Talking and Listening to Children) through a social pedagogy framework. The research explored social workers' communications with children and young people through observing their 'everyday encounters' with children. Researchers observed eighty-two visits to children and talked to the workers before and after the visits. The analysis draws on some key concepts of social pedagogy: 'Haltung', 'head-heart-hands' and 'the common third'. The first of these, 'Haltung', is a German word for the attitude or disposition of the practitioner and involves their use of self in developing relationships. The concept of 'head-heart-hands' refers to the worker's use of intellectual, emotional and practical qualities combined. The 'common third' refers to shared activities and points of interest with children and young people, similar to Winnicott's (1964) ideas discussed later in this chapter, about a 'third object' such as a game or a shared task that the worker and child may use as a focus.

Ruch et al. (2016) describe the way that some social workers were able to establish a connection with children through these kinds of pedagogical approaches. For example, one social worker in the study, 'Maggie', had a car boot with a range of toys she could use to facilitate talking to children so that she could adapt to what might be needed for each unique individual. On a first visit to a family, despite entering a fraught situation, she was able to carve out a space to talk on a sensitive topic with a 7-year-old girl, 'Carly', through a shared activity (threading beads):

> *Maggie managed to turn the difficult initial situation around through a child-centred attitude (haltung) that made sure she spent time discretely in a 'common third' activity with Carly whilst using her 'head, hands and heart' to empathise with all the other parties involved i.e. Carly's mother and brother.*
>
> (Ruch et al. (op. cit., p. 6))

Ruch et al. emphasise that it is not just the use of an activity in itself, but the quality and sensitivity of the worker to each child and their individuality, that helps to establish a positive connection.

Building trust

Fundamental to relationships is trust and this is mentioned by children and young people in many research studies about their views (Bell, 2002; Barnes, 2007; Lefevre, 2010). Distilled from several studies involving children and young people, Lefevre (2010) summarises the qualities that can help them to feel trust as follows:

➤ *Kindness, supportiveness, a caring attitude and showing personal concern for children*

➤ *Empathy, sympathy, showing understanding*

➤ *Comfortable with, containing of and responsive to what children say, feel or do*

➤ *Openness, genuineness, congruence and honesty*

➤ *Accepting and non-judgemental approach*

➤ *Friendly and warm in manner*

➤ *Respectfulness towards children*

➤ *Accessibility and availability*

➤ *Consistency, trustworthiness and reliability.*

Lefevre (2010, p. 34)

In the author's own research with social workers, advocates and young people, the young people said they were able to trust social workers and other professionals who were reliable, honest and confidential. For example, Chris, a 16 year old in residential care, said this was one of the most important things for him. He wanted social workers who *'stick to their promises'* and *'if they say we'll get back to you they do it'*.

Confidentiality, an important factor in building trust, was a difficult issue for the social workers and young people, especially in matters of child protection. This is discussed in more detail in the following chapters since it can give rise to dilemmas that may be a barrier to child-centred practice. The young people in the study were aware that social workers did not keep confidentiality even where there was no risk to them involved. For example, Lucy, a 14 year old in foster care, said:

> *Some things that I've told my workers, my social worker has gone back and told the boss....Young people won't be able to speak their mind if they can't think that you're going to keep it to yourself.*

Winter (2011) recommends a careful attention to the *process* of work for building trust with children. She maintains that it is important at the beginning stage to become a familiar figure to the child. This could involve showing children photographs of yourself at work, in your car or engaged in talking to children. She notes that it is also helpful to leave behind a postcard with your picture as a reminder and all the information about you that a child may need to make contact.

It is very important when working with children to check whether they know what social workers do and why you are there. It may not be obvious to them what, for example, an assessment means, what you will be talking about, how long this will take and so on. Winter (op. cit.) advises that you may begin with conversations that are neutral, about the weather or your journey, rather than introducing more threatening topics immediately. If you are using materials such as puppets or paper and pens or crayons for drawing it helps to let children have a choice whether or not to use them. Here, Winter is describing a process for working with young children, but her advice can be adapted as a useful guide to good practice with older children too.

Communication

Good communication is a basic element of building relationships, and communicating with children and young people of different ages is vital to child-centred practice. Whilst social workers sometimes feel daunted about communicating with children, they do not need to be skilled play therapists. It is important, too, not to attempt complex therapeutic work that will need the skills of a well-trained therapist or child psychologist. The most important thing for social workers is a commitment to try and create trust and understanding sensitively in the best way possible so that children feel able to let their social worker know about things important to them. Social workers do need to communicate well with children and young people to gain an understanding of their wishes and feelings in a variety of circumstances, such as assessments, child protection enquiries and in the planning for looked after children. General communication skills include:

➤ Verbal communication skills

➤ Non-verbal communication skills

➤ Observation skills

➤ Listening skills.

Social work requires us to try to understand another's world by these means in order to do our work, but empathy plays an important role. As defined by Trevithick (2012) this means:

> *trying to understand, as carefully and as sensitively as possible the nature of another's experience, their own unique point of view, and what meaning this carries for that individual.*

> (Trevithick, 2012, p. 194)

The communication skills listed above are used in the service of this empathic understanding. Differences in culture, gender, ethnicity, ability, sexual orientation, class and so on all affect our ability to achieve this understanding. It is important to try to understand people's cultural world, but workers should also show they are aware of the impact of oppression and discrimination on these groups of young people.

We need to understand, for example, how these differences may affect how people express their emotions. In some Asian cultures emotional restraint is expected and service users may not feel able to convey their distress as this may affect their reputation. In some African and African Caribbean cultures it is more acceptable to express emotional distress through physical symptoms rather than through verbal expression (Hwang et al., 2008).

Case example: Baashi

Baashi is a 13-year-old boy from a Somali family. He lived until recently with his mother, father, older brother and two younger sisters. A few weeks ago he made allegations that his 17-year-old brother hit him with a belt. He told his teacher, and a

▶

◀

medical examination confirmed that he had bad wounds from the attack, consistent with his account. He said he was frightened to go home and is now in emergency foster care.

The foster family are White British and Baashi says he likes the foster mother and she tries to cook the food he likes but he misses his mother's cooking. He says that he misses his two younger sisters too but he doesn't want to see his mother or his brother. He has been getting into trouble at school for being badly behaved in class but says he is being bullied.

Baashi says he feels a bit lonely away from his family and sometimes he wishes he had not said anything about his brother's attack.

Comment on the case example

In the above case example, it is difficult to gauge how much of Baashi's distress relates to his being in a family where the culture is different from his own. He has said he misses his mother's cooking and his sisters. However, he is also suffering the fate of many children who disclose abuse in their family, in that he is the one who has been removed although he is not the perpetrator. Further sensitive exploration of Baashi's feelings will be needed to understand about his wish not to see his mother, his loneliness and his behaviour at school. The worker will also need to find out whether contact with his sisters can be arranged and whether better links with his cultural heritage such as attendance at the mosque would help.

Language

Social workers will need to communicate with a diverse range of children and young people in terms of age, language, culture and ability; therefore good preparation is often needed. It is the responsibility of the social worker to plan for communication where there are language differences. For example, an interpreter may be required if a child's first language is not English, or if a child speaks simple English but does not understand more complex ideas in this, their second language. There are pitfalls in using interpreters and it is useful to prepare well and have training in this skill. Kadushin and Kadushin (2013) advise of some important principles. For example, using other family members to interpret can lead to children's words being distorted since they may have an interest in presenting events from their own point of view rather than the child's. Using an interpreter who is from the same community as a family can lead to their concerns about confidentiality amongst their friends and relatives. It is important to talk to the interpreter about a meeting with a child before-hand to explain the context and purpose as well as about confidentiality. In the actual meeting the social worker should always address their words to the child and not to the interpreter. It is also vital to check children's understanding at every stage and bear in mind that this means of com-munication will need longer than usual.

Verbal communications with children clearly need to take account of language development as well as the differences in culture and so on noted above. We may need to adapt or simplify our language when speaking to younger children, and it is always helpful to avoid jargon and check that children understand the everyday terms that social workers take for granted such as 'placement' and 'assessment'. Trevithick (2012) notes that the language used by social workers may often be misun-derstood by service users, adults as well as children. The Social Services Inspectorate (1991) found, for example, that the words 'gender', criteria' and 'networks' were not understood at all by service users, whilst the word 'agency' was interpreted as a second hand clothes shop and 'eligibil-ity' as a good marriage catch. This illustrates the importance of checking with children and young people that they have understood. In practice with disabled children and young people, social workers will need to find out the child's preferred communication style, as is discussed in more detail later in this chapter.

Communication through play and activity

In work with young children, communication that includes some non-verbal activity is often preferable, for example an activity based on play and drawing. This can help build rapport and trust. Even older young people who have the verbal skills may often feel uncomfortable in a face to face interview, being asked questions about their lives, and some more indirect communication through interactive media or playing games may help them feel more able to express their views. Winnicott (1964) talks about a 'third object' being helpful as this gives the worker and the child another focus and takes them from the intensity of verbal interaction.

Examples of methods to communicate through activities and play with a range of ages and abilities are contained in books and guidance such as those of Corrigan and Moore (2011), Lefevre (2010), Fahlberg (2012) and Tait and Wosu (2013). Corrigan and Moore (2011), for exam-ple, give detailed guidance about activities that can be used in a range of situations such as trauma, loss or moving placement, and these come with helpful advice to social workers about basic theories, preparation techniques and listening skills. Corrigan and Moore (2011) recommend a range of materials to use from soft toys and fuzzy felts to simple pen and paper. Simple line drawings of the houses and streets where children have lived can help with discussion about moves in their lives. These can include schools, the social worker's office or a court building. These 'ecomaps' are a useful way of helping children to talk about their lives without direct questioning, which can feel threatening (Figure 4.1).

'The Three Houses' tool in Munro (2011) was first developed in New Zealand (Weld, 2008) and is widely used in the UK and internationally

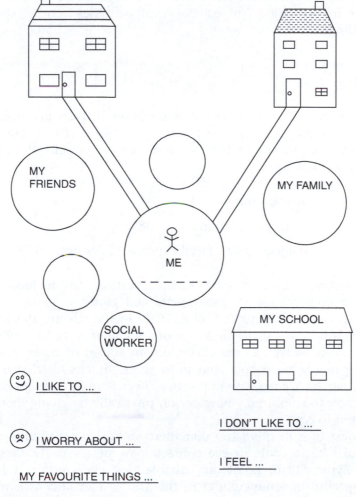

Figure 4.1 Child's ecomap

to help children and young people express their thoughts and feelings. It uses a 'house of worries', a 'house of good things' and a 'house of dreams' where children can draw and write their concerns about home, the nice things about their lives and what they hope for the future.

Lefevre (2010) gives guidance on the use of painting and drawing to communicate and using story books to give children information. There is a growing range of simple story books and online resources to help with specific situations such as going to a foster home, living in a family where there is domestic violence and coping with bereavements. A good example of a book for younger children about domestic violence is *How are you Feeling Today Baby Bear?* by Jane Evans (2014), which tells about 'Baby Bear' hearing violence downstairs when in bed. It is accompanied by notes to help adults talk about the contents of the book with children and open up discussion. There are also fun activities to help express difficult feelings.

Body language

The importance of non-verbal communication is often underestimated. An influential proponent of this finding, Mehrabian (1972) claimed that in face to face encounters between two people typically the predominant communication is:

Verbal:	Words, content – 7%
Vocal:	Tone, pitch, intonation – 38%
Visual:	Body language, facial expression, gestures – 55%

The constituents of non-verbal communication can include features such as physical closeness, movements and gestures. Some writers on the subject (Kadushin and Kadushin, 2013) include in this the setting of communication, that is the ambience of a home or an office and people's personal dress, as well as the effects on the senses of smell and touch. We know that some people tend to be more 'touchy-feely' than others and this may have a negative or positive effect. Should a social worker, for example, try to comfort a young person physically by giving them a hug if they start to cry?

We must bear in mind too that there are different cultural interpretations of what a smile or eye contact may mean. As Henderson and Mathew-Byrne (2016) point out, maintaining eye contact is regarded as disrespectful in some cultures in the Middle East and Asia, whilst in Western cultures it is seen as disrespectful not to do so.

Observation

Of course communication is a two way process and while, as social workers, we must be mindful of our own verbal and non-verbal behaviour, we need to attend to that of children and young people also to understand their situations. Hence it is important to observe and to listen.

Observation of children is regarded as an important part of assessment of children and their care in social work, especially when looking at attachment to parents and carers. Observation studies along the 'Tavistock model' were originally developed by Bick (1964) for training in child psychotherapy. They are now frequently included in qualifying courses for social workers (Fawcett and Watson, 2016). This traditionally involves a student or practitioner in observing a baby or very young child with their parent or carer for an hour at a regular time for several weeks. Originally, in child psychotherapy training programmes, this observation would continue for at least one year. The method requires a reflective approach where the student does not interact with the parent or child, but writes down their detailed observations later to discuss these in seminars and bring in their reactions and their hypotheses about the child and the parent – child relationship. The seminars help students to examine their own values about childhood and parenting. The following excerpt from a student's observation demonstrates the detail observed as well as the student's reactions and hypothesis about attachment behaviour.

Practice example: Excerpt from a student observation of 'C', an 8-month-old baby

Observation

When C's mother left the room he began to cry, but she soon came back and he looked up when she said his name and smiled, waving his arms and legs excitedly. She stroked his face and he moved his mouth towards her hand.

Thoughts and feelings

When C became distressed I felt the need to try and comfort him but didn't because of the observation rules. This was made easier because his mother was so responsive.

Theoretical applications

There was clear anxiety when C's mother left and he remained in the room with me, a stranger. C presented many attachment behaviours such as smiling, tracking his mother's voice and she responded immediately, indicating that she was sensitive to his needs.

It does not come naturally to most of us to simply watch people without interacting with them, so students often find this a very difficult thing to do (Quitak, 2004; Fawcett and Watson, 2016). Nevertheless, we can learn a lot from attending to children and young people. Students and practitioners say that the discipline helps them to step back from their own busy agenda and really attend to what is going on for children and young people in their subsequent work. If observing closely, they find that they notice more, rather than making assumptions about what is happening. They learn about children's development and their relationships through observing play, facial expressions, interactions of touch and tone of voice. The skill of close observation can be helpful in practice situations, especially in initial assessment visits to families. Workers who do these visits in pairs can helpfully check out their observations with one another.

Reflective exercise

To try a mini child observation exercise yourself, watch parents with children you encounter, maybe in a supermarket or on a bus or train.

Afterwards, think about how they appeared, what they said and how they interacted.

Did you have ideas about the quality of the relationships between the parents and children?

Do you think these were based on evidence or your assumptions?

Listening

As already noted in Chapter 1, young people commonly complain that social workers do not listen to them. A good listener is someone who attends to the other rather than being preoccupied with themselves and the impression they are making. It is easy to understand why sometimes the stress and pressure of work in social work can lead to distraction and can result in poor listening. Furthermore, social workers usually see their service users to complete a focused piece of work such as an assessment or an investigation. Therefore some of the matters that their service users talk about may seem irrelevant to their purpose. The skills of 'active' listening demand an alertness and close attention to what the service user is trying to convey (Moss, 2015). Some of the skills needed include:

➤ paying attention to one's own body language with good eye contact and an open posture and being aware of, and controlling, our possibly distracting movements and mannerisms

➤ being responsive in a sensitive way by following cues, checking our understanding and having an empathic response to emotions

➤ tolerating silences and making sure that people find their own words without inappropriate interruption or prompt

➤ listening for emotional content and mood and picking up on what is not being said e.g. through non-verbal behaviours.

Even when a social worker does all the above children may still complain they have not listened. McLeod (2008) describes how in her study *'Listening but not Hearing'* social workers explained that for them listening meant paying attention to what young people said with respect and empathy and nothing further. For the young people in the study listening crucially meant hearing what they said, then actually *doing* something about it. They felt that their social workers, although they listened, did not act on what they heard.

Clearly, social workers cannot always act on the request of a young person. There may be restrictions imposed by resource shortages. They may also be unable to act on a child's wishes if they are aware that this may bring serious risk of harm. For example, a child may wish to go home to his or her family when their abuser is still present and they would not be safe. If this is the case it is vital to explain the reasons why it is not safe, and to demonstrate that as a social worker you want to support and improve their lives.

The young people in the author's study showed that they understood about social workers' concerns for their safety and the shortage of resources. They were realistic in their demands when they were given good information about the restrictions that social workers faced. It was only when social workers did not take the trouble to explain that they found it difficult to accept their situation. Some even accepted that social workers were too busy to see them often but they needed to know that their social worker cared enough to try.

Communicating with disabled children and young people

A social model of disability contends that the concept of disability is constructed by society and provides barriers to the lives of disabled people in the way that it organises the environment, including work, leisure and education (Oliver, 1990). Thomas (2005) recognises that attitudes towards disabled children and young people as well as adults are some of the greatest barriers that they face in life and that we, as social workers, need to recognise our own disablist views. We may value disabled children less and see them less as individuals than through the 'lens of their condition'

(Middleton, 1999). We should remember, as is part of the ethos of the Children Act 1989, that disabled children are 'children first'. Barriers exist also in the realm of communication.

Young disabled people complain that they are not involved enough in decisions about their care and that their views are not heard (Franklin and Sloper, 2009). Quite often workers will not speak to them at all but will talk to their parents or carers about them instead (Turner, 2003). Stalker and Connors (2003) have discussed some of the reasons that workers do not try to engage with disabled children, such as thinking that it will be too time consuming or that they do not have the necessary skills. The most important thing is the worker's positive motivation to try to communicate.

Of course, disabled children are unique individuals and workers will need to prepare by finding out about them in advance, especially about the ways they communicate.

Workers may need to learn some basic words in a communication system such as Makaton to be able to communicate with children with a learning disability, and they may need to use a wider range of aids to communication such as pictures and drawing. Augmentative and alternative communication (AAC) encompasses a range of techniques and equipment that are used to assist speech or instead of speech. These may involve, for example, facial expression, signing, simple pen and paper or, at the other end of the spectrum, complex specialist computer technology.

A parent or support worker may be needed to assist to begin with, especially if young people are using picture boards or specialised computer-assisted communications. However, once the communication systems are understood, workers will need to see children and young people on their own whenever possible, or use an independent person who can interpret. This is especially important where there are child protection concerns since carers may be implicated in abuse. It is important too to appreciate that it can also be frustrating for the young disabled person who is trying to make their views and wishes heard (Lefevre, 2010).

Conclusion

Good communication is the cornerstone of child-centred practice and building good relationships, and demands careful attention and planning from social workers. Training will be helpful and will help build confidence in creative approaches, observation skills and listening skills. One of the difficulties social workers often mention is having the confidence to do this work, but it is not as important to have superior skills as to make the time and effort to try to communicate with children and young people. It must be acknowledged, however, that making this time can be problematic for social workers, who may have pressure to prioritise other work such as child protection and court procedures.

Summary points

➤ Building trusting relationships with children and young people is fundamental to child-centred social work. This involves an attention to the process of work with children.

➤ Social workers can use ideas from social pedagogy about a holistic approach.

➤ Both verbal and non-verbal skills are important, and social workers need to plan carefully for communicating with children whose first language is different from their own and with disabled children.

➤ A creative approach will often be needed in work with children and young people, such as play and activities.

➤ Practice in observing children and their carers is an important skill in understanding children's worlds.

➤ Really listening is vital and something young people frequently mention as the most important.

Further reading and resources

Corrigan, M. and Moore, J. (2011) *Listening to Children's Wishes and Feelings*. London: BAAF.
Provides a wealth of suggestions about activities and materials to work with children and young people.

Lefevre, M. (2010) *Communicating with Children and Young People: Making a Difference*. Bristol: Policy Press.
Good advice about the process of communicating with children and young people in social work with creative ideas.

Ruch, G., Turney, D. and Ward, A. (eds) (2010) *Relationship-Based Social Work: Getting to the Heart of Practice*. London: Jessica Kingsley Publishers.
Argues the case for a return to relationship-based social work.

Trevithick, P. (2012) *Social Work Skills and Knowledge*, 3rd edition. Maidenhead: Open University.
A comprehensive compendium of skills for social work practice.

Jessica Kingsley Publishers produce a wide range of books to use with children, e.g. about coping with loss, such as *A Sky of Diamonds* by Camille Gibbs (2015), and working with autistic children, such as *Robin and the White Rabbit* by Emma Lindström and Ase Brunnström (2017).

Talking and Listening to Children website draws on research across the UK about social workers' communication with children and provides online resources, including films, about four key stages of communicating with children. Available at: http://www.talkingandlisteningtochildren.co.uk/about-tlc/

Social Care Institute for Excellence (SCIE) has a video series on working with disabled children, available at: https://www.scie.org.uk/socialcaretv/topic.asp?t =disabledchildrenandyoungpeople

5

Empowerment, Participation and Advocacy Skills

Introduction

This chapter continues the exploration of skills in child-centred practice through considering some further key elements such as empowerment, the role of participation in decision making and consultation. There is a particular focus on the role of advocacy in social work and on working with children's advocates. This highlights the differences in role between the social work focus on best interests and the advocacy focus on 'voicing'. It draws on some of the author's research findings about social work and advocacy.

Empowerment

The principle of 'empowerment' is a common theme in social work theory and professional standards. As noted in Chapter 1, it is mentioned in the agreed international definition of social work (IFSW and IASSW, 2014), which talks about the 'empowerment and liberation of people', and in the UK Knowledge and Skills Statement for Social Workers in Adult Services (DfE, 2015a). It is usually seen in the context of enabling oppressed groups to gain more power and control of their lives. Yet there is controversy about the ability of one individual to 'empower' another and whether this really makes sense. The question is how power can be transferred from one person to another. As a commitment to anti-oppressive practice, however, it is a meaningful and central value of social work (Dalrymple and Burke, 2006; Thompson, 2016), and social workers can attempt to ensure that their service users have the tools at hand to improve their situation.

General principles and skills needed to 'empower' service users have been usefully outlined by Braye and Preston-Shoot (1995). These include measures for empowering service user groups such as involving key participants, making sure people can attend meetings and having an open agenda, but some measures can also be applied to individuals. These are aspects like giving time and information and clear channels for complaints. They also include offering choice about involvement, but in social work with individual children and their families this is frequently non-negotiable since looked after children and those at risk are automatically allocated a social worker. The limits of empowerment therefore need to be clearly outlined.

Children and young people are relatively lacking in power in relation to adults since, as discussed in some detail in the previous chapters, they are widely seen as immature and incompetent (Lee, 2001; James and Prout, 2015) and are often treated as such by adult professionals. We have also seen how the emphasis on psychological developmental theories in, for example, social work assessments (DoH, 2000) can feed into this view. Children and young people's sense of their personal agency can be weakened by the focus on their vulnerability and weaknesses rather than on any strengths. Rowe's (1989, p. 16) definition of power is helpful in considering children's situation in relation to adults. He defines power as: *'the right to have your own definition of reality prevail over other people's definition of reality'*. Adults, especially professionals, define the reality for children.

Studies of children's views have found that children have felt in a powerless situation in relation to their social workers. McLeod's (2007) study of the communication between looked after young people and their social workers found that some young people stopped engaging with social workers since they felt they had no say in the agendas that were imposed on them.

In the author's own study, young people talked about social workers having a powerful authority role. An 18 year old, Emily, who had been in foster care since the age of 4 said she saw social workers as *'trying to control your life'*. This was borne out by one of the social workers, Sandra, who talked about her work with a 13-year-old boy in residential care, saying, *'He is a child and we are the adults and we make the decisions.'*

McLeod (2008) gives some guidance about how we can give children more control. She explains that children are sensitive to the power dynamics between themselves and adults and that they are so used to the authority of adults that they may suspect any question from an adult, no matter how neutral it may seem to the speaker, as being controlling. McLeod (op. cit.) suggests letting children take the initiative in dialogue where possible and not asking them questions to which we already know the answer since children feel these questions are controlling. Another tactic is to 'act stupid' so that children will feel more powerful through explaining something they know about to the adult.

Minor practical details can help redress the imbalance of power. Children and young people can usually be given some choice about the place and time of a meeting and a choice of activities. They may need to be asked about their need for refreshment and toilet breaks. If they can also be reassured that they do not have to answer questions or may signal if they are upset, this can help them to feel more in control.

Enabling participation

Enabling children and young people to have meaningful participation in decisions affecting their lives is another means of empowering them, and their right to participation, as discussed in Chapters 1 and 3, is outlined in the Children Acts 1989 and 2004 and in the UNCRC. Theories of participation and ways that participation can be meaningful rather than tokenistic also are discussed in Chapter 3.

Studies from that of Thomas (2000) to the more recent one by Pert et al. (2017) have found that young people frequently complain that they are not involved in decisions about their care. This suggests that change in the level of children's participation, if any, has been very slow. Thomas's (2000) research into the participation in decision making of young people in the public care found that they often were not invited to meetings such as statutory reviews about their care and not consulted about their views on important issues regarding their future. Further, when they were present at the meetings they found it difficult to make a meaningful contribution because they had not been properly prepared or they found the situation disempowering. Children and young people's attendance at child protection and statutory review meetings are discussed further in Chapters 7 and 8. Pert et al. (2017) interviewed twenty-five children and sixteen foster carers about children's participation in reviews and concluded the situation had changed little in fifteen years. This was despite the introduction of Independent Reviewing Officers, who were meant to make the meetings more child-centred, and the statutory guidance regarding participation in reviews. With regard to disabled young people in care, Morris (1998) found that they were very little consulted and that their views and wishes were often not even recorded. Research by Franklin and Sloper more recently (2009) found that disabled children were less likely to be involved in decisions than non-disabled children. Besides professionals and carers they interviewed twenty-one disabled children, ages 5–18. The majority of the children interviewed had a learning difficulty, ranging from mild to severe, and six children had a communication impairment. Key messages from the children were that they:

> *often had limited contact or rapport with social workers;*

> *had few opportunities to express their views about services;*

> *often had a limited understanding of what they had been involved in, either they had received no explanation or information had not been given to this in accessible formats;*

> *enjoyed taking part, being listened to and being able to make choices;*

> *particularly enjoyed methods which were creative and fun;*

➤ *enjoyed the socialising associated with being part of a youth forum; and*

➤ *would like more opportunities to undertake participation, and be kept informed of what happens.*

(Franklin and Sloper, 2009, p. 9)

A review of research on children's participation in welfare services by van Bijleveld et al. (2013) concluded that they were less likely to participate in situations where risk of abuse or neglect was involved, where the adults viewed children as vulnerable and immature or they were disabled and where there was not a good relationship between the child and social worker.

These findings were borne out also in the author's research. For instance a 16-year-old young woman, Tamsin, in residential care who had been diagnosed with autism complained that she was not involved at all in a decision to move her from her current placement to a semi-independent hostel that she had not even seen. Tamsin gave an example of her lack of involvement in important decisions about where she would be living in the future. She said of her social worker, Gillian:

Tamsin	*I feel like she's found this placement and that's where I'm heading, basically – where it's like came as a big shock to me – where I actually got told by my social worker where I would probably be staying here till I'm at least 17, cos I'm not fully independent.*
Interviewer	*Mm. This is a semi-independent one is it?*
Tamsin	*Yeah. And then the next thing I know, I get a referral somewhere else.*
Interviewer	*And didn't you take any part in thinking about that?*
Tamsin	*No. She just come with it.*
Interviewer	*Yeah.*
Tamsin	*So I didn't really get a chance to get used to it and stuff but...*
Interviewer	*How would you have liked things to happen then, about finding somewhere else to stay?*
Tamsin	*For me to get more involved in it and for me to make sure it's all right for me, and stuff like that.*

Support for young people to assist them in participating in decisions needs the commitment of workers first and foremost. As Woodhead (2006) has argued, we need to focus on what adults need to do to make participation for children and young people possible.

The skills listed in the previous chapter such as building trust, listening, communicating and giving information and choice are very important in this. Gallagher et al. (2012) maintain that in addition, children and young people will need to be properly prepared for participation. This means taking time to go through their concerns before important meetings and to give them confidence that they will have support when they express their views. Preparation may involve play for younger children and use of information technology for older young people. Young people may appreciate being able to express their views in a familiar online or text format rather than to be questioned face to face by a worker.

Case example: Participating in a meeting: Terry

Terry is 14 and has Down syndrome. He was rejected by his family, who are travellers, when he was 5 and has been fostered since that time. Terry has some speech supplemented by Makaton sign language. He understands simple words and phrases about his home life and school but has limited understanding of more complicated ideas. Terry has never enjoyed his statutory review meetings, which are attended by a chairperson, his teacher and education support worker, a school nurse, a social worker, a foster carer and occasionally his mother. At the last meeting he walked out after five minutes. The adults were mainly talking to each other and occasionally asked him a question but he did not answer.

The social worker is committed to trying to get Terry involved in his meeting so that he will be a part of the decisions that are made. She spends time with him a week beforehand to prepare. To help explain, she brings on an iPad photographs of the people who will be at the review and goes through some matters that people will talk about to get his views. These include the foster home, school and his birth family. Together they draw pictures and stick cut-out pictures to create Terry's views about seeing his mother and brothers and the activities he likes at home and school. Terry draws his garden at home with a swing and the school with a football (his favourite game) and a heart because he loves his school so much.

Terry and his social worker present his book of pictures at the beginning of the review and Terry is happy to remain there answering a few questions. He has since been happy to attend every meeting.

Comment on the case example

The above case example illustrates how careful but simple preparation can make a difference to young people's feelings of inclusion in a process that previously felt unwelcoming, with adults talking to each other about them. Terry was able to contribute to the meeting and to feel at last that these meetings were his.

Group participation and consultation

Since 2006 local authorities in England and Wales have had a duty to consult young people in preparing their planning and development of services. Many groups of young people are now involved in these consultation exercises, for example in Children in Care Councils. There are, however, concerns that this is sometimes mere window-dressing and that young people are being manipulated to satisfy statutory and managerial requirements. As in Hart's (1992) *'ladder of participation'* described in Chapter 3 they may not have been allowed beyond the first few rungs.

There are arguments that consultation is not productive for all children and can reinforce the power and control of adults. Whilst acknowledging the importance of seeking children's views, Moss et al. (2005) argue that this does not always work because adults usually define the parameters of any consultation. Furthermore, more vocal and privileged children will tend to dominate the discussions, leaving out the views of a diverse range of children.

Different methods of consulting children's views can be tried. For example, Coleman and Rowe (2005) have suggested using websites that young people can design themselves to express their views. Local authorities are increasingly using mobile phone 'applications' to consult with young people, such as 'MOMO' (Mind Of My Own) and 'Viewpoint'. These free services give young people the freedom to express themselves in whatever format they wish.

Advocacy

Advocacy can play a key role in promoting children and young people's participation and in making sure a focus is kept on children's wishes and feelings. Here, I consider advocacy by social workers themselves and by independent professional advocates. I also look at the understanding and skills social workers need to work with advocates. Advocacy is defined by Lee (2007) as follows:

> *Advocacy... promotes* **equality**, **social justice** *and social inclusion. It can* empower *people to speak up for themselves. Advocacy can help people become more aware of their own* **rights**, *to exercise those* **rights** *and be involved in and influence decisions that are being made about their future.*
>
> (Lee, 2007)

To compare this with the IASSW–IFSW definition of social work quoted earlier in Chapter 1, I have repeated this below:

> **Social work** *is a practice-based profession and an academic discipline that promotes social change and development, social cohesion, and the* **empowerment** *and liberation of people. Principles of* **social justice**, **human rights**, *collective responsibility and respect for diversities are central to social work.*
>
> (International definition, IFSW and IASSW, 2014)

In order to emphasise the similarities between the two definitions the key words in both definitions above are highlighted. As can be seen, *empowerment, social justice* and *rights* are cited as central to both advocacy and social work.

Advocacy covers a range of activities and roles, some of which are more or less important to social work with children and young people. These include:

> ➤ **Self advocacy** – This involves speaking out on one's own behalf either individually or as part of a group.

> ➤ **Peer advocacy** – Where the advocate has a similar background and experiences.

> ➤ **Non-instructed advocacy** – For those who are, for reasons of lack of capacity or communication, unable to personally instruct their advocate.

> ➤ **Citizen advocacy** – One to one advocacy where the advocate is usually a volunteer. This is used most commonly for people with learning disabilities.

> ➤ **Professional advocacy** – Provided by a trained and paid advocate.

> ➤ **Legal advocacy** – This is usually provided by a solicitor or other legally trained person.

Social workers may encourage children and young people to self advocate and to speak out for themselves, although there is evidence that young people often do not have the confidence to do so and prefer to have a professional advocate (Boylan and Ing, 2005; Dalrymple, 2005). Social workers may also refer young people to some of the advocacy services and professionals listed above. Citizen advocacy and peer advocacy, however, are likely to suit other marginalised groups better, such as adults who have learning disabilities or mental health issues. Legal advocates may be a very useful resource in providing specialist advice to young people, for example about immigration law or housing law. Social workers are most likely to encounter professional advocates, and I discuss their work with these later in this chapter. Professional advocates are also able to provide non-instructed advocacy for young people with learning disabilities.

Advocacy in social work

As we have noted above, there are overlaps between the social work and the advocacy role, so how can social workers act as advocates?

In their work with children and young people, social workers may help them, as required by policy and law, to voice their wishes and feelings (see Chapter 1). They may assist young people, in their transition to independence from foster or residential care, to become more self-reliant and confident in their approach to organisations such as benefits and housing offices. As discussed in the previous section, social workers have a significant role in enabling young people's participation in statutory reviews and child protection meetings. They may also encourage young people to take part in local authority consultations concerning their attitudes and opinions about services provided. Importantly, they should know about their young service users' rights and help to ensure that these are upheld.

Sometimes it is difficult for social workers to uphold the rights and promote the wishes and feelings of young people. There is more discussion of the barriers in the next chapter. A manager may say there are no resources to provide for post abuse counselling, for example, or that a young person must move to a different foster home for organisational reasons. This can make it difficult for a social worker to challenge a decision themselves without being seen as a 'troublemaker'.

One advantage that social workers have in acting as advocates is that they are in a good situation to understand the intricacies of the bureaucratic systems they operate within and, with this knowledge, to challenge for young people from within the organisation.

Skills for advocacy

As noted above, social workers will need to use skills in supporting children and young people's participation in decisions, to enable them to express their views and ensure that these views are properly heard by others. To advocate for children and young people, social workers also need a variety of other specific skills, as follows:

➢ A detailed knowledge of law, policy and rights

➤ Skills in presenting a case

➤ Being able to rally influential allies

➤ Use of appropriate experts

➤ Assertiveness

➤ Negotiation techniques

➤ Persistence.

Children's social workers are all expected to have a good knowledge of, say, the Children Act 1989, but advocacy is likely to demand a more detailed knowledge of specific sections of Acts and policy guidance to support a case on behalf of a young person. For example, they may need to argue for a child to receive funding for expenses in higher education and will need to know the actual wording of relevant law and policy to make their case.

As well as setting out the policy and legal criteria, a balanced presentation to advocate for funding will require highlighting alternatives as well as the favoured course of action, and it should consider the risks and benefits of each alternative. It is important to include in the presentation, especially if the young person is not present, a summary of their views in terms of their wishes and feelings.

It is sometimes possible in advocacy to get the support of allies in the argument. A manager or an Independent Reviewing Officer may support the young person's wishes and add their weight to a proposal. In this, experts may also have a role. As discussed earlier, legal expertise may be required to put specific arguments across. In any challenge on behalf of young people, social workers will often need to be assertive and persistent and be skilled negotiators.

Assertiveness is sometimes misunderstood to mean a stubborn resistance. In fact, it means treading a careful line between being too passive and being too aggressive. Passive behaviour involves expressing our wants and needs indirectly and often apologetically. This allows other people to disregard them easily. Aggressive behaviour, on the other hand, involves ignoring or dismissing other people's wishes and opinions and trying to get what we want through any means. This can easily alienate other people and encourage them to be obstinate in their turn. Persistence, however, can be a useful tool if used assertively. It is easy to give up in the face of rejection but trying again, perhaps armed with further information and argument, can be a good strategy.

Being a skilled negotiator is one of the major skills of advocacy. Wilks (2012) explains in detail that negotiation may involve an element of compromise and it is important to get a clear understanding of the other party's point of view before embarking on any assertive challenge. To summarise, assertive negotiation involves:

➤ Being clear about your negotiating position

➤ Being flexible and open to compromise

➤ Trying to understand the other's position

➤ Responding constructively

➤ Challenging assertively.

Reflective exercise

Can you think of a successful negotiation you have made? This could be any everyday matter such as disputing a bill, declining to take on extra work in your job or deciding with your family where to go on holiday.

This would be a situation where you were happy with the outcome, but you do not necessarily have to have got your own way completely.

Considering the assertive negotiation points above, what helped this process?

Were you clear about what you wanted?

Did you listen to others' points of view?

Were you constructive and assertive?

As pointed out by Trevithick (2012), advocacy requires far more knowledge and skill than just speaking up for children:

> *to act as an advocate for another person requires considerable professional confidence and standing on the part of practitioners, particularly when confronted with officialdom and authority figures.*
>
> (Trevithick, 2012, p. 268)

Working with professional advocates

As noted above, there are issues that may make it difficult for a social worker to act as an advocate for a young person. They may need to refer young people to an independent advocacy service, or the young person or a carer may make the referral. As outlined in Chapter 3, advocacy services are provided by a range of mainly voluntary sector agencies such as Barnardo's and Coram Voice and these provide advocacy services to a range of young people. Most assist children and young people who are looked after or who are young care leavers. Many also support young people involved in child protection issues and young asylum seekers and refugees. They may provide services for young people in institutions such as in mental health, youth offending and secure units.

Advocates deal with a range of individual issues for young people. Those in foster and residential care may require help with restrictions in their placements, having to move or not being happy where they are. One major concern has been restriction on contact with family and friends (Oliver et al., 2006; Barnes, 2012). Young care leavers often want help with difficulties over housing and finance. In relation to their social workers, young people, as already noted, complain about not getting on with them, not being listened to, having difficulty contacting them or not having enough contact. It is the role of these specialist children's advocates to support and represent children and young people at meetings, for example in looked after children's statutory reviews and child protection conferences. They also meet with social workers and other professionals together with young people and help negotiations. They may explain local authority systems and procedures, explain rights and legal issues and support young people with complaints. They may also refer young people to specialist legal advisors.

Case example: Children's advocacy: Sam

Sam is a White British boy age 10 and he has been in foster care since he was 8. His mother was unable to care for him because of severe mental health issues. His father is no longer in contact with the family and there are no other relatives in a position to help.

Sam was settled into a foster home until his foster father died suddenly and violently three months ago. His foster mother felt unable to care for Sam any longer as she was coping with the shock of the bereavement. She was very clear that he would not be able to return to her in the future.

The local authority had to find an alternative placement quickly, and Sam was placed with foster carers from a private fostering agency as no appropriate local authority foster carers were available. This was seen as an emergency placement but Sam's allocated social worker left the department and nothing much was done for ten weeks whilst the case was re-allocated, apart from statutory visits by a duty worker.

The newly allocated social worker, Jenny, has been to see Sam, who is very happy at the placement. He has bonded with both foster carers, their dog and the local

▶

◀

extended family and says he does not want to move. The team manager has said that Sam must be moved to local authority foster carers as this was an emergency placement and he will very likely be able to bond with other foster carers. Jenny suspects that this is a financially motivated decision since these 'in house' carers will be cheaper than the private agency foster carers. She tries to advocate for Sam to stay where he is, quoting the Children Act 1989 about Sam's wishes and feelings, but meets total opposition from the manager.

Jenny puts Sam in touch with a children's advocate, Adrian, who meets with Sam to check what he wants and how he wants the advocate to proceed. Adrian then tries to negotiate with the team manager about Sam remaining where he is but the manager is still adamant that Sam must move. Adrian also tries to negotiate with senior managers in the local authority but to no avail. The advocate then helps Sam to put in a complaint, which immediately 'freezes' his placement so he can stay put at least until the local authority deals with it (within ten working days).

In the meantime a statutory review is held and the advocate helps Sam to express his views in the meeting. The Independent Reviewing Officer also speaks to Sam before the meeting and subsequently supports Sam's wish to remain.

A decision is confirmed that he can stay with his new foster parents.

Many social workers find that having an advocate involved, as in the case study above, is helpful to their work, since this can help to support their own case about proper provision of services for young people with managers and with other agencies. However, there can be difficulties and misunderstandings in working together.

Difficulties in working with advocates

One of the confusions that occurs between social workers and advocates is their different role in relation to the 'best interests' of the child. (Best interests are discussed in detail in Chapter 3.) Whilst, like social workers, they try to empower young people to participate and they try to elicit young people's wishes and feelings, they have a very different role with regard to the best interests of the child.

The Advocacy Standards (DoH, 2002) make it clear that the advocate's role is to '*voice*' young people's wishes and feelings, not to act in their best interests:

*The child or young person leads the advocacy process. The advocate acts only upon his/her express permission and instructions, **even when these are not the advocate's view of the child or young person's best interests**. [My emphasis]*

(DoH, 2002: Standard 1.2)

In the author's research there were conflicts due to lack of understanding of these different roles. One of the advocates, Alan, expressed this clearly:

Social workers get confused from the fact that we don't necessarily come at it from the best interests point of view it purely is voicing the child's wishes and views.

He went on to explain an extreme case:

If the children want a pair of chocolate, white chocolate, trainers then that's what we have to say, you know. And it's not about what's right and what's wrong, the best interests of the child.

This stance can lead to frustration. Some social workers regarded the advocates as naïve and irresponsible. Not appreciating the difference in role, social workers in the study considered that the advocates needed to be aware of the consequences of this 'voicing' since they thought it could place a child at risk. One example of this was a social worker who complained that an advocate had voiced the wishes of a young woman in foster care to have more contact with her family. The social worker, Sally, explained that there were child protection issues that prevented this:

She [advocate] doesn't have insight into the reasons why contact has been reduced and I'm not in a position to reveal the whole background.

Social workers complained that the advocates had not found out the full history of the children they were supporting. However, they had not appreciated that one of the principles of advocacy is to be clear with young people about confidentiality, and that advocates cannot be party to personal background information if the young person does not want this known. Further, social workers need to be aware that advocates have a responsibility to share with young people everything that is said about them, and therefore social workers should not share information of which the young person is unaware.

Confidentiality and sharing information

This highlights the difference for social workers and advocates regarding confidentiality and sharing information. Both groups of professionals are bound by principles of passing on information that they become aware of in relation to risk to young people. Young people in the study were aware of this, but they appreciated that there was a difference in the workers' behaviour. They trusted the advocates because these workers discussed with them at the outset what information they would share and with whom. They knew that social workers routinely shared information with their colleagues and managers. Sue, who was 16, explained her view of the difference,

Sue	*June (advocate) has got more confidentiality than social workers.*
Interviewer	*Can you say a bit more about that?*
Sue	*Obviously she'd have to tell somebody if I was in danger or something like that, but some things you tell a social worker and they all know about it. But if I tell June and she doesn't think I was in danger, she'd keep it to herself.*

Social workers are repeatedly exhorted to share information with other professionals to prevent tragic deaths from child abuse and neglect (Thompson, 2016). Therefore they are caught in a dilemma of compromising children's trust. This issue is explored further in following chapters.

Another issue that gives rise to conflict between advocates and social workers is the impact of complaints and challenges. When an advocate helps a young person to make a complaint, it can feel very uncomfortable for social workers, even if they understand that this may help to provide a better service for the young person. This is particularly uncomfortable for social workers if the complaint is about them personally. One of the social workers said of working with advocates, *'I have this feeling that you're shot down straight away'*.

To work together effectively with advocates, social workers need to understand their different roles and try to promote the welfare of children and young people together. It can help to understand that social workers cannot be everything to the children they work with and that sometimes an advocate, a teacher or a school nurse can provide a service that better suits the young person's needs. They may have more opportunity to listen or to take up issues that for organisational reasons social workers are unable to.

It is important that both professional groups learn from one another and work together. An advocate, Mary, expresses the importance of this way of working, recognising that an aggressive challenge on behalf of children can be counterproductive:

You don't just charge in and get very angry. You sort of try to sit down and say, let's talk about this. Can we work together?

Difficulties faced by social workers in working with advocates are echoed in the barriers social workers face in child-centred practice generally, discussed in the next chapter.

Children and young people's views of advocacy

Studies of independent advocacy services have found that children and young people are overwhelmingly positive about their experiences of advocacy (Oliver et al., 2006; Barnes, 2012; Thomas et al., 2016). Thomas et al.'s (2016) research into the impact and outcomes of advocacy for young people found that they highly appreciated their relationship with advocates. They spoke of this as being open and honest communication that made them feel valued and taken seriously. It felt good to have someone who was on their side. For many young people this relationship was as important as resolving their issues. Some felt they were better able to participate and speak up for themselves, thus growing in self confidence and self esteem.

There were similar findings in the author's study. The young people valued their relationships with advocates and said that they listened and seemed to care about them. In fact, most thought that their advocates cared more about them than did their social workers. They particularly appreciated the *process* of their work together as equal parties and being involved in decisions. Katy, age 14, gave an example of having help from her advocate in writing a letter. Of her advocate, June, she said:

> ...she listens to what I say and instead of putting her own words down on a piece of paper – if we have to write a letter she uses my words instead. So we sort of work together.

This way of working together was much appreciated by young people. They wanted to be involved in the process. Although it can be quicker for a worker to write a letter themselves, this does not help young people to develop the skills and confidence in advocating for themselves.

Conclusion

Child-centred practice is furthered by an understanding of ways that children and young people can be assisted to participate in decisions. Social workers can develop skills in preparing children for taking part in meetings and consultations and making their wishes known. The skills of advocacy can also assist in this, and where it is not possible for social workers to advocate, it may be helpful to children and young people to work with a professional children's advocate.

Summary points

➤ Children and young people lack power in relation to adults and there are ways social workers can address this.

➤ Enabling children's individual and group participation requires good preparation and support.

➤ Social workers can use advocacy to help children and young people to voice their wishes and feelings.

➤ Advocacy requires a good knowledge of law and policy and skills in presenting a case, as well as assertiveness and negotiation.

➤ It is necessary to have an understanding of the professional advocate's role to work effectively with them.

➤ Children and young people appreciate the support of advocates.

Further reading and resources

Bell, M. (2011) *Promoting Children's Rights in Social Work and Social Care: A Guide to Participatory Practice*. London: Jessica Kingsley Publishers.
An overview of theory, policy and research on children's participation.

McLeod, A. (2008) *Listening to Children: A Practitioner's Guide*. London: Jessica Kingsley.
Contains guidance about giving children more control in their relationships with social workers.

Oliver, C. and Dalrymple, J. (eds) (2009) *Developing Advocacy for Children and Young People*. London: Jessica Kingsley.
A guide to children's advocacy in a variety of settings.

Wilks, T. (2012) *Advocacy and Social Work Practice*. Maidenhead: McGraw-Hill.
Practical and detailed advice in the skills of advocacy.

Coram Voice website links to their free children's Helpline and advocacy services for children and young people, plus advice about advocacy for professionals who work with them. Available at: http://www.coramvoice.org.uk/?gclid=CPHF7vm46tQCFVUo0wodLSoAVg

Coram Children's Legal Centre website links to free legal information, advice and representation to children, young people, their families, carers and professionals. Available at: http://www.coram.org.uk/how-we-do-it/coram-childrens-legal-centre-upholding-childrens-rights?gclid=CNDOqoDR6tQCFUO-7QodyXQN8Q

6

Breaking Down the Barriers?

Introduction

As discussed in the previous two chapters, there are many skills and considerations involved for those committed to child-centred practice, but a social worker may have all the necessary skills and still find it difficult to work in a child-centred way. This is set in the context of social work in a climate of 'austerity' that affects the quality of services overall. The chapter examines some of the barriers and dilemmas that social workers face in their everyday practice. It draws on the findings of the author's research about the experiences of social workers who were trying to provide a good quality of service to children and young people and the views of the young people they worked with. The chapter concludes by examining some of the ways that these barriers might be overcome.

The development of social work services

Organisational barriers to child-centred practice need to be seen in the wider context of the development of social work and welfare in the UK. The benign, if paternalistic, welfare state was established after the Second World War in accordance with the Beveridge report of 1942. This provided a universal safety net for poor and sick individuals for the first time and developed social work as a service that Harris describes as, 'the operational embodiment of the welfare state's intervention in individual citizens' lives' (Harris, 2003, p. 9).

By the 1970s, however, spending on welfare was discredited and seen as wasteful and inefficient (Parton, 1998). Since that time social work has undergone transformation to a market led service. Power (1997) traces the foundations of this change back to the establishment of the

Audit Commission in 1982. The Commission measured effectiveness and value of public services against a set of standards and objectives that were not based on evidence from research or professional consensus (Munro, 2004). Despite this, its judgements were accepted and given the highest priority, thus launching procedures and policies for data management, recording and monitoring. Power (1997) argues that organisations became 'constructed around the audit process itself' (p. 51).

Political and economic changes brought in by the New Right affected all aspects of welfare. Social work adopted a business culture and clients were renamed 'consumers', who were to have individual choice, and redress if they were not satisfied with their service. In reality, however, new eligibility criteria meant that services were restricted. The social problems of poverty and disability were individualised and families were expected to be self-sufficient through employment, rather than welfare.

The current policy of austerity, a reaction to the global financial crisis of 2008, has unfairly impacted on those least well off, and cuts to budgets have affected all welfare sectors. A report by the United Nations' Economic, Social and Cultural Rights Committee criticised the 'disproportionate adverse impact' austerity measures were having on disadvantaged and marginalised groups in the UK such as women, children and people with disabilities. This impact was reported on older people's care and treatment, people with disabilities and mental health issues, low income families with children, homelessness and reliance on food banks (Carter, 2016). Ferguson and Lavalette (2013) have argued that the protection of universal welfare is no longer seen by policy makers as a right:

> *What in British social policy is referred to as the imposition of 'higher eligibility criteria' in social care is a polite way of saying that basic services that people require for a decent existence and to which they have been entitled for decades will no longer be available and that they will have to get by, somehow, without support.*

> (p. 96)

Governments have continued the process of 'marketisation' of services in an attempt to address spending levels and to reduce the role of the state in social care. Critics argue that the policy of outsourcing services to private companies adversely affects children's care and protection (Jones, 2015), as discussed further in Chapter 7.

Ideas in this chapter about overcoming barriers to child-centred practice cannot be seen in isolation from the above political and economic climate in the UK.

Organisational barriers to a child focus

Resources

Many organisational barriers to child-centred practice were found in the author's study described in the Introduction. These were outlined by social workers themselves, and the young people spoke of the problems that resulted for them. The main issues for the social workers in terms of their organisation were lack of resources, high workloads, lack of time, bureaucracy and rigid procedures.

As explained above, cuts to children's services have deepened over the last decades. An All Party Parliamentary Group Report (2017), 'No Good Options', found that the use of locum social workers, linked to high staff turnover, meant that children and families are passed from one worker to another. This together with high caseloads meant that workers were unable to forge positive stable relationships with children and families.

Social workers in the author's study maintained that the lack of a range of resources in social care affected their work with children and young people. Staff shortages led to high workloads and meant that they could not provide the quality of service that they wished to. A social worker, Sandra, talked about the lack of choice of placements for Paul, a young man of 13, who was in residential care:

> The most difficulty I find is the system seems to be resource driven not need driven, so we spend a lot of time assessing needs and what the child would benefit from but we can't always find that resource. And that is one of the difficulties because you know you're letting the child down. The child is thinking, 'What have we been doing all this work for if you're going to get me something you know I'm not going to benefit from?'. So that really breaks down the relationship in a sense because they don't trust you any more – that's when it can get very difficult.

Another social worker, Angela, complained about the lack of support she was able to provide for young care leavers because of high caseloads:

> I think sometimes young people are sent out to cope on their own when they're not ready, with enough support. Young people are not properly protected because of social workers' high case loads. Social workers don't have time to do their job properly.

Most of the social workers complained that they were unable to spend enough 'quality time' with children and young people on their caseload because of other demands of their job. Sally, for example, said:

> The difficulty is, as a social worker in a child care team, we're under time constraints. We don't have time to work on a one to one basis and build a rapport so that the young person feels comfortable with us.

Resource shortages were also compounded by the pressure to work in a bureaucratic, impersonal way.

Bureaucracy and managerialism

Max Weber (1947 [1920]) saw bureaucracy as a model of streamlined administrative structure, an efficient machine. It prescribed clear rules understood by all, clear roles and divisions of labour and a clear hierarchy. Its popularity declined in the late twentieth century, and critics of the model have emphasised its tendency to promote rigid behaviours and resistance to change, nowadays denounced as 'red tape'.

Some preferred current models in social work are a 'learning culture' or 'competent workplace'. A learning culture aims to promote opportunities for ongoing learning, inquiry and creativity in the workplace, fostering an environment where sharing ideas and taking risks are safe (Hughes and Wearing, 2013). However, many assert that a managerialist culture prevails. This model, following the lead of business management, aims to strip out the bureaucratic structures of middle management and create a flattened organisation that can be more efficient and responsive to changes in the environment (Fawcett et al., 2010). The organisation should be led by a charismatic, transformational leader. Critics of this model for social care observe that increasingly social workers have to report to a management that is not grounded in social work and does not understand or share its values. Further, professionals' autonomy is limited through constant monitoring, evaluation and control (Hughes and Wearing, 2013).

In the author's study social workers spoke of the constraints they experienced in working with children and young people as a change to their work from former times. David, an experienced worker, commented that it was now unusual to find a social worker spending an hour or two taking children out, as in the past, because of bureaucratic demands on their time. He said:

> There are rules and regulations but you've got to be a human being, really and social work these days is just so bureaucratic – you're just in and out basically. I miss the old type of social work where you can really get involved.

This refers back to a time when the 'casework relationship' (Biestek, 1961) was seen as centrally important. Some of the social workers said they found little time to work with children themselves as they were spending so much time writing assessments and liaising with parents, carers and other professionals and agencies on behalf of children and young people. 'Direct work' with children, if it did happen, tended to be passed on to other specialist workers.

Similarly, research by Winter et al. (2016) for the TLC project (Talking and Listening to Children) described in Chapter 4 found that social workers were constrained in their relationships with children and young people by time pressures in their work. Workers in initial assessment teams were only able to see children a couple of times before having to transfer cases to a team that worked longer term with them. Thus relationships were affected by the way that these organisations and their work were constructed.

In the author's study, relationships with children had also been squeezed out by the demands of increased accountability. The social workers spoke about constant form filling, paperwork and computer recording. Norma said: *'We no longer work as a social worker, we work as an admin officer'*. Thus, the social workers blamed the bureaucratic way their work was organised for preventing them from providing a good service to young people, as social worker. This perceived change to becoming *managers* of care rather than being actively involved with young people reflects the business culture of social work with its focus on targets and auditing.

Gibson's (2016) research, observing social work practice and interviewing social workers in one English local authority with a 'good' inspection rating, explored the workers' experiences of child protection work. He also found that the social workers experienced their jobs as primarily administrative, spending 70%–90% of their time on administration, this being mainly on recording on computer. Gibson found that although this administrative work was closely monitored by managers there was very little oversight of the workers' direct work with service users and they were reprimanded if their 'paperwork' was not up to date. In an interview, it was reported that one social worker was upset:

> ... *she had had an email from [the team manager] which told her to do less visits to families and do more paperwork.*

> (p. 4)

Thus the workers were strongly encouraged in *'prioritising the administrative component of the work at the expense of the relational component'* (p. 5).

The organisation of social work, especially in child protection, is also affected by the 'blame culture' (Jones, 2014) since recurrent scandals of allegedly preventable child deaths lead to social workers having to make sure their every move and decision is documented.

The young people's views

Many young people in the study said they had good relationships with their social workers and some said they understood the pressures on their workers who were busy people. However, they still felt let down when their workers were late, did not return calls or forgot to do things. Vanessa, a 14-year-old girl in foster care, said that she could not get through to her social worker on the phone and he had let her down by not coming to her review meetings:

> He's really let me down in the past – so I'm not giving him stuff that I'd normally ask him to do. He never turns up to my review either. And that was last week and I come home early especially to see him and he never turned up and I got really angry cos I could have hanged out with my friends.

Young people who had these sort of experiences often felt their social worker did not care about them. A young woman of 16, Sue, who was about to move to a hostel from foster care, expresses such views about social workers very clearly in the following excerpt from the study.

Sue	I don't think they really care. I just think they're just there, sort of thing – doing a job.
Interviewer	What makes you think they don't care?
Sue	I dunno. They're just there doing a job, ain't they? – like a person in an office is doing a job.
Interviewer	Mm – so it doesn't feel as if you're important to them?
Sue	Just another name on a computer screen.

Young people in the study said they saw their social workers as having great power and influence over their lives, and yet they were often unavailable and seemed to be uninterested. They held parental responsibility delegated from the local authority's corporate responsibility for children who are looked after. However they did not have the resources to make this relationship a positive experience for young people. Although some young people thought their social workers did not care, evidence from the interviews with social workers suggested that they were very concerned for the young people. It was just that they failed to demonstrate this.

Reflective exercise

Think of an organisation that you know well. This could be one you work in currently or possibly an educational or health organisation such as a school, university or hospital.

Can you think of some of the rules, regulations and habits?

Do these all serve a purpose?

Can you think of any that may work against best practice?

Decisions and procedures

Further barriers to child-centred practice arose from social workers having to make decisions that young people were unhappy with and from the rigidity of procedures, especially in child protection work. Sometimes unpopular decisions were linked to a lack of resources. For example, one social worker explained that she had to discontinue counselling for a young woman in foster care because her management refused to pay for this any longer. Another, Sandra, said that young people often found it difficult to trust the social workers because, for example, having found out what kind of foster home the young people would like to live in, they had to compromise because the resources were just not available:

> *A child may say, 'Look I don't want a family where there's 2 boys or 4 girls because there's too many children there. I want a family where there's only two people'....*
> *So it's unfair when you're seeking their wishes and feelings about where they want to be placed, what kind of family they'd like and then you do the complete opposite because you've got no choice, you've got deadlines, you know. That's when it's difficult.*

Sometimes social workers had to take account of a range of issues and not just young people's wishes and feelings since they had to consider risks to children and their best interests. Sally, for example, explained that she had to limit 14-year-old Katy's contact with her family because of child protection issues within the family and court directions. She said:

> *We have listened to Katy's view and when I placed her in the foster home I told her contact would be every two months. She was very distressed.*

Social workers talked about the rigidity of procedures that they had to follow in child protection and sometimes they felt that this meant children and young people were not listened to. Leanne reflected that this automatic procedural response to risk may not be the best and most child-centred way to work with young people:

> *I'm just thinking of one example where a young person made some allegations about some things in placement – and in my opinion, I think there might have been a bit of a rush to deal with that and the young person felt very lost in it all and actually said to me, 'Actually if you'd have listened to me and what my views were on how it should have been dealt with, I might have felt very differently about the situation now'. Cos I think she feels that things have been made worse really. And I thought at the time, 'Well yes, I wonder if it was all the professionals moving in – and suddenly thinking, "Right, this is how we deal with it" – and moving on.' And I'm wondering how lost she was in that. Or even if it still had to be done that way, which I think it probably did, I think she probably did get lost in that – in terms of – maybe she didn't feel that she was being heard properly.*

This procedural response includes sharing information with other professionals. As discussed in previous chapters, this could also be a barrier to child-centredness because it led young people to feel they could not trust their social worker. Social workers in the study said they were frequently preoccupied with the networks of professionals and carers around children and with managing these networks to ensure children had a safe and stable life. The young people, however, wanted to maintain the quality of their relationships with family and friends and were less concerned about risk. Leanne, quoted above, acknowledged that young people were sometimes forgotten in the process. She said: *'I do think sometimes we do have to remind ourselves who's at the centre of this'.*

Policies and guidance for social workers in child protection emphasise the importance of sharing information since numerous high profile child death inquiries (from that of Maria Colwell in 1973 to that of Daniel Pelka in 2013) have highlighted the need for good communication between the professional and agency workers involved in children's lives. Nevertheless, this may be at the expense of their relationship with a young person if it leads to loss of trust.

The young people's views

Some of the young people said they were frustrated that decisions were made *for* them and that their views were not properly taken into account. Fourteen-year-old Katy, for example, was angry that her social worker, Sally (quoted above), would not let her have more contact with her family:

I think she's trying to do what's best for me in her eyes but not listening to what I think's best for me.

Sixteen-year-old Tamsin, quoted in the previous chapter, talked about a decision to move her from residential care to semi-independent living without her knowledge. Young people also said that the onus on social workers to share information made them reticent. Timothy, 15, in foster care, said he found it difficult to trust social workers because he did not feel they would keep things he said confidential:

They have to tell their manager and then they have to look at your file and then all the other social workers might see your file and then you think, 'Well who else sees this file?'

Clearly, social workers are not always able to meet the wishes of children and young people for a number of reasons, such as lack of resources or potential risks. They have to take a holistic view of young people's situations and take into account other family members, carers and other professionals. They have a duty to keep children safe and to ensure that they have stability in caring arrangements. Social workers need to take time to explain these matters and involve young people more in the process so that they may feel less alienated.

Attitudes to children and young people

Finally, workers' attitudes to children and young people have a role to play in the barriers to child-centred practice. In Chapters 2 and 3 we considered the various social attitudes to children and young people ranging from the protectionist to the liberationist.

Few of the social workers in the study said they regarded young people as competent, and they talked about assessing competence in terms of the 'Assessment Framework' (DoH, 2000) or *'Gillick competence'*. As discussed in Chapter 1, the latter is an assessment of young people's maturity used originally to determine whether they were capable of making decisions about their health. Some social workers in the study said that children and young people often did not know what they needed or what was best for them. Sharon, for example, said:

I think that young people, not to patronise them, but sometimes will not know what the best thing is, what they need. Well we know through research and our job and having been through the stage of being a young person and that – what children do need at a certain age.

Social workers in the study, whilst saying they favoured young people's participation, explained that sometimes children were too young to be involved in decisions or unable to participate because of their learning disabilities. Other workers did perceive the need to try and involve them but then talked about needing to make the decisions themselves.

With regard to children's rights, several of the social workers commented that it was more important to attend to children's needs rather than their rights. Others said they agreed with rights principles and tried to uphold them, but most of the social workers said they felt that children did not understand rights fully. Sally said children were likely to abuse their rights by insisting on behaviour that might put them at risk; she gave an example of a young person on her caseload who wanted to go to Wales to visit someone they had encountered on the internet. David said that children could abuse rights to try and get out of doing housework. He commented, *'the pendulum has swung too far the other way'*.

Some young people said they felt that they were underestimated by their social worker and treated as small children rather than young people. Liz, 14, said her social worker *'treats me like a five year old'* and Katy, also 14, said of her social worker, *'I reckon that she still thinks that I'm a little girl and she needs to make all my decisions for me'*.

Although there were exceptions, the young people did complain that they were not enough involved in important decisions about their lives and futures.

The social workers emphasised young people's immaturity and need for protection and they tended to have a paternalistic view of the young people they worked with. This is understandable when we consider their central role in child protection and risk assessment. However, this protectionist viewpoint was not appreciated by the young people, who wanted to be seen as competent and able to decide themselves what was in their own best interests.

Barriers to good relationships

Winter (2011) found similar barriers to those discussed above that social workers in her study experienced in making good relationships with children and young people. She discusses the following '7 Ts' as some of the more common barriers that occurred:

> *'tasks, trust, threats, theories, training, tools and time'.*

> (p. 38)

I summarise some of her discussion here. As found in the studies discussed above, Winter explains that social workers are frequently preoccupied with bureaucratic *tasks* such as the demands of meeting targets, filling in forms, computer work and completing assessments and these get in the way of a focus on children and young people. Young people may lack *trust* in their social workers, especially when they are unable to meet young people's wishes, for example to remain in a placement. Sometimes social workers feel *threat*ened and have anxieties about personal risk of violence from parents or carers who may feel compromised if they insist on talking to children.

Winter explains further that *theories* about the incompetence of children may pose a barrier to communication and social workers may underestimate young children's feelings and understandings. A lack of *training* in communicating with children and young people can add to this problem as can the lack of resources (*tools*) such as play materials or appropriate physical spaces to see children. Finally, high caseloads sometimes led to social workers delegating work with children and young people to other workers because they could not make *time* for this themselves.

Reflective exercise

Besides barriers faced by social workers, young people may also experience barriers to relationships.

Can you think what barriers to their relationship with a social worker may be faced by:

a 14-year-old young woman who has experienced sexual abuse by a close family member?

a 10-year-old boy who has been in several foster homes since he was 6?

Breaking down the barriers?

The next question is: how can we try to overcome these barriers to relationships and child-centred practice? Can we change a culture that many children and young people see as remote and uncaring, where social workers do not listen but make decisions for them and treat them as incompetent? Some of the barriers are very difficult to remove, especially those of the lack of resources in local authority services. This is a major political issue that individual workers will only be able to influence marginally. However, there are efforts that individuals and teams can make.

Changing the culture

The structure of social work, its hours, processes and workplaces, are arguably designed to suit adult professionals, not children and young people. Social workers normally work from around 9am till 5pm. The majority of this time is when children and young people are at nursery, school or college. Meetings are planned in social workers' normal working hours so that children who wish to attend must miss school or not attend at all. It would be most unusual for case conferences in particular to be planned to suit children's free time in the evening or weekend.

Meetings themselves, even those that children and young people are expected to attend such as statutory reviews of children looked after, are more geared around adults' needs. Commonly, adults sit around talking about children for a lengthy period of time. Child protection meetings are even less child friendly since they involve large numbers of adult professionals, very often people that the children have never met, representing agencies such as the police and legal advisors. They adhere to rigid procedures and are often very long. Chapters 7 and 8 discuss such meetings in more detail and young people's views about them.

Winter (2011) describes a social worker's reaction to a chairperson of a children's review meeting, taken from her study with social workers, parents and young children. The social worker describes the behaviour of this new review chair who wanted to make meetings more child friendly. She made efforts to get to know the children and young people through visiting them at home prior to meetings. She brought in cartons of juice and sweets to meetings and paid for these herself. Social workers initially ridiculed this practice but, *'it began to act as a catalyst for change. It made social workers reflect on their own professional practices that hindered relationships with young children.'* The social worker reported, *'We are family and childcare but we have no provision for children being in the office. You know and that's, that's quite disturbing'* (Winter, 2011, p. 55).

It can be seen from this that very small steps can make a difference to the culture of social work practice.

There are some social work offices that are child and young person friendly, but many are not welcoming for children. There are some with play areas, but many offices are adult rather than child friendly. Some of the inner London offices are vast and daunting even for adults. If there is no office facility that is child friendly then it is often preferable to meet elsewhere such as home, a family centre or school, depending on the child's preference and the possibilities of privacy. Older young people may prefer to meet in a quiet café.

Challenging the organisational ethos

Some commentators argue that social workers, given their understanding of deprivation and disadvantage, should be more active in challenging the oppressive systems in which they work (Becker, 1997; Jones, 2001), but can an individual worker challenge a powerful organisation? Organisational cultures have a strong influence over their members and people are easily sucked into the prevailing ethos (Johnson and Scholes, 2008). An individual worker, trying to resist the culture of extensive recording, for example, is likely to provoke criticism or worse from managers, even if the argument is made that we should put children first.

Gibson and O'Donovan (2014) have outlined a method of rethinking organisational practice under which permission was obtained to jettison the restrictions of government performance measures and IT in order to redesign services for children in care in several children's services departments in England and Wales. This was based on rethinking the purpose of the service by putting children at the centre and working out changes in the systems needed, so that the service was designed around the children's needs, rather than the demands of administration and bureaucracy.

Munro (2011) acknowledges the bureaucratic demands on social workers and recommends:

> ...an operational structure and systems (practice and managerial) which enable all social workers to spend most of their time undertaking effective work that directly benefits children and families and which values continuity of social worker with children and families.
>
> (p. 108)

It is not clear, however, how these aims will be achieved without social workers, both as individuals and as lobbying groups, opposing the current culture. Social work does not have a strong professional body like the medical profession's British Medical Association, but organisations such as Social Work Action Network try to rally opposition against further cuts in social care and privatisation.

Child-centred supervision

Professional supervision performs a number of functions. It is a key tool in worker accountability, in aiding reflection, and in checking our values and perceptions with an experienced other. Howe and Gray (2013), for example, see its dimensions as:

➤ work/case discussion,

➤ professional development,

➤ the supervisee's relationships with others,

➤ managerial issues, and

➤ the supervisory relationship.

The case discussion dimension includes '*critical and reflective value based analysis and exploration*' (Howe and Gray, 2013, p. 6).

The model is a generic one but there is little mention of the service user, whether adult or child. Much of the literature giving guidance for supervisory practice focuses on the relationship between supervisor and supervisee. The Munro Review (2011) with its emphasis on child-centred child protection recommends that practitioners should have:

> *frequent case consultations to explore and reflect on service effectiveness and case decision-making, separate from arrangements for individual pastoral care and professional development.*

> (p. 108)

Ferguson (2016) also recommends that workers should have regular opportunities for critical reflection on their practice. His research observing social workers' home visits to families where there were child protection concerns found that failures to focus on children resulted partly from the lack of such reflection. Research by Hunt et al. (2016), outlined in more detail in Chapter 7, found that social workers also needed support through supervision to deal with threats and hostility from parents.

Both social work supervisors and supervisees will have experience of rushed meetings where cases are checked one by one to ensure that the worker is meeting the minimum requirements of the organisation. Some of this is about keeping the organisation free from blame, in the same way that managers may orchestrate Ofsted inspections to get good ratings.

As a contrast, it is interesting to speculate what child-centred supervision could look like. There is little literature or research on this topic. McPherson and MacNamara (2016), though, propose a model for supervision in child protection drawing on literature and research to '*strengthen the quality of the service that the child experiences through the vehicle of the supervisory relationship*' (p. 3). This model suggests a proforma for supervision for each child, to include a photograph of the child as '*a powerful means of "bringing the child into the room"*' (p. 36). There are questions about child development, parenting capacity and environmental factors as would normally be expected in child protection cases. This model also brings in consideration of the impact of abuse on the child and the following questions that are critical in promoting child-centred practice:

➤ *What type of relationship do you have with the child/young person?*

➤ *To what extent does the child/young person trust you?*

➤ *In what ways have you provided information to the child/young person?*

➤ *In what ways have you encouraged the child/young person to be involved in decision making?*

This kind of focus on children in all child care cases could make a significant difference to social workers' practice and to the children who rely on them.

Making and spending time

Analyses of the time social workers spend with children, young people and their families demonstrate the continuous demands of indirect work such as recording, report writing, attending meetings and liaising with other agencies. Holmes et al. (2009) found that 80%–90% of social workers' time was spent in this 'indirect work'. There was no breakdown of the time spent with children themselves as opposed to their parents and carers. As discussed above, Gibson's (2016) research also found that child protection social workers spent 70%–90% of their time on administration.

Reflective exercise

If you are working with children and young people:
  Can you calculate:

➤ How much time you spend communicating with adults (parents, carers, other professionals and agency workers, colleagues and managers) in comparison with the people a children's service is for – namely children and young people?

➤ How much time you spend on administrative procedures such as computer work, report writing, case notes etc.?

(You could try this exercise also if you are working with a different group of service users – in which case you could calculate how much time you spend with individual service users in comparison with other professionals etc. as well as the administrative work.)

Social workers should be aware of the need to try to prioritise time with children and young people. If combined with trying to change to a more child-friendly culture and child-centred supervision this step could make positive changes. Training can also play a part.

Training

Good social work education and training can build social workers' confidence in child-centred practice. In Chapter 4 we look at the different and creative ways of working with children and young people. Ideas from social pedagogy literature and resources can help this process and enable social workers to use these methods more routinely in their work with children and young people.

O'Reilly and Dolan's (2016) study with social workers who were involved in child protection and welfare assessments found that they developed increased enthusiasm and confidence in their work with children from participation in a Play Skills Training programme of twenty hours' duration. The training incorporated theory, techniques and use of a range of play materials, books and worksheets. Participants said that the training had helped their practice to be more child-centred and child friendly although there were still difficulties for some in being able to take the time needed to work in this way.

Training can also help social workers to develop a reflective awareness of social attitudes and prejudices about children and young people, especially teenagers. This should include examining our own values, grounded in our culture and upbringing. It is important to be aware how these can affect judgements when working with children and young people.

Training about children's advocacy and rights can be helpful to social workers in their work to help children participate in decisions and to ensure that they receive a fair and child-centred service from organisations.

Conclusion

This overview of the organisational and attitudinal barriers to child-centred practice in social work also considers some ways of challenging these. To overcome the resource shortages requires a political will; this is a barrier that an individual social worker cannot challenge alone. Other ways of making a difference include changing to a more child-friendly culture in offices and meetings, child-centred supervision and training.

Summary points

➤ Barriers to child-centred practice are governed by the political and economic climate of social care provision.

➤ Social workers experience resource shortages and bureaucratic procedures that affect the quality of their work with young people.

➤ Social workers sometimes have to make decisions that children and young people are unhappy with, but these need to be carefully explained.

➤ Some social workers have paternalistic attitudes, which children and young people find upsetting.

➤ Changing the culture of an organisation can be difficult, but small measures can help services to be more child friendly.

➤ Prioritising time with young people, child-centred supervision and training can all help to break down some barriers.

Further reading and resources

McPherson, L. and Macnamara, N. (2016) *Supervising Child Protection Practice: What Works?: An Evidence Informed Approach*. Cham: Springer.
Includes child-centred ideas for supervision.

Winter, K. (2011) *Building Relationships and Communicating with Young Children: A Practical Guide for Social Workers*. Abingdon: Routledge.
Some helpful ideas about overcoming the barriers to trusting relationships between social workers and young children.

Social Work Action Network (SWAN) website gives information about the campaigns, conferences and resources of this group. It aims to unite social work students, service users, carers, practitioners, and academics in combating welfare cuts and managerialism and marketisation. Available at: http://www.socialworkfuture.org/

PART 3

Specific Fields of Child-Centred Practice

7

Child Protection and Safeguarding

Introduction

Whilst safeguarding children is everyone's concern, social workers have more specific duties in child protection. Hence the term 'safeguarding' is broader in its meaning. It is defined in 'Working Together' (DfE, 2015b, p. 92) as:

> *protecting children from maltreatment;*

> *preventing impairment of children's health or development;*

> *ensuring that children are growing up in circumstances consistent with the provision of safe and effective care; and*

> *taking action to enable all children to have the best life chances.*

Child protection is defined as:

> *part of safeguarding and promoting welfare. This refers to the activity that is undertaken to protect specific children who are suffering, or are likely to suffer, significant harm.*

> (DfE, 2015b, p. 92)

Safeguarding can be very rewarding but it is one of the most complex areas of work for social workers and one where they come under the most scrutiny. This applies whether their work is with children or with adults who have mental health issues or who lack capacity. The extra pressure on social workers who work in children's services is clear from the media uproar when a child's death from abuse hits the headlines. Jones (2014) has documented the furore that arose following the death of 'Baby P.' (Peter Connelly) and the effects this had on the professionals who were involved.

This chapter considers briefly the history of safeguarding law and policy in the UK up to the present. Changes have been influenced by numerous child death inquiries that have led to developments in policy and practice. I shall focus particularly on the role of child-centred practice where there have been attempts to improve this, including the guidance in the Munro Review (2011).

The chapter considers the processes involved in child protection and how child-centred practice can be promoted in these. This includes assessments of risk, including the impact of domestic violence and parental misuse of drugs and alcohol. It examines how children and young people can be involved in forums such as case conferences that consider individual safeguarding plans. Research about children's views and experiences in child protection inform this discussion.

Finally, it considers particular aspects of child-centred practice where there are different kinds of suspected or actual abuse, for example child sexual abuse, neglect, physical and emotional abuse as well as recently highlighted concerns about child sexual exploitation, cyber-bullying and internet abuse.

Findings of public inquiries: two strands: information sharing and focus on the child

Sharing information

Due to the findings of official inquiries into child deaths from the 1970s to the present there has been a strong emphasis in social work on sharing information about children and families effectively with other professionals and agencies. The lack of shared information has been regarded as a major factor in professional workers missing signs of serious risk to children, leading to tragic outcomes. Lord Laming, who conducted the inquiry into the death of 'Baby P.', commented of the professionals involved as follows:

> *It is evident that the challenges of working across organisational boundaries continue to pose barriers in practice, and that cooperative efforts are often the first to suffer when services and individuals are under pressure.*

> (Laming, 2009, p. 36)

Thompson (2016) highlights the complexity of information sharing, focusing mainly on this exchange in referrals. She considers the information held and given by professionals, agencies and lay people and their differing interpretations of its meaning, although this does not include information from children and young people.

Despite the obvious importance of sharing information about children at risk, as discussed in the previous chapter, children and young people have concerns about confidentiality, which can lead them to be unwilling to trust professional workers. Enabling children and young people to talk about their concerns is therefore vital.

Focus on the child

Another major finding from inquiries and Serious Case Reviews, as discussed briefly in Chapter 1, has been that social workers have failed to see and talk to children and young people when there are child protection concerns. Social workers were sometimes preoccupied with all the adult professionals surrounding a child's care and sometimes intimidated by adult carers from insisting on seeing a child (Ofsted, 2010a). Ferguson's (2016) research involved observations of social workers' interviews with families where there were child protection concerns. He found many examples of good practice, but where social workers did not engage with the children this was often due to anxiety and feelings of menace from adults present:

> *They are overcome by the sheer complexity of the interactions they encounter, the emotional intensity of the work, parental resistance and the tense atmospheres in the homes.*

(p. 11)

Research by Hunt et al. (2016), which consisted of a survey of 590 workers in children's services (72% in child protection), found that there was a high proportion of these who were working with hostile or intimidating parents or clients and that 61% of the participants had been threatened in the past six months. The survey found that workers felt unsupported by supervision and management to the degree that they felt they were hampered in protecting children.

Examples of the failure to engage with children abound throughout the last forty years – from 7-year-old Maria Colwell whose stepfather abused and killed her in 1973 to the death of 4-year-old Daniel Pelka in 2012 from physical abuse and neglect by his mother and stepfather. Recommendations from these inquiries repeat the finding that social workers and other professionals need to see and communicate with children as well as with each other.

The inquiry into the death of Victoria Climbié at age 8 in 2000 illustrates with particular clarity the need to talk to children (Laming, 2003). She died from hypothermia, malnutrition and physical abuse perpetrated by her great aunt and the aunt's cohabitee. Victoria was seen in hospital where there were concerns that she may have been hit with a belt, deliberately scalded, bitten or burnt. The allocated hospital social worker went to Victoria's hospital ward five times but did not speak to Victoria. Neither did a social work home visit shortly after this involve talking to Victoria herself. She appeared to be well dressed and was playing on the floor with a doll. A further home visit, as reported in the Inquiry, said:

> Victoria seems to have been all but ignored during this visit as she sat on the floor playing with a doll. The fact that she was still not attending school was raised during the conversation, but no questions were asked about how Victoria was spending her days.

(Laming, 2003, p. 33, para 3.59)

Although allegations of sexual abuse were also made, Victoria was never given the chance to speak to the police or to a social worker and she died two weeks after this.

Developments in law and policy

The following section describes developments in law and policy mainly in England and Wales. Fundamental law governing child protection in Northern Ireland, the Children (Northern Ireland) Order 1995, follows a similar pattern and wording to the Children Act 1989. In Scotland, the Children (Scotland) Act 1995 has similar regulation for child protection enquiries and case conferences to that in the rest of the UK, but the legal system differs. In Scotland, the children's hearings system decides mainly on welfare matters in child protection, while the court system is used where facts are disputed.

Changes in policy and law over the forty-year period from the 1970s have followed the shifting concerns of Inquiries. Reforms were instigated after the inquiry into the death of Maria Colwell (DHSS, 1974), which brought in multi-agency child protection conferences, now called 'case conferences', and the child protection register, which no longer exists but has been replaced by 'child protection plans'. One of the main aims in this change was better information sharing between professionals. Further high profile child deaths in the 1980s such as those of Jasmine Beckford and Tyra Henry in 1984 and Kimberley Carlile in 1986 led to further reforms such as the categorisation of abuse including 'physical injury', 'emotional abuse', 'physical neglect' and 'failure to thrive'. The emphasis in the Beckford Report (London Borough of Brent, 1985) and the inquiry into the death of Kimberley Carlile (London Borough of Greenwich, 1987) shifted attention to a focus on the child and his or her protection ('holding the child in mind') and away from the rights of parents.

The allegations of large scale sexual abuse of 121 children in Cleveland in 1987 added a different focus and ensured that sexual abuse became central to child protection policy considerations. Unlike in previous inquiries, commentators criticised social workers for acting too precipitately and without valid evidence. The lack of care about children's involvement in planning and assessment in intrusive medical examinations prompted the chair of the subsequent inquiry to comment, *'the child is a person not an object of concern'* (Butler-Sloss, 1998, p. 12).

Another attempt to transform the child protection system resulted from the range of concerns expressed in the inquiries of the 1980s. The first 'Working Together' guidelines were published in 1988 (DHSS and Welsh Office, 1988) and these led to more emphasis on inter-agency cooperation. The publication laid down strict procedures for social workers and other professionals to follow. The Children Act 1989 was published shortly after this and was key in promoting a focus on children and their wishes and feelings, although as discussed in detail in Chapter 1, this was largely in respect of court proceedings rather than in child protection processes. The Children Act 1989 is still the basis of principle and procedure in child protection in England and Wales. It introduced the concept of 'significant harm' and a 'duty to investigate' under Section 47(1), where a local authority had *'reasonable cause to suspect a child who lives or is found in their area is suffering, or is likely to suffer from significant harm'*. The Act also introduced legal processes for protecting children such as Emergency Protection Orders under Section 44(1) and Police Protection Orders under Section 46. New court orders including Care Orders and Supervision Orders (Section 31) introduced legal backing to compulsory local authority care for children suffering significant harm.

The publication of several research studies in 1995 provided evidence that child protection had become too procedural and had drawn too many families into investigations unnecessarily (DoH, 1995). A more holistic approach to assessment was outlined in the Assessment Framework (DoH, 2000), discussed in Chapter 1. This has now been incorporated into 'Working Together' (DfE, 2015b).

After the Victoria Climbié Inquiry (Laming, 2003), the five principles of 'Every Child Matters' (DfES, 2003) – *'being healthy, staying safe, enjoying and achieving, making a positive contribution, and economic well-being'* – aimed to improve outcomes for children. Local Safeguarding Boards and the creation of Children's Trusts aimed to integrate services through common management structures. This was implemented through The Children Act 2004 but the plans for a multi-agency database, subsequently launched under Section 12, were criticised by many for their element of surveillance and for infringement of privacy and confidentiality (Penna, 2005; Shepherd, 2009).

The Munro Review and a child-centred system

Following the tragic death of 'Baby P.' (Peter Connelly) in 2007, the same concerns as in previous inquiries were raised by the Laming Report (2009) about the failures of professionals. Baby P. died at the age of 17 months having suffered chronic neglect and physical abuse by his mother and stepfather. The subsequent Munro Review (2011), a comprehensive overview of the child protection systems in place, advised improvement in the same strands as discussed above: those of professionals sharing information and 'a child-centred system'. With regard to the latter, the primary focus of this book, Munro cites the UNCRC (1989) as a helpful framework for child-centred practice in child protection since its core principles are *'non-discrimination; devotion to the best interests of the child; the right to life, survival and development; and respect for the views of the child'* (Munro, 2011, p. 16). On this foundation, Munro recommended her 'child-centred system':

> *everyone involved in child protection should pursue child-centred working and recognise children and young people as individuals with rights, including the right to participation in decisions about them in line with their age and maturity.*
>
> (p. 23)

The report quotes findings from an analysis of sixty-seven serious case reviews between 1 April and 30 September 2010, which identified five key themes:

> ➤ *The child was not seen frequently enough by the professionals involved, or was not asked about their views and feelings.*
>
> ➤ *Agencies did not listen to adults who tried to speak on behalf of the child and who had important information to contribute.*
>
> ➤ *Parents and carers prevented professionals from seeing and listening to the child.*
>
> ➤ *Practitioners focused too much on the needs of parents, especially on vulnerable parents, and overlooked the implications for the child.*
>
> ➤ *Agencies did not interpret their findings well enough to protect the child.*
>
> (Ofsted, 2011, p. 6)

Munro (op. cit.) emphasises the importance of early intervention in families and stresses the importance of the relationships between professionals and children, as well as with other family members. She recognises that there are barriers to these relationships from the demands of managerialist systems for accountability in the form of extensive recording of contacts, assessments and plans. She recommends a shift from more proceduralised to more professionalised practice.

The Review gives some guidance on how to achieve increased child-centredness although, as noted in Chapter 1, child-centredness is not fully defined. Munro draws attention to the need for professionals, and social workers in particular, to communicate effectively with children and young people, to find out their wishes and feelings and to include them in decision making where this is possible, according to their age, understanding and so on. To support this practice, she recommends that social workers should have good training in communicating and building relationships with children and young people. The Review also provides an illustration of ways that social workers may communicate more creatively with children and young people in the form of 'The Three Houses' tool for interviewing children, which invites children to draw a 'house of worries', a 'house of good things' and a 'house of dreams', as described in Chapter 4.

Munro presents details from a submission to the Review of children's views on child protection services from the Office of the Children's Commissioner, discussed in more detail below. To summarise here, young people said they wanted more information, honesty and emotional support. They wanted to be heard separately and involved in decisions. The Review also showed that children appreciated continuity in relationships with their workers and the support of independent advocates.

After Munro

Parton's (2012) appraisal of the Munro Review, whilst commending the call for child-centred practice and professionalism rather than proceduralism, is sceptical about its success. This, Parton argues, is partly because the systems in place are so strongly embedded, but also because of government cuts to local authority services. Parton writes that the constant 'trial by media' of social work also militates against the success of the Review since it leads to professional defensiveness and a rigid adherence to procedures for fear of blame. Child-centredness is not something that is appreciated by the tabloid press.

The analysis of serious case reviews from 2011 to 2014 (Sidebotham et al., 2016) supports this view and advocates a move from blame to 'progress and hope':

> ...we would suggest an approach that steers away from trying to pronounce on whether a death or serious harm could have been predicted or prevented, to acknowledging that there is always room for learning and improvement in our systems, and therefore we owe it to children and their families to identify those lessons, disseminate the learning, and implement appropriate actions for improvement.
>
> (p. 247)

Jones (2014) has examined in detail the effects on social work of the media storm around Baby P.'s death and reaches the conclusion that child protection systems were adversely affected by the coverage. He argues that the shifts created in political attitudes and consequent changes in policy and practice were not beneficial to children or their families and led to decline in recruitment and retention of social workers as well as increased workloads.

Another effect, well documented, was the increase in care proceedings immediately after the Baby P. inquiry. There was an immediate effect in numbers of care applications, which increased by 36.1% between 2008–09 and 2009–10 (CAFCASS, 2012). Figures from CAFCASS (the Children and Family Court Advisory Service) have shown a consistent increase in applications to 14,597 in 2016–17. (There were 6,488 in 2008–09.) Dickens and Masson (2016) argue that the numbers of care proceedings have also been fuelled by shortened court time limits and a drive to adopt children from care. The statutory time limit on care proceedings was set at 26 weeks in the 'Public Law Outline' in 2014 (Children and Families Act, 2014, Section 14). This, they argue, has led to less family support or prevention of care proceedings and more focus on the court process, a move which is not in children's interests. Similarly, Featherstone et al. (2013) complain about the climate of early child protection intervention and early removal of children, which has led to lack of support for children and families and an increase in care applications. There has also been a drive to get more children adopted quickly, and 'adoption scorecards' on local authorities' performance on placing children for adoption are published by the Department for Education.

In the meantime local authority cuts have continued with more severity to the present. Jones (2015) quotes alarming figures from 2014:

> *The National Audit Office (2014) states that there will be 37% estimated real-terms reduction in government funding to local authorities between 2010–11 and 2015–16. This is at a time when between 2008 and 2014 child protection investigations have increased by 60% and child protection plans by 50% (based on Department for Education, 2014a) and local authority care proceedings applications to the courts by 76% (Based on CAFCASS, 2014).*

(Jones, 2015, p. 13)

Jones (2015) reports on the incipient privatisation of children's services including child protection, which he argues will not be in children's interests since it fragments services and undermines accountability. A move to outsource child protection by the then Education minister, Michael Gove, was shelved, influenced by the opposition of leading social work academics (Butler, 2014). However, some local authorities have already outsourced children's services 'by stealth'.

Subsequently, the Children and Social Work Bill 2016 aimed to allow the government to 'exempt' local authorities from legal duties under certain pieces of children's social care legislation, including some sections of the Children Act 1989 and the Children Act 2004. They were to be allowed to innovate if better outcomes could be achieved by doing so. This was, however, opposed and not included in the final Children and Social Work Act 2017.

Processes of child protection and children's views

In this climate of an increase of work and of funding cuts, how can social workers be more child-centred in the processes of child protection? There is guidance from law, policy, theory and research, but the views of children and young people are key to this and are included in this section. Studies have looked specifically at children and young people's experiences of child protection and its processes. I shall consider the main areas of this research. These focus on children and young people's views about being able to tell someone about abuse and being involved in decisions and meetings.

Principles of child protection

Statutory guidance for professionals in child protection, 'Working Together to Safeguard Children' (DfE, 2015b), states two key principles that still reflect the two strands of concern, outlined in child death inquiries over the last forty years, discussed at the beginning of this chapter:

> ➤ *safeguarding is everyone's responsibility: for services to be effective each professional and organisation should play their full part*

> ➤ *a child-centred approach: for services to be effective they should be based on a clear understanding of the needs and views of children.*

(p. 9)

The guidance sets out the principles of a child-centred approach to safeguarding:

> *Failings in safeguarding systems are too often the result of losing sight of the needs and views of the children within them, or placing the interests of adults ahead of the needs of children.*

Children want to be respected, their views to be heard, to have stable relationships with professionals built on trust and to have consistent support provided for their individual needs. This should guide the behaviour of professionals. Anyone working with children should see and speak to the child; listen to what they say; take their views seriously; and work with them collaboratively when deciding how to support their needs.

(pp. 9–10)

Willow (2009) talks about children being 'invisible' in child protection, and we have noted above the many similar comments from inquiries into child deaths from abuse. Clifton (2014) also makes a strong argument for children and young people to be seen and heard in child protection processes, but what do children themselves say?

Some of the views expressed by children about their participation and involvement in social care generally (cited in Chapter 5) are relevant here. 'Working Together' (DfE, 2015b) provides a summary of children's views about child protection and what they have said they need:

> ➢ Vigilance: to have adults notice when things are troubling them
>
> ➢ Understanding and action: to understand what is happening; to be heard and understood; and to have that understanding acted upon
>
> ➢ Stability: to be able to develop an ongoing stable relationship of trust with those helping them
>
> ➢ Respect: to be treated with the expectation that they are competent rather than not
>
> ➢ Information and engagement: to be informed about and involved in procedures, decisions, concerns and plans
>
> ➢ Explanation: to be informed of the outcome of assessments and decisions and reasons when their views have not met with a positive response
>
> ➢ Support: to be provided with support in their own right as well as a member of their family
>
> ➢ Advocacy: to be provided with advocacy to assist them in putting forward their views
>
> **(DfE, 2015b, p. 11)**

Cossar et al. (2011) conducted a day workshop and interviewed 26 children, ages 6–17, about their views of the English child protection system. The study found that the worries of children who were involved in child protection procedures may be different from concerns that brought the family to the professionals' attention. For example, they included worries about bullying and other problems in school and in their community.

Initial enquiries and assessments

Whilst safeguarding children is a general duty that is the concern of everyone, social workers have a duty to lead the child protection process with specific responsibilities under the law:

> Local authorities, with the help of other organisations as appropriate, also have a duty to make enquiries under section 47 of the Children Act 1989 if they have reasonable cause to suspect that a child is suffering, or is likely to suffer, significant harm, to enable them to decide whether they should take any action to safeguard and promote the child's welfare. There may be a need for immediate protection whilst the assessment is carried out.
>
> (DfE, 2015b, p. 18)

Section 47 (and Section 17) of the Children Act 1989 was amended by Section 53 of the Children Act 2004 to specify that the wishes and feelings of the child should be ascertained and given consideration in the child protection process.

Talking to children and young people at the stage of initial enquiry under Section 47 may be more limited because of time constraints than during a longer assessment, and statutory guidance and local safeguarding procedures should be followed. Consent to talk to younger children should be approved by both parent and child unless this might place a child at risk of significant harm, but a court order may be needed if parents refuse this. A strategy discussion with police and other professionals involved may recommend a special investigative interview. These interviews with children for evidential purposes require specialist training and need to be conducted according to Ministry of Justice Guidance (2011) 'Achieving Best Evidence'. For helpful detailed advice about the process of evidential interviewing, see also McLeod (2008), who outlines the stages and processes of setting up and conducting these interviews.

Social workers are sometimes unsure about talking to children at the initial enquiry stage when evidence may necessary for criminal proceedings, but it is still vital to listen to children and make it possible for them to express their views. However, leading questions should be avoided and children's words recorded accurately in case these are needed for court proceedings.

Being able to tell someone

Child protection procedures and the courts are not geared up to enable children and young people to feel comfortable to talk about their abuse. It is often not until many years after the events that people are able to talk about the traumatic abuse that happened in their child-hood and adolescence.

Studies have looked at children and young people's difficulties in being able to talk about the abuse they have suffered so that this can be stopped. In general terms, young people have said that they find the stigma and shame of abuse a difficulty in itself. Several studies have found that young people tended to blame themselves (Buckley et al., 2011; Cossar et al., 2013; Katz, 2013). In the study by Buckley et al. (2011), 67 young people in Ireland ages 13–23 were interviewed about their experiences of child protection processes. It found that they felt embarrassed by their involvement with Social Services and tried to conceal this from others, saying it was their 'big secret' (p. 104).

Even recognising that abuse is happening can be a barrier to receiving help. Cossar et al.'s (2011) study, previously described, found that children and young people were sometimes not sure whether the abuse was 'normal', especially children in the younger age range. Sometimes they did not have the words to describe what was happening to them. This was also found by Adamson and Templeton's (2012) study into children living with parental alcohol abuse.

Loyalty to the abuser, especially if this was a member of the family, prevented some young people from telling but also fear of them and of what might happen such as being taken into care (Cossar et al., 2013; Jobe and Gorin, 2013). Jobe and Gorin (2013) interviewed 24 young people ages 11–17 about their experience of seeking and receiving help for maltreatment in England. This study also found that young people were unsure about the safeguarding process. They were more likely to tell a friend or a relative about the abuse and were unsure which professional they should talk to, although the study found that teachers were most likely to receive their confidence. A 15-year-old girl said:

> It's all about trust, isn't it – some people you get on with and some people you don't like – some people you can trust and some people you can't.
>
> (Jobe and Gorin, 2013, p. 433)

She advised that professionals should *'keep trying to be approachable'* – to enable children to turn to them.

In Cossar et al.'s (2011) research, children and young people said that it helped them to talk about the abuse if a trusted person was sensitive to their being upset and asked them about this. Young people in this study said they needed to build a consistent relationship with their social worker to be able to open up to them and they needed to feel safe. For them disclosure was not a one off event but a longer process.

Reflective exercise

Think about a personal difficulty you had in your own life.

How did you decide who to talk to about this – of family and friends? Did you tell the whole story to everyone?

If you spoke to a professional about this how did it feel?

The above exercise may help to remind us how difficult we all find it sometimes to trust other people with our personal problems. For children, who lack the wisdom gained from experience of the world, it can be even more difficult since they are unlikely to know how others will react and what the outcome will be.

Assessments

Guidance on assessments in safeguarding and child protection have built on the 'Framework for Assessment' (DoH, 2000) outlined in Chapter 1. 'Working Together' (DfE, 2015b) gives principles for high quality assessments, many of which are child focused:

High quality assessments:

➢ *are child centred; Where there is a conflict of interest, decisions should be made in the child's best interests;*

➢ *are rooted in child development and informed by evidence;*

➢ *are focused on action and outcomes for children;*

➢ *are holistic in approach, addressing the child's needs within their family and wider community;*

➢ *ensure equality of opportunity;*

➢ *involve children and families;*

➢ *build on strengths as well as identifying difficulties;*

➢ *are integrated in approach;*

➢ *are a continuing process not an event;*

➢ *lead to action, including the provision of services;*

> *review services provided on an ongoing basis; and*

> *are transparent and open to challenge.*

(p. 21)

The Ofsted report (2011) on serious case reviews held during 2010 highlights, and gives examples of, positive practice in child-centred assessment. The overall findings are quoted earlier in this chapter. The report cites cases where children and young people had only been able to talk about their abuse when their carers were not present. One case involved children who could only talk about longstanding neglect and physical and sexual abuse once they were removed from home. The report advises that children need to be seen on their own, in a place they find familiar and where they can relax. It acknowledges that communication is not always straightforward and direct observation will be important with babies and young children, whilst an appropriate means needs to be found to communicate with disabled children to find out their views. In addition, young carers may need an assessment in their own right since the needs of adults with mental health issues or alcoholism may lead them to be overlooked.

Lefevre (2010) outlines a helpful process for conducting child-centred assessments. Many of the issues about good communication with children and young people discussed in Chapter 4 apply here. I summarise Lefevre's advice here with some additions:

> Firstly it is key to give the young person information and explain what an assessment is, why it is happening and how, and what kind of things will be the focus.

> Young people's consent and an agreement are useful here.

> All this needs to be conveyed in a way that is appropriate to the individual child, bearing in mind their age, language, disability and so on.

> It is important to build up a trusting relationship, as noted above, and different kinds of communication including play may be helpful, as well as a range of questions and prompts.

> Attentive listening, as described in Chapter 4, will be essential to interpret what children are trying to say.

Children's views about assessments

Once involved in child protection assessments and procedures, young people said they appreciated the continuity of having the same social worker and, very importantly, being able to build up a relationship where they felt trust and safety (Jobe and Gorin, 2013; Cossar et al., 2016). They wanted workers who were relaxed, took time with them and were easy to talk to (Buckley et al., 2011). A 17-year-old young woman in Jobe and Gorin's (2013) study said:

> I think one of the main things is that when a social worker is designated, you should keep that social worker for as long as possible... I really think that they should try and keep that same social worker with that child for as long as possible, so then a relationship can get built up, the trust can get built up. And then at the end of the day the social worker will find out a lot more...I think if they expect children to tell them things and put trust in them, then you need to put the work in and be with them for a long period of time, and just make a relationship with them.
>
> (p. 434)

Young people were frustrated by having to wait a long time for assessments (Buckley et al., 2011) and the lack of contact with their social workers who sometimes seemed remote (Jobe and Gorin, 2013; Cossar et al., 2016). In the latter study young people talked about feeling interrogated by their social workers and about struggling to understand the child protection process. They appreciated being given information by the social worker and seeing reports and assessments that had been written about them. They also needed to know the outcome of these assessments.

Child protection meetings: case conferences and core groups

Case conferences and core groups are important decision making forums that include key professionals involved with a family and usually parents and carers. They frequently do not include children and young people themselves. Good child-centred practice should dictate that children and young people are able to participate in decisions about themselves and their future and thus be able to represent their views at child protection meetings. Bruce's (2014) study in Scotland examined the extent of participation of young people ages 7–14 in case conferences and the representation of their views in reports. The vast majority of the children did not attend their conference and many of the meetings took place without the views of the child being represented. Quite often the child's view was 'filtered' through the interpretation of professionals. Bruce concluded that social workers needed to be more committed to children's participation to enable a change in practice.

Horwath and Tarr's (2015) study of conferences and core groups pertaining to neglect in England and Wales found that children's wishes and feelings were overall poorly represented at these meetings. From evidence in the study, they attributed this firstly to social workers not getting to grips with the meaning and the impact on children of the neglect they experienced. Further, the children's perception of self and their *'lived experience'* were not adequately conveyed (p. 1389). Children were represented in terms of their parents' failures rather than as unique individuals affected by these. In sibling groups there was some difficulty in being able to focus on individual children.

Another aspect found by Horwarth and Tarr (op. cit.) was that social workers engaged only superficially with the children, partly because of the strict timescales imposed for the conferences (fifteen days from the beginning of an assessment). As in Bruce's (2014) research, in this study it was found to be rare for the children to attend conferences themselves. Only one set of older siblings attended with an advocate. Professionals gave various reasons for their omission, such as that children may not wish to attend, that they may be overwhelmed by having to hear difficult discussions and that adults might feel unable to speak as freely if children were present. Further obstacles reported were the lack of child friendly set ups and venues for meetings and the timing of these, usually during school hours. Also there was recognition that a lot of preparation would be needed for children to attend and that this would be time consuming.

Horwath and Tarr (2015) highlighted areas of good practice in understanding and presenting children's viewpoints. These included social workers sharing with children photographs of routine daily activities, like watching television, in order to understand a child's daily life. One social worker was able to describe a child's identity as *'a protector of her mother from domestic abuse, a young carer and a bullied child'* (p. 1385). Such descriptions were able to help child protection meetings to be more child-centred in their considerations and plans.

Lefevre (2010) highlights the importance of good preparation for children and young people attending child protection meetings, including explanations of the purpose of the meeting, who else will be present and what the child's own role will be. They will want to know also about the nature of the information that will be shared at the meeting, especially any sensitive topics. Lefevre discusses the usefulness of an advocate to support young people through the process.

Different models for assessments and conferences have been introduced to attempt to build on family strengths and to work more in partnership. The 'Signs of Safety' model developed by Turnell and Edwards (1999) aims to be more transparent with families about risks and protective factors to children and to set goals jointly about what needs to change. Family Group Conferences, which were first developed in New Zealand in the 1980s, aimed to involve children and their extended family networks to work with professionals in seeking their own solutions to protecting children in their care. Both these models aim to involve children and young people more in decisions but need careful attention to family power dynamics to enable children to have a voice (Morris and Connelly, 2012).

Children and young people's views about their involvement in decisions and meetings

Young people's participation in decision making and in child protection meetings is not universal (Bruce, 2014), and studies of those young people who had attended case conferences, for example, often found this was a difficult and emotional process. Children have talked about their experiences of case conferences in research studies (McLeod, 2008; Buckley et al., 2011; Cossar et al., 2016). Young people in Cossar's study said they found the process *'nerve wracking'*. One said of the meetings:

> *I did go once but it was awful... they were just all talking and I didn't understand what they were saying. It was about me. I didn't really enjoy it that much.*
>
> (p. 109)

Young people said they found it difficult to be heard or to ask questions. Both young people and their families appreciated being properly prepared for meetings by their social worker (Buckley et al., 2011).

The Office of the Children's Commissioner's submission to the Munro Review (2011) provided evidence from children that supports many of the findings in the studies above about children's need for information about child protection processes and consistent support from the same worker. It also found that young people appreciated advocacy support. Studies such as that by Scutt (1999) have found that children felt better prepared and supported at conferences when they had an advocate present, someone who could also represent their views if they chose not to be present.

Case example: Mira and Sam: Case conference

Mira moved to the UK from Algeria when she was 15 as a young asylum seeker. She is now 18 and has a baby boy, Sam, 9 months old. Mira was looked after in a foster home, then in semi-independent living, before moving to privately rented accommodation, but she is still supported as a young care leaver by her social worker, Jonathan. Mira had been living with Sam's father, Nick, but he assaulted her when

▶

◀

Sam was just 4 months old and she sustained bad facial injuries, which she tried to disguise from children's services, fearing that they might take Sam away from her. Mira's social worker discovered the domestic abuse and reported this to the police. A case conference was held to assess the risk to Sam and he now has a child protection plan because of the risk from his father Nick. The health visitor is happy about Mira's general care of Sam.

Mira says she has now broken up with Nick, who was prosecuted for the assault but is out on bail and has tried to visit Mira and Sam. The police were called but children's services are not sure that Mira will keep Nick away as she has said that Sam should get to know his father in the future.

A review conference is due, and Mira wants support from Jonathan, her leaving care social worker, to remove the child protection plan, which she finds oppressive because of the regular checks on her by Sam's social worker.

Comment on the case example

In the above scenario Jonathan, the leaving care social worker, has a duty to offer support to this young care leaver and he feels that it is unfair that she is being punished for the violence of her ex partner. This is a familiar story that women are held responsible for the safety of their children when they have not contributed to any abuse. Jonathan is, however, also concerned about Sam's safety. He is aware that social workers need to focus on the safety of very young children in any family. He decides that the best course to support Mira is to put her in touch with a young person's advocate who can help her express her views at the conference.

The importance of relationship

One thing the studies cited in this section all have in common is their emphasis on the importance of children and young people's relationship with professionals, in particular their social worker, and this is at the heart of child-centred practice. This finding has been repeated in studies dating from Bell's (2002) research into children's relationships with their social worker when involved in child protection (described in Chapter 4), to those conducted most recently.

Specific issues in child protection

It is not within the scope of this book to go into detail about the prevalence, causes, symptoms and effects of abuse or the detailed guidance about procedures for response to these and child protection enquiries.

Here I shall deal with some specific issues affecting child-centred practice in relation to different forms of abuse.

The statutory guidance 'Working Together to Safeguard Children' (DfE, 2015b) gives definitions of the four main categories of child abuse. These are physical abuse, emotional abuse, sexual abuse and neglect. I give the brief definitions here but for the full detail see DfE (2015, p. 92–94).

➤ *Physical abuse: A form of abuse which may involve hitting, shaking, throwing, poisoning, burning or scalding, drowning, suffocating or otherwise causing physical harm to a child.*

➤ *Emotional abuse: The persistent emotional maltreatment of a child such as to cause severe and persistent adverse effects on the child's emotional development.*

➤ *Sexual abuse: Involves forcing or enticing a child or young person to take part in sexual activities, not necessarily involving a high level of violence, whether or not the child is aware of what is happening.*

➤ *Neglect: The persistent failure to meet a child's basic physical and/or psychological needs, likely to result in the serious impairment of the child's health or development.*

It is important to note that the definition of emotional abuse includes witnessing the ill treatment of another (as in domestic violence) and bullying. The definition of sexual abuse includes non-contact activities such as being involved in seeing sexual images, grooming via the internet and child sexual exploitation. The definition of neglect includes that to the unborn child, e.g. through substance misuse.

Emphasis on particular aspects of child protection changes over time. For example, the prevalence of child sexual abuse was not recognised by professionals until after the Cleveland scandal in 1987 (Butler-Sloss, 1988). The effects on children of witnessing domestic violence were not universally recognised in the UK until at least the 1990s. More recently, concerns about internet safety and child sexual exploitation have featured strongly in the news and now receive increased professional attention. These latter concerns will be discussed further at the end of this chapter. There are also differing emphases in child protection depending on place. As discussed in Chapter 2, in the 'Global South' concerns for children's safety centre around issues such as poverty, child labour and forced marriages.

Some commentators have raised fundamental concerns about the UK society's values regarding children's safety. Walker (2011) notes the inherent difficulties in promoting children's rights and child-centredness and in protecting children under current law and policy in England. For example, there is a clear link between child protection interventions and poverty and deprivation, especially in cases of neglect (Walker, 2011; Hood et al., 2016). Fundamental changes in society's priorities would be needed to lift children out of poverty, but this is not likely in a political climate where welfare cuts are seen as more important. A government briefing paper reported a rise in child poverty figures for 2016, to 3.9 million (House of Commons, 2016).

Regarding physical abuse, whilst many other European countries have outlawed smacking for years, in England parents still have the right to smack or hit their child. Under Section 58 of the Children Act 2004 they can use the defence of 'reasonable chastisement' where a physical assault does not cause wounding, grievous bodily harm, actual bodily harm or cruelty. The law protects adults from similar violence, so that the different rules for hitting children and adults make the whole legal system far less child-centred.

The impact of parents' issues

Bruce (2014) reports that professionals dealing with neglect often focus on parents' failings rather than the effects on children. This is similarly the case with other parental behaviours or issues that adversely affect children. For example, when there is domestic violence or substance misuse by family members, there is a tendency for professionals to focus on this adult behaviour and overlook the impact on children and on what they want from professionals. Sidebotham et al.'s (2016) analysis of serious case reviews emphasises the cumulative effects that a range of parental issues such as mental ill health, substance misuse and domestic violence can have on children.

It has been increasingly recognised that children are affected by witnessing domestic violence and may suffer emotional damage even when they themselves are unharmed physically. We also need to understand the impact of ongoing coercive control on children and other family members rather than just considering isolated incidents (Sidebotham et al., 2016). Children have frequently been regarded as passive members of the family where this coercion and violence takes place, but Katz (2015) argues for a more sophisticated understanding of children's agency in situations of domestic violence, one that takes account of their wishes to support themselves and others in their family. Mullender et al. (2002) also found that children wanted to be listened to and involved in solutions for their families. They wanted a dialogue with their mothers and others about this and to help make decisions.

Adamson and Templeton's (2012) research showed the importance of considering children's individual experience and the impact on them of their parents' problem drinking. It found that many children of parents and carers who abused alcohol did not feel they could talk to anyone because of the stigma of this and they could not always rely on friends and neighbours for respite. One young person explained how difficult their situation could be:

I need somewhere safe to go quickly when mum starts drinking and cutting herself but where can I go?

(p. 24)

Young people experienced violent scenes and often neglect, or having to take responsibility for their parents' care and for the running of the household. Many parents did not see their drinking as a problem or understand the impact on their children since drinking is widely socially accepted.

Similarly, professionals need to understand the impact on individual children of parental abuse of other substances (Cleaver et al., 2011). Cleaver et al. (op. cit.) chart the range of possible effects on children and young people of living with parents who misuse substances or perpetrate domestic violence and parents who have a learning disability or mental illness. These effects can vary depending on the age of the child. For example, babies may be affected by a parent's depression if the parent is emotionally unavailable, and this can lead to poor bonding and insecure attachment. Older children may feel isolated and have low self esteem if their parent has a mental illness, especially if they feel unable to talk to anyone about this. It is important to learn from children themselves what the impact on them might be, and professionals need to respond accordingly.

Some children become young carers in these circumstances. These young people often take pride in their role as carer for parents with mental or physical ill health, or drug or alcohol misuse. Aldridge and Becker (2003) found that these young carers wanted to be able to get practical help and good information and be involved by professionals in their parents' care and treatment. Sometimes the divisions between the services for children and those for adults, however, led to them being overlooked and not given adequate support (Cleaver et al., 2007).

Case example: Young carer: Natalie

Natalie is 7 and she lives with her mother, Sarah. Sarah is a lone parent whose relationship with Natalie's father ended soon after Natalie was born. Sarah had a car accident four years ago and she is consequently in a wheelchair because of injuries to her legs and hips. Periodically she goes for inpatient hospital treatment. Sarah's

▶

◄

mother looks after Natalie at such times but Sarah does not get on with her and sees her as little as possible.

Natalie's school has reported to children's services on several occasions that Natalie's attendance is irregular and she sometimes turns up at school with inappropriate clothing, e.g. no coat in cold weather or no socks. When asked about this Natalie says that she gets herself ready for school as her Mum is not up. She has also said, when late, that she had to help her Mum get dressed and get her breakfast.

The school nurse has visited home to talk to Sarah about this. She could not get a reply on a couple of occasions. Then one time she looked into the main room since the door was open and she could hear music. She saw Sarah slumped in front of the gas fire asleep, her trousers scorching and about to burn. Neighbours have reported to the school that Sarah uses illegal drugs, partly, they think, as painkillers.

Comment on the case example

Whilst there is clearly an element of risk to Natalie in this scenario, of neglect, she is a young carer, and children's services will need to consider how they can support her. They will need to ask her sensitively about her daily experience of living with her mother. We do not know whether she is happy about her responsibilities as a young carer or whether she needs more support with this. We also do not know how her mother's drug use (if true) is having an impact on her life.

Older children: child sexual exploitation, cyber-bullying and internet abuse

Working Together (DfE, 2015b) gives a definition of child sexual exploitation:

> *Child sexual exploitation is a form of child sexual abuse. It occurs where an individual or group takes advantage of an imbalance of power to coerce, manipulate or deceive a child or young person under the age of 18 into sexual activity (a) in exchange for something the victim needs or wants, and/or (b) for the financial advantage or increased status of the perpetrator or facilitator. The victim may have been sexually exploited even if the sexual activity appears consensual. Child sexual exploitation does not always involve physical contact; it can also occur through the use of technology.*

> (DfE, 2015b, p. 93)

The scale of such abuse has been more widely appreciated through inquiries such as those in Rotherham and Rochdale. Jay's (2014) independent inquiry found that for years the authorities tended to minimise or ignore the evidence of sexual grooming and violence, some preferring to believe that the young people were willingly involved.

The attempts by professionals to deal with child sexual exploitation, gang violence and online grooming and abuse illustrate the difficulties and dilemmas of child-centred practice in child protection. These protection issues occur most frequently with older children and young people. Pearce (2014) argues that the Munro Review with its emphasis on relationship-based practice in child protection overlooks the needs of vulnerable older children since its focus is on abuse of younger children in the home. The abuse of older children in child sexual exploitation and gang violence is normally focused *away* from the family home. Young people who are involved may reject help and support that is offered through their feelings of lack of trust, or they may feel that they do not need help. They may fear the power of the perpetrators or they may wish to exercise choice and control over their associates.

Research by Beckett et al. (2013) on child sexual exploitation in gang affected neighbourhoods found that young people may be too terrified of the consequences from perpetrators to tell anyone, and when they finally do, the response may put them further at risk. This was explained by a young woman in the study who told the police about her rape, only to find that her abuser was let out on bail and came to threaten her. Pearce (2014) explains:

Children who have been sexually exploited want to be trusted, want to be believed and want supported workers to stay with them throughout the process of identification, engagement and eventual prosecution of the abuser.

(p. 132)

She argues that a 'social model' helps to understand these young people's pressures better than individualising their 'consent' to abusive sexual activity. This involves understanding the context of the impact of grooming on young people and the social climate that normalises sexual violence.

Case example: Sonay

Sonay is a 15-year-old young woman whose family are of Turkish origin. All her immediate family live in North London. She has two sisters, and her mother has mental health issues. She has no contact with her father. Until two months ago she lived with her maternal grandparents but there were concerns that they were not able to provide adequate boundaries as Sonay was staying out overnight with members of

▶

◄

a gang who were dealing drugs, and it was thought that she was at risk of sexual exploitation. A Care Order (s31, Children Act 1989) was sought and made and Sonay was moved to a residential home just outside London whilst a further assessment was made.

Sonay has made progress at the residential home, having had some counselling about drug use and risks around sex and relationships. However, she has absconded several times, returning to her home area. She says she misses her family and friends, and her grandparents are not able to travel to see her easily because of infirmity. She says she is no longer seeing the gang where she was thought to be at risk, and anyway, they would no longer accept her into their group after the police and children's services questioned her.

The team manager in children's services has suggested that Sonay should move to a foster placement well away from London to keep her safe. A placement in rural Wales has been identified but Sonay has said she is horrified at the thought of living in a rural area so far from home and her community. She is also clear that she does not wish to be fostered as she says she has a family of her own and does not feel she could make relationships with foster carers. Sonay really wants to be able to go back and live in her home area but if not, to remain in the residential home where she feels well supported by staff.

Comment on the case example

Sonay's social worker has the difficult job of weighing up the risk to Sonay from absconding to her home area and being back with the gang, against her wishes to stay near enough home to visit her friends and family. The social worker also needs to consider Sonay's views about foster care and about being in a rural area, something she feels she would be unable to adjust to after living in an inner city area all her life. A model that builds on partnership and shared learning, as suggested by Pearce (2014) below, is most likely to help keep her safe since at 15 she can absent herself from any placement however far away.

Internet abuse and cyber-bullying

Bailey's independent review of the commercialisation and sexualisation of childhood (DfE, 2011), involving parents and young people, reported that children and young people are exposed to a pervasive sexual culture that he termed *'the wallpaper of children's lives'* (DfE, 2011, p. 9). This culture is prevalent in television, film, advertising, music videos and print and online media. Against this background, the scope for abuse of children and young people via the internet is now widely understood and safeguards have been difficult to achieve. Increasingly, younger children have unlimited access through computers and smartphones. Research in 2014 found that 74% of children in the UK ages 9–16 used mobile phones and that 95% of these accessed the internet on their phone (NTT DOCOMO, 2014). These children and young people may view sexually explicit material inadvertently though 'pop-ups' or through accidentally accessing 'adult' websites. They may also view such material deliberately when there is no filtering software in place.

On the internet, grooming of a young person by an adult can take place, for example through social networking sites or chat rooms. Children and young people may be encouraged to engage in sexually explicit conversations or in sexual acts and can leave themselves vulnerable to blackmail or extortion. They may be led to meet their contact in person and thereby risk physical and sexual abuse. Often young people are misled to think that they are communicating with someone of a similar age to themselves, rather than the actual adult groomer.

In a study by Katz (2013) on internet-related child sexual abuse, young people said they had difficulty in talking about this abuse because of their embarrassment and feelings that they were themselves partly to blame for it happening. They said they felt guilty but also overwhelmed by the perpetrator's power. One of the young people said of the abuser, '*He can do anything*' (p. 1539).

Children and young people are also exploited and abused in the making of illegal video material for the sexual gratification of paedophiles. Much of this is accessed via the 'dark web' and not easily traceable by law enforcement agencies. In the UK the Child Exploitation and Online Protection Centre (CEOP) works to try to eradicate this abuse and has a safety centre to encourage people to report online abuse and cyber-bullying.

Communication between young people themselves may have a sexual content that may be verbal but may also include sexualised images of themselves. This 'sexting' has exposed many young people to humiliation and bullying, when their message has been shared by a boyfriend or girlfriend without their permission. Sexting may also lead to criminal prosecution for abuse if a younger person is involved by one slightly older. This may have serious consequences for these young people, who can end up on the Sex Offenders Register. According to the National Crime Agency (2015), sexting has become increasingly the norm for teenagers in the UK and there are concerns about the criminalising of many young people because of this.

Cyber-bullying has also become an increasing problem for children and young people, as many of them are constantly on social networking sites, such as Facebook and Twitter. Cyber-bullying can be defined as '*the repeated harassment, degradation or abuse of another through or with technology'* (Giant, 2013, p. 25). This can be through texts, phone calls, pictures, videos, email, online chat rooms, social networking sites and websites generally. There are major concerns about the links between this form of bullying and young people's depression and suicide (Kowalski et al., 2012). Whilst bullying has long been recognised as a problem in schools, the difference with cyber-bullying is that young people cannot escape it when they go home since they are still linking in through the networking sites that are a central part of their peer relationships.

Pearce (2014) suggests the use of 'Learning Action Partnerships' (LAPS) in helping to protect older young people from abuse. The model was originally developed by the Oak Foundation in work to prevent child abuse and is based on a relationship-based model that respects young people's agency and their willingness or otherwise to engage with the process. The process involves shared learning between professional and young person about abusive behaviours, shared actions for potential change and a genuine partnership that respects the young person's choices.

Conclusion

This overview has attempted to consider child protection from the perspective of children and young people as far as possible and to emphasise the importance of placing children at the centre of practice. It is a challenging time for social workers in this field of work, when they are vilified for any failures in protecting children and resources are reducing. It is tempting to adhere strictly to procedures to 'cover one's back' and make sure that everything is recorded and information shared with other professionals. However, this can be at the expense of supporting children and young people who are caught up in the child protection process and who want to be involved in decisions and kept informed. Research has consistently found that children and young people are helped through the trauma of abuse and neglect through good relationships with professionals and through being understood as unique individuals with views of their own.

Summary points

➤ Inquiries into avoidable child deaths from abuse repeatedly report two major failures in child protection: that of not adequately sharing information and that of not focusing on the child. Subsequent law and policy has recommended more child-centred practice.

➤ There has been a recent increase in referrals and a reduction in resources for social work in child protection.

➤ Children and young people say they want respect, information and support. A good stable relationship with their social worker is vital.

➤ It can be difficult for young people to tell of their abuse, and they need good preparation and support with their participation in assessments and meetings.

➤ Protecting children and young people from parental abuse and neglect requires a focus on the impact of these on each individual child.

➤ Older young people involved in sexual exploitation or internet abuse may need a response that involves them more in partnership with professionals.

Further reading and resources

Blyth, M. (ed.) (2014) *Moving on from Munro: Improving Children's Services*. Bristol: Policy Press.
Contains useful chapters including the child's experience of child protection and working with older children who have been sexually exploited.

Brammer, A. (2015) *Social Work Law,* 4th edition. Harlow: Pearson Longman.
Helpful for further detail of the law relating to social work with children.

Department for Education (2015b) *Working Together to Safeguard Children*. London: DfE.
This outlines the government guidance and the major principles and practice for professionals in child protection.

Munro, E. (2011) *The Munro Review of Child Protection: Final Report: A Child-Centred Approach*. London: The Stationery Office.
Some helpful advice about implementing child-centred practice.

Cleaver, H., Unell, I. and Aldgate, J. (2011) *Children's Needs–Parenting Capacity: Child Abuse, Parental Mental Illness, Learning Disability, Substance Misuse, and Domestic Violence*, 2nd edition. London: The Stationery Office.
Considers the impact on children of parental difficulties at different ages, including children's views and experiences.

The Child Exploitation and Online Protection Centre (CEOP) website provides a range of information about keeping children and young people safe online, including videos for different age groups of children and for carers and professionals. Available at: https://ceop.police.uk/safety-centre/

The NSPCC website is a useful resource about all aspects of child protection in the UK, including information about services, research and statistics. It also gives details of the NSPCC Helpline – advice for professionals and families, and Childline – a counselling service for children themselves. Available at https://www.nspcc.org.uk/

8

Children and Young People Who are Looked After

Introduction

I just think they're a much misunderstood bunch are looked after children. They're some of the most amazing, intelligent children in our city, if uneducated! But very intelligent children and with the most amazing skills and talents and it's just over-looked for the simple reason that they're looked after.

(Children's Advocate)

The above excerpt from the author's research interview with a children's advocate shows his appreciation of these young people and of what they have to overcome, but children who are looked after in the public care are some of the most disadvantaged in our society.

This chapter starts with a brief outline of law and policy in this field, looking at how this may guide child-centred practice. It includes an examination of developments over time, for example the increased use of foster care, the pressure for adoption and special guardianship, and asks whether this is driven by child-centred concerns. It then considers the various disadvantages of young people in the care system and how young people's experience may be ameliorated by child-centred practice.

The chapter considers children and young people's experiences of public care, from the stage of entering care, through their time in foster or residential placements and then to moving out. It also looks at evidence about young people's views of the care system and their continuing dissatisfaction about their lack of involvement in decisions, considering how they can be meaningfully involved in, for example, statutory reviews and other meetings.

As noted in the Introduction, I use the terms 'in care' and the 'care system' as well as the more clumsy, but technically correct, 'looked after'.

Law and policy

Looked after children and the Children Act 1989

The main framework of the law regarding children who are looked after remains the Children Act 1989, with subsequent amendments. Chapter 1 discusses aspects of the law that contribute to child-centred practice such as consultation with children about their wishes and feelings through a 'welfare checklist' (Section1(3)(a)) in court proceedings. Social workers are also required to ascertain children's views when making decisions about their care (Sections 22(4) and (5)) and before statutory reviews (S.26). Similar participatory principles were enacted in Scotland and Northern Ireland in 1995 (the Children (Scotland) Act 1995 and the Children (Northern Ireland) Order 1995).

The Children Act 1989 made attempts to remove some stigma from the previous legislation involving 'reception into care' by making a clear distinction between children who were 'voluntarily accommodated' (Section 20) at the wish of their parents or carers and those who were in care through a court order. A court order could be made if children were found to have *'suffered significant harm or to be at risk of significant harm'* (Section 31). Prior to the Children Act 1989, local authorities could apply to 'assume parental rights' and keep children in care against parents' wishes even where the parents had originally requested care. The new legislation was intended to create more of a partnership model between parents and local authorities, although as Goodyer (2011) argues,

> *the foregrounding of the partnership between birth parents and local authorities effectively marginalised children's rights, relegating children to a position of having a say, rather than being listened to or being heard.*
>
> (Goodyer, 2011, p. 22)

Hence this was not a particularly child-centred change in the law. However, children and parents were permitted by the Children Act 1989 to take a more active role in care planning. Local authorities now have duties to consult children, parents and relevant others before making decisions. They have to take account of children's religion, culture and linguistic background and place them near home and with siblings, if practicable and consistent with the children's interests. Guidance for planning, review and complaints was clarified and there was an explicit presumption of maintaining children's contact with their birth family.

Subsequent law

As discussed in Chapter 1, amendments were made to the Children Act 1989 in the Children Act 2004 and the Adoption and Children Act 2002. These both extended the participation rights of children and young people through the appointment of a Children's Commissioner and through limited rights to advocacy. The Adoption and Children Act 2002 provided legislation for the role of the Independent Reviewing Officer (introduced in 2004) who would be separate from the local authority management structure and therefore in more of a position to hold the local authority to task if children's care was not up to a required standard.

The Children and Young Persons Act 2008 was enacted following the White Paper, 'Care Matters: Time for Change' (Department for Education and Skills, 2007). This acknowledged some of the failings in provision for looked after young people. These included the lack of choice in placement provision, the number of moves between placements young people had to make and their poor educational achievements. It also recognised the importance for young people of positive relationships with social workers.

The new Act aimed to achieve a better quality of care and greater consistency and stability of placements through ensuring children and young people appropriate accommodation with better support, both personal and financial. To achieve this, it included such measures as extending the role of Independent Reviewing Officers. There were also measures to try to improve young people's school achievement and improved access to, and support in, higher education. The Act clearly had good intentions for young people looked after but there were concerns that the additional resources needed for its implementation were not being earmarked for this purpose.

Subsequent guidance (DCSF, 2010a) aimed to be more child-centred in terms of care planning and reviewing children's care, acknowledging the importance of continuity of relationships and of placements and education. There was also emphasis on the importance of children's participation, listening to children's wishes and feelings, and ensuring advocacy services for young people who had difficulty in expressing these. The practical reasons for ascertaining wishes and feelings were summarised in Section 1.11 as follows:

> *Many children have an understanding of what is causing their problems and what underlies their needs;*

> *They may have insight into what might or might not work in the context of their current circumstances and environment;*

> *They often know what sort of support they would most value and be able to access.*

(DCSF, 2010, p. 4)

However, as noted in Chapter 5, research by Pert et al. (2017) has found that little has changed in terms of children's satisfaction with their participation in care planning.

Forms of care

The scope of this book does not allow for lengthy discussion of different forms of care so below is a brief overview of fostering, residential care, adoption and kinship care, incorporating children's views.

Law and policy emphasises that children and young people should remain with their family of origin where this is in the children's best interests, and support should be provided to facilitate this. Many children enter care for short breaks and then return to their families, a form of care that is commonly used for families with disabled children and young people. The rationale for this was often to provide a break for parents or carers, but it has been increasingly recognised that the impact of staying away from home on the children themselves could be negative and, if used, should be part of a positive package of activities for disabled children (Simcock and Castle, 2016).

Foster care

According to the statistics, on 31 March 2017 there were 72,670 looked after children in England, an increase of 3% from 2016 (DfE, 2017). Three quarters of these were placed in foster care and this proportion of young people in care who are fostered has remained more or less stable over several years (DfE, 2016a). Fostering is often seen as the placement of choice for children and young people who cannot remain with their birth family or with relatives.

Morgan's (2005) national survey of foster care explored the views of 410 children and young people in foster care from the age of 4 to 18. These views of children, although from some time ago, are similar to other more contemporary findings, and this suggests that little has changed. In summary Morgan's main findings are:

➤ One third of foster children said they were not told enough about the foster family before moving there.

➤ Two thirds said they had no choice in the decision about which foster home they moved to.

➤ Over one quarter said they were not asked about their care plan and did not know what it said.

> The 'best things' about foster care were receiving care and support, having good opportunities and liking the foster family.

> The 'worst things' were missing one's birth family and friends, new rules in the foster home and feeling 'odd' because of being in care.

Goodyer's (2011) research with twenty-two children and young people in foster care found that these young people had differing senses of belonging. Some felt they were a permanent part of their foster family whilst others still felt they really belonged with their birth family. Some had an allegiance to both families whilst others, worryingly, felt they belonged to neither. In Happer et al.'s (2006) study of thirty-two young people and adults who had been looked after, a young person expressed the importance to her of feeling fostered by the whole family, not just the foster parents:

So it was the whole family that fostered you, it wasn't just mum and dad. It really has to work that way.

(Happer, 2006, p. 15)

Love, care and affection in foster care were important but so too was feeling that you were treated in the same way as the other children in the family (Holland et al., 2010). The children in Goodyer's (2011) research appreciated good amenities in their foster home but disliked being disciplined in ways they were not used to. The study also found that the children had little understanding of their rights or entitlements.

Residential care

On the whole, older children, especially those with challenging behaviour, are more often placed in residential care (Kendrick, 2012). It is important to remember that there is a diverse range of residential care, some of it provided by health or education as well as by private providers. Children and young people may prefer residential care to foster care if given a choice. Young people who have a strong sense of belonging to their family of origin say they find it hard to be part of a small family unit and prefer the looser ties of residential care (as in the case example of 'Sonay' in the previous chapter). Having said this, some young people have found the care they received in residential units too distant. In Duncalf's (2010) survey of 310 care leavers, some young people spoke of the lack of affection they received from residential staff. A 26 year old who had been in residential care said:

Way too institutionalised children's homes. Do you know how much we needed a hug?

(Duncalf, 2010, p. 26)

Young people also talked about bullying and violence in residential units. In Holland et al.'s (2010) study some young people said that they found that the boundaries were too lax and the behaviour of other young people threatening. Frequently, young people found they were placed a long way from their friends and family, which made keeping in touch more difficult.

The standards in children's homes vary considerably. Ofsted (2011) reported on those that provided 'outstanding' care. In summary, the characteristics of these were:

➢ leaders who are hands-on and who unite their staff behind a shared purpose and pursuit of excellence;

➢ a clarity of vision, which is focused on the experience of children and young people and a commitment to continual improvement;

➢ staff who are deeply committed to their work, supported to grow and develop;

➢ understanding which young people will benefit from living in the home and creating the conditions to make the placement a success;

➢ meticulous planning that engages young people and responds in detail to their individual needs, combined with a commitment to never 'give up' on a child or young person;

➢ time spent with the children and young people individually and in groups;

➢ absolute consistency in the management of behaviour so that young people understand and respect the boundaries that are set;

➢ an unwavering commitment to support children and young people to succeed;

➢ working with each child or young person to build their emotional resilience and self-confidence.

Adoption

Where there are no long-term prospects of children returning to their family of origin, adoption may achieve a more stable future for children and young people. In 2017, 71% of such adoptions were of children ages 1–4 years (DfE, 2017). Adoption is often seen as a solution to providing a stable and permanent home for children in the care system. This view was influenced in the 1970s by research conducted by Rowe and Lambert (1973), who found that many young children were then left to 'drift' in care with no real plans made for their future. The push for adoption has also been influenced more recently by findings from neuroscientific research, as discussed in Chapter 2, about critical periods for babies and young children to be able to form attachments to their carers (Cozolino, 2014). This critical period is disputed by some commentators, who argue that it is exaggerated and used by government to plan permanent alternatives for children when support of the birth family could be offered (Wastell and White, 2012).

Morgan (2006) conducted research on the views of young people themselves about adoption. These were 208 children between the ages of 6 and 22 who responded to a questionnaire. Young people said that the best things about being adopted were being part of a family and joining a new family, whilst the worst things for some were leaving their old family and being separated from brothers and sisters. In summary, children's ideas for improving adoption included:

➤ making it quicker and involving children more;

➤ giving children more information about adoption and about what is happening;

➤ not changing social workers;

➤ not separating brothers and sisters;

➤ having more trial days with the new family; and

➤ being able to make the final decision themselves.

An increase in numbers of children adopted from care has been set as a target for local authorities along with tighter timescales for achieving this through court proceedings (DfE, 2016a). This is a contentious issue and some see it as an inappropriate 'rush to permanency'. The condensed timescales for achieving adoption, as discussed in Chapter 5, have been regarded as infringing parents' rights and denying children the chance of family support to remain in their birth family (Dickens and Masson, 2016).

The Department of Education's *'Adoption a Vision for Change'* (DfE, 2016c) has proposed to boost the numbers of adoption decisions in court, reduce children's time in waiting for adoption, provide more support for adopters and give adopters more of a voice in the process.

Special guardianship

There has been increased use of Special Guardianship Orders since their introduction in 2005. These are permanent arrangements for children but, unlike in adoption, the legal link with birth parents remains. An order shifts full responsibility for decisions about children's upbringing from the local authority to a child's foster carers or kinship carers. One of the issues that has arisen with Special Guardianship is that social services may withdraw from a family once the order is made, and some families would like at least to keep a link in case of difficulties (Wade et al., 2014). Children were on the whole positive about the arrangement especially where they had a strong link to the family before an order was made.

Kinship care

'Kinship care' (placement with relatives) is an important option for children and is one that research has shown has varied but often favourable outcomes (Farmer, 2010). Already, under the Children Act (1989) (Section 23(2)ii), there was a requirement to give preference to placement with family members. More recent amendments in 2011 and the requirements of the 'Public Law Outline' (which came into effect in 2014) to consider care by relatives in care proceedings have led to an increase in the use of kinship care.

Being different in care

Children and young people in the public care are faced with disadvantage and discrimination in their lives, as is evident both from research and from regular governmental statistics. Disadvantage commonly occurs at every stage of their lives: in their birth family, in their experiences within the care system, through to their lives after leaving care. These processes of leaving and entering care and children's experiences whilst in care are considered in more detail later in this chapter.

Young people are individuals with varying experiences, and Parker (1987) warned against generalising about looked after young people, concerned that this could add to the stigma. However, research suggests that these children and young people come disproportionately from families living in poverty (Thomas, 2005; DCSF, 2009; Bywaters, 2015). Black children and those of mixed ethnicity are over-represented in the statistics (Barn, 2006; Bywaters et al., 2016) and there has been a rise in the number of unaccompanied asylum seeking children in care in recent years. These latter accounted for 6% of the looked after children population in 2016 (DfE, 2016a). Disabled children and young people are frequently in the public care, although many are there for short periods (Stein,

2005). Taken together, the evidence suggests many of these young people already experience a range of intersecting oppressions.

In terms of their family life, statistics provide evidence that in 2016, 60% of children had come to the attention of social services because of abuse or neglect prior to entering care (DfE, 2016a).

Effects of poverty and class

Although it is a very old study from 1989, there is little to suggest that the composition of young people in care has changed in respect of poverty. Bebbington and Miles' (1989) research found that nearly three quarters of families of the 2500 children and young people in care they studied relied on state benefits, at that time 'income support'. More recent statistics bear out the continued relationship between care and poverty:

> On 31 March 2012, a child living in Blackpool, England, was eight times more likely to be 'looked after' out of home—to be in the care system—than a child in Richmond upon Thames, an outer-London borough.
>
> (Bywaters, 2015, p. 7)

This, as Bywaters points out, is due to the relatively high levels of deprivation in Blackpool. Besides the associated stigma, poverty is accompanied by poor provision of education, health care and housing, and these children entering care are therefore disadvantaged in many respects from the outset.

Disabled young people

As noted above, disabled children and young people are over represented in the statistics of children in care. Although some of the reasons for them entering care, such as abuse or neglect, are similar to those for other children there are additional routes into care for disabled children. These can be through the provision of short breaks, as discussed above, or through placement in residential schools. Frequently local schools do not cater for children's particular needs and they are placed in boarding schools at a distance from their family.

There are few studies of the views of disabled children about their experiences in care. However, research that has been conducted suggests that they have many of the same concerns as other young people in care about keeping in contact with their birth families and being involved in decisions. Connors and Stalker (2003) found that disabled young people found it more difficult to keep friendships as they got older when activities became less frequently organised by adults. Research by Morris (1998) also found that disabled young people had difficulty in keeping in touch with friends. Sometimes this was due to their residential unit or school being distant from their home area and this meant that family contact could be irregular too. Young people in Morris's (1998) study said that being able to communicate well with others was a prime consideration and they valued continuity of care with carers who had learnt to understand them and to help them communicate their views. Some talked about abuse and bullying in care, but few had sought help as they were not confident that they could communicate their abuse adequately to be believed. Social workers need to develop means of communicating with disabled children, as discussed in Chapter 4, and be committed to involving them in decisions and finding out their wishes.

Young people from minority ethnic groups

As noted above, it is widely held that Black and minority ethnic children are over represented in the care system but in fact the picture is more complex. Some groups such as children with a Black African or Caribbean heritage and those of mixed heritage are more represented in the care statistics, whilst children with an Asian heritage such as Chinese or those from the Indian sub continent are under-represented. Research by Bywaters et al. (2016) found that the over-representation of Black children was connected to socio-economic disadvantage:

> *Overall – Black children are more likely than White to experience separation from their parents through state action, because so much larger a proportion of Black children compared to White live in very disadvantaged neighbourhoods.*

(p. 16)

Social workers need to help children and young people who are separated from their families and sometimes removed from their culture to develop a positive identity. These young people are likely to need support to appreciate their cultural heritage and to deal with racism and discrimination. Black and minority ethnic carers may be able to help with this but contact with young people's birth families, where this is possible, should better help them to make sense of their cultural history.

Social workers cannot be experts on every culture, race and religion but they can work with sensitivity to these. O'Hagan (2001) outlines the basics of cultural competence for professionals and recommends that they apply the following principles:

> *Respect on initial contact*

> *Appreciation of why culture is important to the individual and awareness of crucial components*

> *Genuine, friendly curiosity*

> *Ability to admit ignorance and respond appropriately to mistakes they make.*

(O'Hagan, 2001, p. 254)

Abrams and Moio (2009) argue that it is not sufficient to consider 'cultural competence' in relation to race and culture only, but that social workers should consider the individual's unique personal and social identity as a whole taking account of their gender, ability, sexuality, nationality and so on.

Young people have reported that their views about the ethnicity or religion of the families where they were to be placed were not sufficiently considered (Gaskell, 2010; Oliver, 2010). Black young people said that they did not necessarily want to be placed with Black carers. They complained that professionals did not make an effort to understand their individual wants and needs but made assumptions about this without asking them (Barn et al., 2005). They wanted respect for their culture and ethnicity and proper support during placements.

Case example: Rosie and Stella

Rosie and Stella, now in their thirties, were both fostered as young children by the same family. Stella's father and mother were born in Jamaica. Rosie's mother was born in Jamaica and her father in Pakistan. Both were placed with White foster carers in a middle class, predominantly white, area of a large English town.

They both retain strong links with their foster carers and have great affection for them but, looking back, recognise the problems they faced of being in a transracial placement.

They both attended a primary school where they felt different as there were few other Black children. Stella remembers being bullied by a girl in her class about her colour and being in care and she became very shy. Her father used to visit her at first in the foster home but she felt embarrassed when he came as he looked odd, wearing a woolly hat pulled down to his eyes and he talked sometimes in patois which she couldn't understand. She asked for him to stop visiting and this wish was granted.

▶

◄

Rosie was granted her wish to change her name by deed poll to that of the foster carers as this made her feel she belonged more. She found it difficult to accept that her father was of Asian descent as she wanted to identify with, and be accepted by, a group of teenagers who were of Black Caribbean heritage.

They both felt that their foster carers had tried hard to help them with their culture and had tried to introduce them to Black families. Their foster mother attended a course on multi-culturalism and found out about suitable hair and skin care products. Their social worker tried to get them involved in groups of young people in care where there were other Black children. Rosie attended but Stella was too shy.

Comment on the case example

Although some young people in the studies cited above said they did not necessarily want to be placed in foster families with the same ethnicity as themselves, the experiences of Stella and Rosie demonstrate some of the problems that children face when they have this double oppression of being from an ethnic minority and being in care. It is not clear that if given a choice of placement as younger children, they would have been able to express a preference, and certainly there is no guarantee that a suitable placement would be available. However, children's services would nowadays try hard to avoid this kind of long-term transracial placement in a predominantly White area and adoption would be considered.

Young refugees and asylum seekers

Young refugees and asylum seekers have increasingly featured in the statistics of young people in the care system in the UK. Between 2015 and 2016, there was an increase of 54% in the numbers of asylum seeking children, who accounted for 6% of the looked after population at 31 March 2016 (DfE, 2016a). These young people have often suffered trauma and abuse in their country of origin as well as en route to Britain. Once arrived, they are likely to be unfamiliar with the language, culture and systems of the host country and have difficulties negotiating the complex immigration procedures.

Wade et al. (2005) examined the case files of 212 young asylum seekers and interviewed 31 of these and their support workers. The study found that, as these young people were separated from family members back home, they often felt isolated. Sixty-two per cent had no contact with their family and those that did mainly had links with their siblings. Retaining contact with siblings was therefore vital, as well as making and keeping friendships they made after arrival.

An example of this isolation is described by a young asylum seeker in the author's study. Ben spoke of his first experiences in the UK when he was placed in foster care at age 15. He recalled that the foster carer locked him out of the house all day without any money when she went to work. She told him to go to school although he spoke no English at the time and could not find the school. He said:

> I didn't know even Malcolm [social worker] then. I didn't know no one. I didn't have any friends even. I was just on my own.

Matthews (2011) found that these young people encountered racism because of their status as asylum seekers, especially in largely white communities where they arrived in Kent. Prejudice increased after the UK's EU referendum in June 2016, which led to an increase in hate crime. Home office figures for July 2016 showed a 41% increase in hate crime that month from July of the previous year (Weaver, 2016). There has also been a rise of support for the anti-immigration policies of far right politicians in Europe overall because of the usually false association of migrants and refugees with terrorist activities on mainland Europe and in the UK.

Young refugees and asylum seekers requiring support who have no documentation to prove their age have to undergo 'age assessments'. If it is accepted that they are under 18 years of age they are entitled to be treated as looked after children under Section 20 of the Children Act 1989 and provided with the support afforded to all such children in the UK. Otherwise they will be treated as adults and offered far less support. Crawley's (2010) research with young people whose age was disputed said they felt disempowered and abused by the questioning of immigration officials who treated them as 'guilty'. Young people also said they found it difficult to relate to social workers there to support them when the social worker was involved in an age assessment (Chase et al., 2008; Matthews, 2011).

Processes of care

This section of the chapter looks at children and young people's journey through care and their experiences of this. Children and young people's moves into care can mean a very positive change from a previous situation of abuse or neglect. However, the process of entering care is often a bewildering and confusing experience (Thomas, 2005; Winter, 2014). The move can be prompted by a family emergency and children are not always informed why they are leaving or for how long. Once in the care system many young people suffer negative labelling and stigmatisation

(Duncalf, 2010). Many also experience bullying and abuse (Utting, 1997; Waterhouse, 2000; Clough et al., 2006; Kendrick, 2012). Children and young people often have numerous moves in foster and residential care, which affect their education and close relationships (DfE, 2016a). They may find it difficult to access services because of changes of social worker and resource shortages. Research about young care leavers provides further evidence of their disadvantage, for example their low level of educational attainment and high unemployment levels (Stein, 2012).

Entering care

Young people's transitions into care can be extremely traumatic events for them, and are frequently life changing. Whilst many children and young people experience the move as a positive one, removing them from difficult or abusive situations at home, research studies show that young people face many emotional difficulties with the process and that social workers can help make this easier for them.

Research by Goodyer (2011) explored in detail young people's first experiences of being in foster care. Some of these young people expressed feelings of shock at the suddenness of events. An 11-year-old girl who had moderate learning disabilities said:

> They just came to school and took me. They just took me...that was Sandra (social worker), really strange, really upset.
>
> (Goodyer, 2010, p. 89)

Many of the young people said they had very little information about where they were going and how long this would be for. Worryingly, some said they had been told they were just going to visit a foster home but had then had remained for months or even years. The young people talked about feeling scared, rejected and bewildered by what was happening, especially when it was their first move and even when they were relieved to be leaving home. They still experienced feelings of loss in a number of ways. These included loss of contact with familiar people such as family and friends, loss of their routines and possessions and loss of their familiar locality and community.

Practice points

Young people wanted to be involved in all aspects of decision making about their placement (McMurray et al., 2011). Thomas (2005), however, acknowledges the difficulty for social workers in involving children and young people in the planning of care when local authorities have limited choice of the foster and residential care placements available.

Mitchell et al.'s (2010) research with twenty young people about their experiences of foster care asked them to highlight what they needed from practitioners to help with these transitions. They listed the need for more time over the transition, more information and the support and space to develop a relationship with their new carers in order to overcome feelings of anxiety. Winter (2014) emphasises the importance of practice that supports children and young people's coping mechanisms in transition and ways of helping them to feel in control. Key in this is providing factual information, accessible after the event, that is in written not just oral format. Also important is preserving children's histories and their links with the past and providing carers with information about their tastes and routines. This can involve social workers in negotiation and advocacy with new carers.

Life story work with children and young people can help them to make sense of the past and the present. This can involve a book of pictures and photographs and video material, as well as objects that are mementos of the past. The work needs to go at the child's pace and take account of their stage of development as well as of their emotional 'readiness' for this, since any reminder of the past is likely to evoke strong feelings, for example about loss or previous abuse. A small-scale study by Willis and Holland (2009) found that the young people interviewed who had experienced life story work found it useful for giving them factual information about the past and for providing emotional support.

Ryan and Walker (2007) provide practical ideas for carrying out life story work, such as how to talk to children about where and how they were born, the strong impact of sharing their birth certificate and ideas about creating family trees and diagrams that children can understand. They also cover some important principles, such as establishing and honouring a regular commitment to meeting and carrying out this work with children.

Reflective exercise

Imagine if you suddenly had to move away from your friends, family and home to live with strangers.

What would you miss?

What would you want to take with you to help?

Being in care

Being in care can be a positive experience for many children, who may receive better education, freedom from abuse and neglect and a loving relationship with their new carers. However, there are downsides for many. Amongst these are facing stigma from people who do not understand the reasons why children may have to leave their birth families. They may suffer bullying and abuse, particularly in residential care. As mentioned above, they may feel the loss of familiar family members, friends and places. They may not feel they have sufficient contact with loved ones and they may face frequent moves between placements. Young people therefore sometimes feel isolated. As noted above, Goodyer's (2011) study of young people in foster care found that young people had varied experiences of feeling they 'belonged' or not to the foster home or their birth family.

Stigma, bullying and abuse

Studies have documented the stigma that young people in the care system often face (Buchanan, 1995; Duncalf, 2010; Goodyer, 2011). They complain about hating the fact that people felt sorry for them or that people thought they were in care because they were causing trouble. As one young person in Duncalf's (2010) study put this, *'All people have certain views about children in care. They think we're troublemakers'* (Duncalf, 2010, p. 29).

This was particularly a problem for young people in residential care who felt they were labelled as 'tramps' or criminals and found it difficult to make friends (Buchanan, 1995; Gallagher and Green, 2012). In foster care too, this stigmatisation could be a problem for young people. In her study, Goodyer (2011) found that young people went to great lengths to hide from their school friends the fact that they were fostered, for example by changing their birth name to that of the foster carers by deed poll (as in the case example above) or by keeping their carers away from contact with their school. Some said they experienced bullying about their status. An 11-year-old girl said she had been taunted about being abandoned by her mother. This bullying at school and being treated differently was also reported by Barnardo's (2006). From conducting a survey of parents and carers of year 11 pupils ages 15–16, they found that bullying was more prevalent in a group of young people who had been in care. They also surveyed sixty-six young care leavers and found that over half said they had been bullied at school. These young people said that they did not receive the support they needed with this, especially when they experienced multiple placement moves as was often the case.

Young people have suggested that there should be more awareness of the issues they face in the care system through education, discussion and literature for children (Martin and Jackson, 2002), and there should be more emphasis on their strengths rather than on their problems (Duncalf, 2010). A study by Rogers (2016) with young people in foster care found that they were helped to cope with the stigma they faced by being helped to maintain friendship groups and by getting peer support from other young people in care. One of the young people, 'Jack', explained how he felt close to a friend and 'like family' even though they were not related:

> *There was a girl at school called Jess, she was older than me. And she was in care and me and her, we treat each other like family, so I was her cousin, she's my cousin.*

Abuse of young people in care has been the subject of major reports (Utting, 1997; Waterhouse, 2000) and this has led to greater scrutiny of staff and better training and procedures, especially in residential care. Abuse, however, still continues both in residential and foster care.

Identity

McMurray et al. (2011) emphasise the importance of identity for children and young people who are looked after. Their research was a longitudinal study with fifty-two young people and their parents, social workers and carers. The study found that some of the young people were fighting against the negative identity and stigma of being in care or having social services involved in their family. Some founded their identity on former relationships with their birth family or with friends. 'John', for example, presented himself to most people as an angry young person. He explained that he could only be himself with a few old friends from primary school:

> *I don't talk about myself, I talk about others. I do talk about myself but it is only certain people that I talk to. Couple of mates from primary know the real John. One really good mate from primary school. I grew up with him from day one like.*
>
> (McMurray et al., 2011, p. 215)

Young people who are looked after need to have a positive narrative about their lives to help them develop a strong positive identity. This can be very difficult if their life experiences have involved trauma in their birth family and moves between placements in foster and residential care. Life story work as described above can help with this. Social workers can also help young people to formulate an alternative story about their lives that they feel happy about. This 're-storying' draws on a narrative approach as expounded by White and Epston (1990).

Put simply, a narrative approach is founded on the premise that people use stories to give meaning to their lives and to represent themselves to others. These stories are selective – we do not tell people everything – and may be changed according to our audience. Certain stories in society are more accepted and valued than others. Abel and Abel (2001) explain that stories are used to devalue certain groups. They also point out that these negative stories are frequently internalised by those who are the subjects.

> In most cultures, and certainly in all times, there have been sustained beliefs that certain groups of persons are more valued than others. Stories are told about these 'lesser' groups that are intended to promulgate their 'inferior nature'. In our time, in our country, these groups have included ethnic minorities, religious groups, women, gays and lesbians and those with some form of disability.
>
> (Abel and Abel, 2001, p. 22)

As discussed above, young people in the care system also face such stigma expressly because of their care status. A narrative approach is especially helpful since it encourages these young people to explore positive alternative stories about their lives. For example, a young woman in care may have been sexually abused by her stepfather and feel that she is vulnerable and a victim, which is the dominant discourse in our society about sexual abuse. Her social worker can explore ideas with her and help create a new positive story about how she overcame this problem and what this says about her as a person having successfully achieved this. Other facets of her life can be jointly explored to add detail to this new story, such as her relationships with other family and friends, her successes at school and so on. Some of these stories can be adapted to present to other young people and adults. Ryan and Walker (2007, p. 11) call these 'cover stories', essential stories for a child when meeting new people that are '*a clear, understandable, acceptable explanation of his [sic] circumstances, which he must be able to use at will and comfortably'*.

Moves and contact with family

Young people in the care system have repeatedly told adults such as social workers and researchers that they need stability in their lives (Gaskell, 2010; Morgan, 2010a). Having to move out of foster homes or residential care can give rise to feelings of rejection and loss of self-esteem (Barnardos, 2006). However, annual statistics continue to chronicle placement instability (DfE, 2017). In the statistics for March 2016–March 2017, 32% of looked after children had more than one placement during the year and 10% had three or more. In the survey by Timms and Thoburn (2003) young people talked about not knowing where they would be next and not being able to settle properly. Besides having to form new relationships with carers, placement moves often entail changes of school and mean that young people have to make new relationships with other students and teachers. As with their first move into care, young people wanted better planning for moves, with proper introductions to carers and to schools (Gallagher and Green, 2012).

The report 'Putting Children First' (DfE, 2016b) has outlined a vision for 'a safe and stable home for every child' when the state becomes the 'corporate parent' and forthcoming principles are promised to govern this stability. However, the cuts in government spending on local authority provision for these young people may mean that the funds needed to provide this stability will be difficult to find.

As noted above, young people felt the loss of family and friends when coming into care, and keeping in contact with loved ones is very important for many of them, although not all young people want to have regular contact. Social workers need to keep children and young people safe, and their contact with family members who have abused them may need to be supervised.

In Goodyer's (2011) research, young people complained that social workers made decisions about contact with their family that they were not happy with. This theme runs through other studies including that of the author. A survey by Shaw (1998) found that over one third of the 2000 children looked after who were surveyed said they wanted to see their birth families more, both parents and siblings. Young people wanted to be kept informed about events in their families even where contact had decreased. Irregular contact with family members could be a problem for young people who found that with time and loss of everyday contact, they felt increasingly ill at ease with their family since they had fewer common experiences to talk about as time went on.

Decisions: Meetings and reviews

As discussed in Chapter 5, children and young people's participation in decisions about their care is very important to them. Decisions should normally be discussed and care plans made at regular statutory reviews and these should include young people if they wish to be involved. Sometimes young people choose not to attend and their views can be represented at the meeting by an adult, by the social worker, Independent Reviewing Officer or an advocate. Young people who are looked after have a right to have an advocate who may help support them through their review meetings.

The children and young people in Goodyer's (2011) research usually talked about meetings and reviews negatively. One young person in the study complained that she was 'heard' at a review but not listened to about receiving her clothing allowance. As discussed in Chapter 4, McLeod (2008) found that for young people listening meant hearing them and then actually taking action on what is heard.

Independent Reviewing Officers (IRO) were introduced in the Adoption and Children Act 2002 to ensure that reviews are properly conducted and that children are meaningfully involved in the process. This role was extended in the Children and Young Persons Act 2008 and the Independent Reviewing Officers' Handbook (DCSF, 2010b). Ofsted's (2013) survey into the effectiveness of IROs reviewed 111 cases, and solicited the views of children and young people, carers, and professionals. They reported that children had little understanding of the role of the IRO and were generally dissatisfied with their reviews, a finding supported in an extensive survey by Jelicic et al. (2014). Children's experiences were varied. Some felt that IROs had listened to them, explained things and tackled their concerns whilst others felt they had made no difference.

Pert et al.'s (2017) study that included the views of twenty-five children and young people found that they experienced barriers in engaging in their review meetings despite the role of the IRO. They did not all understand the purpose of reviews and did not feel adequately prepared or able to contribute significantly to the agenda, nor did they feel that they had a choice about who would attend. Overall, they wanted better preparation, fewer people at their meeting and their request for parents to attend to be honoured. Whilst some felt listened to others found the meetings boring, saying that these seemed mainly conducted for the adults present and that they felt like outsiders. Pert et al. (2017) commented that reviews should be more child friendly and fun to enable them to engage and participate.

A survey of looked after children (Morgan, 2010b) found that many did not know what a 'care plan' was, although this should be discussed at each review and is a statutory requirement for all looked after children. Between one quarter and one third of the young people said that they did not know that they had a care plan, and of those that did, fewer than three quarters of them agreed with the contents.

In Chapter 6 I describe some findings from Winter's (2011) study with social workers, parents and young children, where a chairperson made efforts to make meetings more child friendly. It is this cultural change that is needed to enable children and young people to feel more involved and in control.

Case example: Lidia: A good review meeting

Lidia, 17, whose family is of Polish origin, has been placed in a residential home a long way from her family. Her mother was unable to cope with her aggressive behaviour when she was 15 and initially she went into foster care. This broke down and she was placed in semi-independent living. She had little support in this placement and started taking drugs, stopped going to college and there was evidence that she was at risk of sexual exploitation. Lidia says she hates it where she is now – far from family and in a boring town. She absconded several times at first. She wants to move nearer home, see her family more and have more independence.

Lidia's review meeting is well planned and she has several opportunities to talk about her views beforehand. The Independent Reviewing Officer sent her an email so she could respond with her views electronically, which she did. He also takes time to see her, check out her views before the review and talk to her about what she wants from the meeting. She also has an advocate who talks to her before the meeting and provides support with presenting her views. Her social worker visits early, brings her a present of a new T-shirt and spends a lot of time talking to her.

The review papers have a lovely picture on the front, of Lidia with a piece of birthday cake at her recent party. The papers have a positive tone and are based on the 'Every Child Matters' outcomes. The residential team try to make the review fun for Lidia. They provide soft drinks and biscuits and talk about some of the outings they have done together and make her laugh. They are positive about Lidia's relationships, talk about her exam achievements and her activities such as boxing, but still outline what she needs to work on such as getting up in time for college and trying to control her anger. Even though she does not agree with all the recommendations, such as limits to her free time away from the unit, she is made to feel that all present care about her and so she is able to commit to a phased plan, including therapy, towards independence.

Comment on the case example

The key to this good review, apart from trying to help Lidia feel it is *her* meeting and making it as fun and age appropriate as possible, is that Lidia is able to feel that those there really care about her, listen to what she says and negotiate about the future with her best interests in mind.

Practitioners may also consider, where possible, enabling young people to set their own agendas and to chair the meetings themselves. It may be appropriate also for young people to decide about who is invited and on the venue and time of the meeting.

Leaving care/After care

Around 10800 young people left care aged 16 or over in the year ending March 2015,
an increase of over 40% in the last decade.

(DfE, 2016d, p. 14)

The figures have increased in England through factors such as young
homeless people of 16 or 17 legally becoming looked after children
(under the Southwark Judgement: *R (on the application of G) v London*
Borough of Southwark [2009] UKHL 26), and there are increases in the
numbers of young people who were unaccompanied asylum seeking children leaving care.

Child-centred practice needs to be extended to young care leavers,
including those who are beyond the age of 18. Concerns about the experiences of these young people at the end of the twentieth century led to
the Children (Leaving Care) Act 2000 in England and Wales. In Scotland
the Support and Assistance of Young People Leaving Care (Scotland)
Regulations 2004 established a similar system. Prior to the Children
(Leaving Care) Act there was no requirement for a local authority to support young people who had been in the care system after the age of 16
unless they were on a care order, and many young people had the trauma
of being faced with trying to make their way in the world on their own
with no support from family or from social services (Broad, 1998).

This plight was highlighted in the publication 'Me Survive, Out
There?' (DoH, 1999), a consultation paper about young care leavers that
documented the research into the poor outcomes for children and young
people in terms of their education, employment, housing, mental health
and over representation in the prison population.

The Children (Leaving Care) Act 2000 considerably extended the
responsibility of local authorities to young care leavers although there
are complex eligibility criteria. 'Eligible', 'relevant' and 'former relevant'
children are entitled to services. A 'pathway plan' should be drawn up
for these young people from the age of 16 to 21 and should include an
assessment of their health and development, family and social relationships, financial situation, education and employment. Provision has
been extended in subsequent guidance (DfE, 2014c). A Personal Advisor
(who is not necessarily a social worker) should be appointed to support
young people and monitor their progress. Financial support is part of this
package and is provided for higher education and costs associated with
employment and training beyond the age of 21.

Subsequently, it has been recognised that young care leavers need
additional support through their early adulthood. 'Staying Put' guidance (DfE, 2013) proposed that young people should be able to remain

with foster carers with financial support until the age of 21 where this was practicable. This came into force in 2014. A similar arrangement for young people in residential care called 'Staying Close' has also been proposed so that they may settle near their residential unit and receive support from staff at their former home base (DfE, 2016b). Under the Children and Social Work Act 2017 local authorities must publish information about their services for care leavers and a Personal Advisor should continue to support young care leavers until they are 25.

Young care leavers have been vocal about their situation and the support they need from social services. They have often found themselves ill prepared for independence, both practically and emotionally. Many have suffered from feeling isolated (Duncalf, 2010). For example, this young person in Barn et al.'s (2005) research had been used to living in company and was anxious about being alone:

> I still, up to now, find it difficult to be in the house alone...I get a bit scared in the night, I sleep with the lights on around the house.

Young people say they need both practical and emotional support with their transition from care. Many young people have reported difficulties with finances and with suitable housing (Duncalf, 2010; Holland et al., 2010). Suitable housing options continue to concern young care leavers. Morgan's (2009) survey of care leavers found that one quarter of young people thought they were in the wrong accommodation for them and 1 in 10 rated the standard of their accommodation as bad or very bad.

Case example: Gina

Gina is 20 and is pregnant with her first baby. She spent years in a range of residential and foster homes during her childhood but still has some contact with her mother and sister. She is currently in semi-independent living accommodation provided by social services and has the support of a leaving care social worker. She will have to leave this accommodation soon because they are unable to provide for young mothers and babies.

The social worker has helped Gina to apply to the Housing Department for social housing for her and her baby since she has priority rights as a young care leaver.

This application failed as the housing official says she cannot be considered since she has rent arrears of around £100. He says she would have to present herself as homeless when she leaves the semi-independent accommodation and be housed in a hostel with shared bathroom and kitchen facilities. The manager of the leaving care team says they are only able to assist with providing accommodation until Gina is 21 – just before the baby is born.

▶

◀

As the leaving care social worker you are concerned about Gina and her baby's welfare in any local hostels, where you know that there is illegal drug use and frequent fights. How could you help Gina to put her case forward for suitable housing for her and her baby?

➤ With the housing department

➤ With your manager

➤ Who else might be able to help?

Young people who are care leavers are still less likely than those in the general population to be in post 16 education. To continue in education and thereby increase their chances of good employment, young people need financial help. There have been initiatives to support young care leavers to continue in education post 18, such as the Aim Higher scheme. Universities now have special support schemes for young care leavers in terms of bursaries, accommodation, advice and study support.

Overall, child-centred practice with care leavers involves

➤ good preparation;

➤ choice of when and where to go;

➤ a smooth transition; and

➤ keeping in touch.

This latter may be difficult when the young person has had bad experiences in the care system. Initially, on leaving residential or foster care and with the prospect of no longer having the statutory involvement of a social worker, many young people report a feeling of freedom but this may be short lived when the reality of their situation kicks in.

Conclusion

This chapter has summarised law, policy and practice with children and young people in the care system, documenting their views about placements, transitions in and out of care and their experiences of being in care. Children and young people who are looked after can be helped to achieve their goals in life with good support from their social workers. This demands an understanding of them as unique individuals and a commitment to involving them in decisions and giving them choices about their future. Being in care can provide love and stability if all goes well but many young people face stigma, isolation and instability. Social workers can help young people to formulate a positive identity and keep important links with their friends and family.

Summary points

➤ Law and guidance on looked after children promote their participation in decisions and continuity of care.

➤ Different forms of care for children and young people should involve them in real choices about their placement and help them to feel they belong.

➤ Children and young people in care face multiple disadvantages, which are compounded by experiences of difference, e.g. poverty, disability, race and culture.

➤ Transition into care can be traumatic and young people need support and time to adjust.

➤ In care young people face stigma, instability and loss of contact with loved ones. They need support to build a positive identity.

➤ Children and young people need to be involved in decisions, and the culture of meetings needs to change to accommodate this.

➤ Young people leaving care need good preparation, choice and ongoing support.

Further reading and resources

Brammer, A. (2015) *Social Work Law,* 4th edition. Harlow: Pearson Longman.
Helpful for further detail of the law relating to social work with children who are looked after.

Davies, M. (ed.) (2012) *Social Work with Children and Families.* Basingstoke: Palgrave Macmillan.
Chapters 16–20 provide a detailed discussion of residential care, law, policy, theory, research and practice.

Goodyer, A. (2011) *Child-Centred Foster Care: A Rights-Based Model for Practice.* London: Jessica Kingsley Publishers.
Advice concerning child-centred work with children and young people in foster care based on their views.

Ryan, T. and Walker, R. (2007) *Life Story Work: A Practical Guide to Helping Children Understand their Past.* London: BAAF.
This is a very practical guide with ideas about life story work with groups, with Black children and with disabled children.

Stein, M. (2012) *Young People Leaving Care: Supporting Pathways to Adulthood.* London: Jessica Kingsley Publishers.
An overview of the challenges faced by young care leavers and ways to support them.

SCIE has produced a series of videos about young people's experiences in the care system and leaving care. Available at: https://www.scie.org.uk/socialcaretv/topic.asp?t=lookedafterchildren

Conclusion

Chapters in this book have documented the many calls for child-centred practice in UK legislation, policy and guidance for social workers. These include expectations that social workers will listen to children and young people, find out their wishes and feelings and help them to participate in decisions. On an international scale, children's rights to provision, protection and participation are recognised under the United Nations Convention on the Rights of the Child (1989).

Since the late twentieth century, social work with children and young people has progressed and there are many examples of good practice. Many social workers bring creativity into their work with children and young people and recognise the importance of communicating through activity and play. Effective Independent Reviewing Officers help young people to feel their views are valued and that they can share in decision making. Children's advocates are available to support young people in getting their needs met and in making complaints when they feel that they are not being heard.

However, this book is in part an examination of social work's failures in child-centred practice. Inquiries into tragic child deaths from abuse still find that social workers have not seen or spoken to children. The analysis of serious case reviews provides a strong message that social workers have focused too much on the needs of vulnerable parents or were intimidated into not seeing children (Ofsted, 2011). They have consequently missed opportunities to find out from children themselves about the abuse they were suffering. Young people, especially those in the care system, still complain that social workers do not listen and do not involve them enough in decisions. Often they experience a frightening lack of control in their lives, for example when not given choices or information about placement moves.

In Chapter 6 we found that there were strong barriers to child-centred practice in social work such as resource shortages of staff and money, organisational cultures that are not child friendly, rigidly bureaucratic procedures and paternalistic attitudes to children.

In examining the background to child-centred practice it appears that adults' attitudes to children and young people have changed through the ages. Children are no longer regarded as the 'property' of parents, but the boundaries and restrictions we set around children are still there. There is still some scepticism and ambivalence about children's rights. Some of this may be due to adults' need to control and protect children 'for their own good'. We regard them as immature and therefore unable to make good choices for themselves. We may not agree with the child liberationists of the 1970s such as Farson (1974) and Holt (1975) who thought that children should have complete control of their lives and do exactly as they please, but we may need to reflect on our attitudes. As some of the children quoted in this book have said, we need to respect the fact that children at least have superior knowledge about themselves. Children in care know what kind of foster family or residential care they want to live in (Gaskell, 2010). Children with severe health issues have a valid view about their medical care since they have experienced the effects of various treatments (Alderson, 2007). Young people deserve to have their strengths and skills recognised. They have resources of creativity and energy and are often more skilled in working with the technology of the future than are adults.

Doris Lessing's novel from the 1970s *Memoirs of a Survivor* provides a thought provoking reflection on our attitudes to children and young people. In the book the old order of society in 'the city' is collapsing. Electricity no longer functions and water becomes scarce. All the usual means of getting food supplies from shops are becoming unreliable and waves of 'tribes' leave the city for destinations unknown. A (presumably) middle aged woman, the narrator, is given charge of a 13-year-old girl, Emily, by a stranger, knowing nothing about her. Whereas in the old order adults took the lead in society, gradually it emerges that adolescents like Emily have the skills and knowledge to survive. Emily knows where to find food and how to get transport and has the practical skills necessary to use whatever resources come to hand. With this change, morality itself changes and the young people dictate the moral order. For instance, Emily's sexual relationship with a young male leader cannot be questioned as before and the packs of very young children, ages from 4 to 10, who go about randomly looting and sometimes killing are not policed. They have assumed the power once held by adults.

At the beginning of the book Emily is clearly the dependent child, the narrator providing her with food, shelter and understanding as she goes through periods of lethargy, over-eating, becoming self-conscious about her appearance and falling in love. However as the book progresses the narrator becomes the one being protected, provided for, informed and understood by Emily. The narrator observes Emily and waits for some kind of destiny to be fulfilled. Halfway through the book she recognises herself as having the usual view of an adult that Emily will mature to a 'biological summit' but says she had to stop herself,

> *to make myself acknowledge that this stage in her life was every bit as valid as the one ahead of her.*

(p. 85)

This view of children and young people as individuals here and now rather than what they will become as adults in the future can alter our perspective on relationships with them and on our professional practice. The change in the moral order in Lessing's book, though fictional, helps to remind us that the value society places on certain qualities is arbitrary. This can change and power can change hands.

One of the main messages from children and young people in this book is that a good relationship with social workers is very important to them and they want workers who care. Skills in child-centred practice require a time commitment by social workers to get to know children and young people. Although bureaucratic procedures for assessment require social workers to do their job in as short a time as possible, it is impossible to win a child's trust in a typical one hour social work interview. Ideally, there should be time to get to know children through activities and fun as well as talking. Ideas from social pedagogy about working with the whole child can be helpful in this.

Social workers, however, cannot do it all by themselves. They are likely to need help from other professionals in health and education or from advocates. Social workers are, though, in a unique position to assist the whole child, especially when working with looked after children and in child protection services. In other roles such as in youth justice, social workers may have a more specific role.

In 2016 child poverty increased to 3.9 million (House of Commons, 2016) and poverty has a positive correlation with many measures of deprivation including child neglect, ill health, poor housing and poor educational outcomes. Looking to the future, cuts in funding for health, welfare and education bode an uncertain time for social work with all service user groups. Local authorities have contracted out children's services already in some areas including in child protection. Jones (2015) sees this as a dangerous move and it is one that no other nation has attempted. He argues that we should oppose the 'marketisation' of such services because of the poor track record of the private companies who are in this 'business' for profit, rather than for the protection of children.

In view of all these negative developments for children and young people, can social workers make a difference? Successful opposition to such policies is likely to be through collective action rather than individual protest. Nevertheless, small changes by the individuals in social work teams can help change the culture to one that is more child friendly and make a difference to children's lives.

References

Abel, P. and Abel, S. (2001) *Understanding Narrative Therapy: A Guidebook for the Social Worker*. New York: Springer Publishing Company.

Abrams, L.S. and Moio, J.A. (2009) Critical Race Theory and the Cultural Competence Dilemma in Social Work Education, *Journal of Social Work Education*, 45 (2): 45–261.

Adamson, J. and Templeton, L. (2012) *Silent Voices: Supporting Children and Young People Affected by Parental Alcohol Misuse*. London: Office of the Children's Commissioner.

African Committee of Experts on the Rights and Welfare of the Child (ACERWC) (1990) *African Charter on the Rights and Welfare of the Child*, available at http://www.acerwc.org/the-charter/, accessed 8 July 2017.

Ainsworth, M., Blehar, M., Waters, E. and Wall, S. (1978) *Patterns of Attachment: A Psychological Study of the Strange Situation*. Hillsdale, NJ: Lawrence Erlbaum.

Alderson, P. (2007) Competent Children? Minors' Consent to Health Care Treatment and Research, *Social Science and Medicine*, 65 (11): 2272–2283.

Alderson, P. (2008) When Does Citizenship Begin? Economics and Early Childhood. In Invernezzi, A. and Williams, J. (eds), *Children and Citizenship*. London: Sage.

Aldridge, J. and Becker, S. (2002) Children who Care: Rights and Wrongs in Debate and Policy on Young Carers. In Franklin, B. (ed.), *The New Handbook of Children's Rights*. London: Sage.

Aldridge, J. and Becker, S. (2003) *Children Caring for Parents with Mental Illness: Perspectives of Young Carers, Parents and Professionals*. Bristol: Policy Press.

All Party Parliamentary Group for Children (2017) *No Good Options: Report of the Inquiry into Children's Social Care in England*. London: NCB.

Archard, D. (2015) *Children, Rights and Childhood*, 3rd edition. London: Routledge.

Ariès, P. (1962) *Centuries of Childhood*. London: Jonathan Cape.

Arnstein, S. (1969) A Ladder of Citizen Participation, *Journal of the American Planning Association*, 35 (4): 216–224.

Axline, V. (1964) *Dibs In Search Of Self*. New York: Ballantine.

Barn, R. (2006) *Research and Practice Briefings: Children and Families: Improving Services to Meet the Needs of Minority Ethnic Children and Families*. London: Department for Education and Skills.

Barn, R., Andrew, L. and Mantovani, N. (2005) *Life after Care: The Experiences of Young People from Different Ethnic Groups*. York: Joseph Rowntree Foundation.

Barnardo's (2006) *Failed by the System: The Views of Young Care Leavers on Their Educational Experiences*. London: Barnardo's.

Barnes, V. (2007) Young People's Views of Children's Rights and Advocacy Services: A Case for 'Caring' Advocacy?, *Child Abuse Review*, 16 (3): 140–152.

Barnes, V. (2012) Social Work and Advocacy with Young People: Rights and Care in Practice, *British Journal of Social Work*, 42 (7): 1275–1292.

Barnes, V. (2013) *Inter-professional Ethics and Professionals' Attitudes to Children and Young People*. Kingston University: Institute of Child Centred Inter-professional Practice.

Bebbington, A. and Miles, J. (1989) The Background of Children Who Enter Local Authority Care, *British Journal of Social Work*, 19: 349–368.

Beck, U. (1992) *Risk Society: Towards a new Modernity*. London: Sage.

Becker, S. (1997) *Responding to Poverty*. London: Longman.

Beckett, H., Brodie, I., Factor, F., Melrose, M., Pearce, J.J., Pitts, J., Shuker, L. and Warrington, C. (2013) *'It's Wrong – but You Get Used to it': A Qualitative Study of Gang-Associated Sexual Violence Towards, and Exploitation of, Young People in England*. Luton: University of Bedfordshire.

Bell, M. (2002) Promoting Children's Rights through the Use of Relationship, *Child and Family Social Work*, 7: 1–11.

Bell, M. (2011) *Promoting Children's Rights in Social Work and Social Care: A Guide to Participatory Practice*. London: Jessica Kingsley Publishers.

Beresford, P., Fleming, J., Glynn, M., Bewley, C., Croft, S., Branfield, F. and Postle, K. (2011) *Supporting People: Towards a Person-Centred Approach*. Bristol: Policy Press.

Bessant, J. (2008) Hard Wired for Risk: Neurological Science, the Adolescent Brain and Developmental Theory, *Journal of Youth Studies*, 11 (3): 347–360.

Bick, E. (1964) Notes on Infant Observation in Psychoanalytic Training, *International Journal of Psychoanalysis*, 45: 484–486.

Biestek, F.P. (1961) *The Casework Relationship*. London: Unwin University Books.

Blyth, M. (ed.) (2014) *Moving on from Munro: Improving Children's Services*. Bristol: Policy Press.

Boddy, J. and Statham, J. (2009) *European Perspectives on Social Work: Models of Education and Professional Roles*. London: Thomas Coram Research Unit/ Institute of Education, University of London.

Bowlby, J. (1969) *Attachment and Loss, Vol. I: Attachment*. London: Hogarth Press.

Bowlby, J. (1973) *Attachment and Loss, Vol. II: Separation: Anxiety and Anger*. New York: Basic Books.

Boylan, J. and Dalrymple, J. (2009) *Understanding Advocacy for Children and Young People*. Maidenhead: McGraw-Hill/Open University Press.

Boylan, J. and Ing, P. (2005) 'Seen But Not Heard' – Young People's Experience of Advocacy, *International Journal of Social Welfare*, 14: 2–12.

Bradford, S. (2012) *Sociology, Youth and Youth Work Practice*. Basingstoke: Palgrave Macmillan.

Bradley, S. (2001) Suffer the Little Children: The Influence of Nurses and Parents in the Evolution of Open Visiting in Children's Wards 1940–1970, *International History of Nursing Journal*, 6 (2): 44–51.

Brady, L. (2011) *Where is My Advocate? A Scoping Report on Advocacy Services for Children and Young People in England*. London: Office of the Children's Commissioner.

Brammer, A. (2015) *Social Work Law*, 4th edition. Harlow: Pearson Longman.

Brandon, M., Bailey, S., Belderson, P., Gardner, R., Sidebotham, P., Dodsworth, J., Warren, C. and Black, J. (2009) *Understanding Serious Case Reviews and Their Impact: A Biennial Analysis of Serious Case Reviews 2005–07*. London: DCSF.

Braye, S. and Preston-Shoot, M. (1995) *Empowering Practice in Social Care*. Buckingham: Open University Press.

Broad, B. (1998) *Children Leaving Care: Life After the Children Act 1989*. London: Jessica Kingsley Publishers.

Bronfenbrenner, U. (1979) *The Ecology of Human Development*. Cambridge, MA: Harvard University Press.

Brown, W. (1995) *States of Injury: Power and Freedom in Late Modernity*. Princeton, NJ: Princeton University Press.

Bruce, M. (2014) The Voice of the Child in Child Protection: Whose Voice?, *Social Sciences*, 3 (3): 514–526.

Buchanan, A. (1995) Young People's Views on Being Looked After in Out-Of-Home-Care Under the Children Act 1989, *Children and Youth Services Review*, 17 (5–6): 681–696.

Buckingham, D. (2000) *After the Death of Childhood: Growing Up in the Age of Electronic Media*. Cambridge: Polity Press.

Buckley, H., Carr, N. and Whelan, S. (2011) 'Like Walking on Eggshells': Service User Views and Expectations of the Child Protection System, *Child and Family Social Work*, 16 (1): 101–110.

Butler, I. and Williamson, I. (1994) *Children Speak: Children, Trauma and Social Work*. London: Longman/NSPCC.

Butler, I., Robinson, M. and Scanlan, L. (2005) *Children and Decision Making*. London: National Children's Bureau.

Butler, P. (2014) Child Social Services for Sale: Experts Denounce Gove Proposal to Outsource Children's Protection to Private Firms, *The Guardian*, 17 May: 1–4.

Butler-Sloss, Lord Justice E. (1988) *Report of the Inquiry into Child Abuse in Cleveland 1987*, Cmd 412. London: HMSO.

Bywaters, P. (2015) Inequalities in Child Welfare: Towards a New Policy, Research and Action Agenda, *British Journal of Social Work*, 45 (1): 6–23.

Bywaters, P., Kwhali, J., Brady, G., Sparks, T. and Bos, E. (2016) Out of Sight, Out of Mind: Ethnic Inequalities in Child Protection and Out-of-Home Care Intervention Rates, *British Journal of Social Work*, doi: 10.1093/bjsw/bcw165.

Cameron, C. and Moss, P. (eds) (2011) *Social Pedagogy and Working with Children and Young People*. London: Jessica Kingsley Publishers.

Carter, B., Bray, L., Dickinson, A., Edwards, M. and Ford, K. (2014) *Child-centred Nursing: Promoting Critical Thinking*. London: Sage.

Carter, R. (2016) Vulnerable Hit 'Disproportionately' by UK Austerity Measures, UN Warns. *Community Care Online*, 30 June 2016, available at http://www.communitycare.co.uk/2016/06/30/vulnerable-hit-disproportionately-uk-austerity-measures-un-warns/

Chase, E., Knight, A. and Statham, D. (2008) *The Emotional Well-Being of Young People Seeking Asylum in the UK*. London: BAAF.

Children and Family Court Advisory Service (CAFCASS) (2014) *Annual Report and Accounts 2013–2014*. London: CAFCASS.

Children and Family Court Advisory Service (CAFCASS) (2014) National Picture of Care Applications in England for 2013–14, available at https://www.cafcass.gov.uk/news/2014/may/national-picture-of-care-applications-in-england-for-2013-14.aspx, accessed 17 February 2017.

Children's Commissioner's Office (2015) Report of the UK Children's Commissioners, available at http://www.niccy.org/media/2461/uk-childrens-commissioners-final-recommendations-crc-examination-of-the-uk-2016.pdf, accessed 17 January 2018.

Children's Commissioner's Office (2017) *Child Participation*, available at http://www.childrenscommissioner.gov.uk/learn-more/child-participation, accessed 12 August 2016.

Children's Rights Alliance for England (2008) *Survey Children's Rights*. London: CRAE Publications.

The Children's Society (2007) *Reflections on Childhood: Friendship*. London: The Children's Society.

The Children's Society (2016) *The Good Childhood Report*. London: The Children's Society.

Chung, S and Walsh, D.J. (2000) Unpacking Child-Centredness: A History of Meanings, *Curriculum Studies*, 32 (2): 215–234.

Cleaver, H., Nicholson, D., Tarr, S. and Cleaver, D. (2007) *Child Protection, Domestic Violence and Parental Substance Misuse: Family Experiences and Effective Practice*. London: Jessica Kingsley Publishers.

Cleaver, H., Unell, I. and Aldgate, J. (2011) *Children's Needs – Parenting Capacity: Child Abuse, Parental Mental Illness, Learning Disability, Substance Misuse, and Domestic Violence*, 2nd edition. London: The Stationery Office.

Clifton, J. (2014) Children Should be Seen and Heard: Understanding the Child's Experience. In Blyth, M. (ed.), *Moving on from Munro: Improving Children's Services*. Bristol: Policy Press.

Clough R., Bullock, R. and Ward, A. (2006) *What Works in Residential Child Care: A Review of the Research and Implications for Practice*. London: National Centre for Excellence in Residential Care and National Children's Bureau.

Cockburn, T. (2005) 'Children and the Feminist Ethic of Care', *Childhood*, 12 (1): 71–89.

Cockburn, T. (2007) Partners in Power: A Radically Pluralistic Form of Participative Democracy for Children and Young People, *Children and Society*, 21: 446–457.

Cohen, S. (1972) *Folk-Devils and Moral Panics: The Creation of the Mods and Rockers*. London: McGibbon and Kee.

Coleman, S. and Rowe, C. (2005) *Remixing Citizenship: Democracy and Young People's Use of the Internet*. London: Carnegie Trust.

Colle, L., Baron-Cohen, S. and Hill, J. (2006) Do Children with Autism Have a Theory of Mind? A Non-Verbal Test of Autism vs. Specific Language, *Journal of Autism and Specific Language Disorders*, 37 (4): 716–723.

Connors, C. and Stalker, K. (2003) *The Views and Experiences of Disabled Children and Their Siblings: A Positive Outlook*. London: Jessica Kingsley Publishers.

Cooper, D. (1998) More Law and More Rights: Will Children Benefit? *Child and Family Social Work*, 3: 77–86.

Corrigan, M. and Moore, J. (2011) *Listening to Children's Wishes and Feelings*. London: BAAF.

Corsaro, W. (2009) Peer Culture. In Qvortrup, J., Corsaro, W. and Honig, M.S. (eds), *The Palgrave Handbook of Childhood Studies*. Basingstoke: Palgrave Macmillan.

Cossar, J., Brandon, M. and Jordan, P. (2011) *'Don't Make Assumptions': Children's and Young People's Views of the Child Protection System and Messages for Change*. London: Office of the Children's Commissioner.

Cossar, J., Brandon, M., Bailey, S., Belderson, P., Biggart, L. and Sharpe, D. (2013) *'It Takes a Lot to Build Trust'. Recognition and Telling: Developing Earlier Routes to Help for Children and Young People*. London: Office of the Children's Commissioner.

Cossar, J., Brandon, M. and Jordan, P. (2016) 'You've Got to Trust Her and She's Got to Trust You': Children's Views on Participation in the Child Protection System, *Child and Family Social Work*, 21 (1): 103–112.

Cozolino, L. (2014) *The Neuroscience of Human Relationships: Attachment and the Developing Social Brain*, 2nd edition (Norton Series on Interpersonal Neurobiology). London: W. W. Norton & Company.

Crawley, H. (2010) 'No One Gives You a Chance to Say What You are Thinking': Finding Space for Children's Agency in the UK Asylum System, *Area*, 42 (2): 162–169.

Cregan, K. and Cuthbert, D. (2014) *Global Childhoods: Issues and Debates*. London: Sage.

Dalrymple, J. (2005) Constructions of Child and Youth Advocacy: Emerging Issues in Advocacy Practice, *Children and Society*, 19: 3–15.

Dalrymple, J. and Burke, B. (2006) *Anti-Oppressive Practice: Social Care and the Law*, 2nd edition. Maidenhead: Open University Press.

Davies, K. and Jones, R. (eds) (2016) *Skills for Social Work Practice*. London: Palgrave Macmillan.

Davies, M. (ed.) (2012) *Social Work with Children and Families*. Basingstoke: Palgrave Macmillan.

Department for Children Schools and Families (2009) *Statutory Guidance on Promoting the Health and Wellbeing of Looked After Children*. Nottingham: DCSF.

Department for Children Schools and Families (2010a) *The Children Act 1989 Guidance and Regulations. Volume 2: Care Planning, Placement and Case Review*. London: The Stationery Office.

Department for Children Schools and Families (2010b) *IRO Handbook: Statutory Guidance for Independent Reviewing Officers and Local Authorities on Their Functions in Relation to Case Management and Review for Looked After Children*. London: HMSO.

Department for Education (2011a) *Fostering Services: National Minimum Standards*. London: DfE.

Department for Education (2011b) *Letting Children be Children: Report of an Independent Review of the Commercialisation and Sexualisation of Childhood*. London: DfE.

Department for Education (2013) *Staying Put: Arrangements for Care Leavers Aged 18 Years and Above*. London: DfE.

Department for Education (2014a) *Knowledge and Skills Statement for Approved Child and Family Practitioners*. London: DfE.

Department for Education (2014b) *Characteristics of Children in Need*. London: DfE.

Department for Education (2014c) *The Children Act 1989 Guidance and Regulations Volume 3: Planning Transition to Adulthood for Care Leavers*. London: DfE.

Department for Education (2015a) *Knowledge and Skills Statement for Social Workers in Adult Services*. London: DfE.

Department for Education (2015b) *Working Together to Safeguard Children*. London: DfE.

Department for Education (2015c) *Children's Homes (England) Regulation.* London: DfE.

Department for Education (2015d) *The Children Act 1989 Guidance and Regulations. Vol. 2: Care Planning, Placement and Review.* London: DfE.

Department for Education (2016a) *Children Looked After in England (Including Adoption) Year Ending 31 March,* available at https://www.gov.uk/government/uploads/system/uploads/attachment_data/file/556331/SFR41_2016_Text.pdf, accessed 12 December 2017.

Department for Education (2016b) *Putting Children First: Delivering Our Vision for Excellent Children's Social Care.* London: DfE.

Department for Education (2016c) *Adoption: A Vision for Change.* London: DfE.

Department for Education (2016d) *Keep on Caring: Supporting Young People from Care to Independence.* London: HM Government.

Department for Education (2017) *Children Looked After in England Including Adoption: 2016–2017,* available at https://www.gov.uk/government/statistics/children-looked-after-in-england-including-adoption-2016-to-2017, accessed 12 December 2017.

Department for Education and Skills (2003) *Every Child Matters.* London: DfES.

Department for Education and Skills (2007) *Care Matters: Time for Change.* London: DfES.

Department of Health (1995) *Child Protection: Messages from Research.* London: The Stationery Office.

Department of Health (1998) *The Quality Protects Programme: Transforming Children's Services.* London: HMSO.

Department of Health (1999) *Me, Survive, Out There? New Arrangements for Young People Living in and Leaving Care.* London: DoH.

Department of Health (2000) *Framework for the Assessment of Children in Need and Their Families.* London: The Stationery Office.

Department of Health (2001a) *Planning with People: Towards Person-Centred Approaches: Guidance for Implementation Groups.* London: DoH.

Department of Health (2001b) *Valuing People: A New Strategy for Learning Disability in the 21st Century.* London: The Stationery Office.

Department of Health (2002) *National Standards for Agencies Providing Advocacy for Children and Young People in England.* London: DoH.

Department of Health (2007) *Putting People First.* London: HM Government.

Department of Health and Social Security (1974) *Report of the Inquiry into the Care and Supervision Provided in Relation to Maria Colwell.* London: HMSO.

Department of Health and Social Security and Welsh Office (1988) *Working Together: A Guide to Arrangements for Inter-agency Co-operation for the Protection of Children from Abuse.* London: HMSO.

Department of Health, Social Services and Public Safety Northern Ireland (DHSSP-SNI) (2011) *Understanding the Needs of Children in Northern Ireland.* Belfast: Department of Health, Social Services and Public Safety Northern Ireland.

Dickens, J. and Masson, J. (2016) The Courts and Child Protection Social Work in England: Tail Wags Dog? *British Journal of Social Work,* 46 (2): 355–371.

Doddington, C. and Hilton, M. (2007) *Child-Centred Education: Reviving the Creative Tradition.* London: Sage.

Duncalf, Z. (2010) *Listen Up! Adult Care Leavers Speak Out: The Views of 310 Care Leavers Aged 17–78.* Manchester: The Care Leavers Association.

Dworkin, R. (1978) *Taking Rights Seriously*. London: Duckworth.

Ennew, J. (1994) Time for Children and Time for Adults. In Qvortrup, J., Brady, M., Sgritta, G. and Wintersberger, H. (eds), *Childhood Matters: Social Theory, Practice and Politics*. Aldershot: Avebury.

Entwistle, H. (2012) *Child-centred Education* (Originally published 1970). Abingdon: Routledge.

Erikson, E. (1950) *Childhood and Society*. New York: W. W. Norton.

Evans, J. (2014) *How are You Feeling Today, Baby Bear?* London: Jessica Kingsley Publishers.

Fahlberg, V.L. (2012) *A Child's Journey Through Placement*. London: Jessica Kingsley Publishers.

Farmer, E. (2010) What Factors Relate to Good Placement Outcomes in Kinship Care? *British Journal of Social Work*, 40: 426–444.

Farson, R. (1974) *Birthrights*. New York: Collier Macmillan.

Fawcett, B., Goodwin, S., Meagher, G. and Phillips, R. (2010) *Social Policy for Social Change*. London: Palgrave Macmillan.

Fawcett, M. and Watson, D. (2016) *Learning Through Child Observation*, 3rd edition. London: Jessica Kingsley Publishers.

Featherstone, B., Morris, K. and White, S. (2014) A Marriage Made in Hell: Early Intervention Meets Child Protection, *British Journal of Social Work*, 44 (7): 1735–1749.

Ferguson, H. (2016) How Children Become Invisible in Child Protection Work: Findings from Research into Day-to-Day Social Work Practice, *British Journal of Social Work*, doi:10.1093/bjsw/bcw065.

Ferguson, I. and Lavalette, M. (2013) Crisis, Austerity and the Future(s) of Social Work in the UK, *Critical and Radical Social Work*, 1 (1): 95–110.

Fern, E. (2014) Child-Directed Social Work Practice: Findings from an Action Research Study Conducted in Iceland, *British Journal of Social Work*, 44 (5): 1110–1128.

Fortin, J. (2002) The Human Rights Act 1998: Human Rights for Children Too. In Franklin, B. (ed.), *The New Handbook of Children's Rights*. London: Routledge.

Fortin, J. (2006) Accommodating Children's Rights in a Post Human Rights Act Era, *Modern Law Review*, 69 (3): 299–326.

Foucault, M. (1975) *The Birth of the Clinic: An Archaeology of Medical Perception* (Translated by A.M. Sheridan Smith). New York: Random House.

Franklin, A. and Sloper, P. (2009) Supporting the Participation of Disabled Children and Young People in Decision-Making, *Children and Society*, 23 (1): 3–15.

Franklin, B. (ed.) (2002) *The New Handbook of Children's Rights*. London: Routledge.

Freeman, M. (2002) Children's Rights Ten Years After Ratification. In Franklin, B. (ed.), *The New Handbook of Children's Rights*. London: Routledge.

Froebel, F. (1826) *Die Menschenerziehung, die Erziehungs-, Unterrichts- und Lehrkunst, angestrebt in der allgemeinen deutschen Erziehungsanstalt zu Keilhau. Erster Band*. Keilhau-Leipzig. Translated by W. Hailmann in 1887 The Education of Man. New York: D. Appleton and Co.

Gallagher, B. and Green, A. (2012) In, Out and After Care: Young Adults' Views on Their Lives, as Children, in a Therapeutic Residential Establishment, *Children and Youth Services Review*, 34 (2): 437–450.

Gallagher, M., Smith, M., Hardy, M. and Wilkinson, H. (2012) Children and Families' Involvement in Social Work Decision Making, *Children and Society*, 26 (1): 74–85.

Gaskell, C. (2010) If the Social Worker Had Called at Least it Would Show They Cared'. Young Care Leaver's Perspectives on the Importance of Care, *Children & Society*, 24 (2): 136–147.

Gerhardt, S. (2004) *Why Love Matters: How Affection Shapes a Baby's Brain*. Hove: Brunner-Routledge.

Giant, N. (2013) *E-Safety for the i-Generation: Combating the Misuse and Abuse of Technology in Schools*. London: Jessica Kingsley Publishers.

Gibson, J. and O'Donovan, B. (2014) The Vanguard Method as Applied to the Design and Management of English and Welsh Children's Services Departments, *Systemic Practice and Action Research*, 27 (1): 39–55.

Gibson, M. (2016) Social Worker or Social Administrator? Findings from a Qualitative Case Study of a Child Protection Social Work Team, *Child and Family Social Work*, doi:10.1111/cfs.12335.

Gilligan, C. (1982) *In a Different Voice*: *Psychological Theory and Women's Development*. Cambridge, MA: Harvard University Press.

Gittins, D. (2015) The Historical Construction of Childhood. In Kehily, M.J. (ed.), *An Introduction to Childhood Studies*, 3rd edition. Maidenhead: Open University Press.

Goodyer, A. (2011) *Child-Centred Foster Care: A Rights-Based Model for Practice*. London: Jessica Kingsley Publishers.

Hadow Report (1931) *The Primary School*. London: HMSO.

Happer, H., McCreadie, J. and Aldgate, J. (2006) *Celebrating Success: What Helps Looked After Children Succeed*. Edinburgh: Social Work Inspection Agency.

Haringey Local Safeguarding Children Board (LSCB) (2009) *Serious Case Review: Baby Peter*. Haringey: Haringey LSCB.

Harris, J. (2003) *The Social Work Business*. London: Routledge.

Hart, R.A. (1992) *Children's Participation: From Tokenism to Citizenship*. Florence: UNICEF.

Health and Care Professions Council (HCPC) (2012a) *Standards of Conduct, Performance and Ethics*. London: HCPC (revised 2016).

The Health and Care Professions Council (2016) *Standards of Conduct Performance and Ethics*. London: HCPC.

Heard, D. and Lake, B. (1997) *The Challenge of Attachment for Caregiving*. London: Routledge.

Henderson, K. and Mathew-Byrne, J. (2016) Developing Communication and Interviewing Skills. In Davies, K. and Jones, R. (eds), *Skills for Social Work Practice*. London: Palgrave Macmillan.

Hendrick, H. (2015) Constructions and Reconstructions of British Childhood: An Interpretative Survey, 1800 to the Present. In James, A. and Prout, A. (eds), *Constructing and Reconstructing Childhood*. Abingdon: Routledge.

HM Government (2007) *Putting People First,* available at http://webarchive. nationalarchives.gov.uk/20130104234649/http://www.dh.gov.uk/ prod_consum_dh/groups/dh_digitalassets/@dh/@en/documents/digitalasset/ dh_081119.pdf, accessed 8 July 2017.

Holland, S. (2001) Representing Children in Child Protection Assessments, *Childhood*, 8 (3): 322–339.

Holland, S., Floris, C., Crowley, A. and Renold, E. (2010) *'How Was Your Day?' Learning from Experience: Informing Preventative Policies and Practice by Analysing Critical Moments in Care Leavers' Life Histories*. Cardiff: Voices from Care Cymru and Cardiff University School of Social Sciences.

Hollis, F. (1964) *A Psycho-Social Therapy*. New York: Random House.

Holmes, L., McDermid, S., Jones, A. and Ward, H. (2009) *How Social Workers Spend Their Time*. Research Report DCSF-RR087. Nottingham: DCSF.

Holt, J. (1975) *Escape from Childhood*. Harmondsworth: Pelican.

Hood, R., Goldacre, A., Grant, R. and Jones, R. (2016) Exploring Demand and Provision in English Child Protection Services, *British Journal of Social Work*, 46 (4): 923–941.

Horwath, J. and Tarr, S. (2015) Child Visibility in Cases of Chronic Neglect: Implications for Social Work Practice, *British Journal of Social Work*, 45 (5) 1379–1394.

House of Commons (2016) *Poverty in the UK*. Briefing Paper Number 7096, 14 November 2016, available at http://researchbriefings.parliament.uk/ResearchBriefing/Summary/SN07096#fullreport, accessed 12 July 2017.

Houston, S. (2003) A Method from the 'Lifeworld': Some Possibilities for Person Centred Planning for Children in Care, *Children and Society*, 17: 57–70.

Howe, D. (2011) *Attachment Across the Lifecourse: A Brief Introduction*. Basingstoke: Palgrave Macmillan.

Howe, K. and Gray, I. (2013) *Effective Supervision in Social Work*. London: Learning Matters, Sage.

Hughes, M. and Wearing, M. (2013) *Organisations and Management in Social Work*, 2nd edition. London: Sage.

Hunt, S., Goddard, C., Cooper, J., Littlechild, B. and Wild, J. (2016) 'If I Feel Like this, How Does the Child Feel?' Child Protection Workers, Supervision, Management and Organisational Responses to Parental Violence, *Journal of Social Work Practice*, 30 (1): 5–24.

Hwang, W.C., Myers, H.F., Abe-Kim, J. and Ting, J.Y. (2008) A Conceptual Paradigm for Understanding a Culture's Impact on Mental Health: The Cultural Influences on Mental Health (CIMH) Model, *Clinical Psychology Review*, 28 (2): 211–227.

IFSW and IASSW (2014) *Definition Approved by the IFSW General Meeting and the IASSW General Assembly*, available at http://ifsw.org/policies/definition-of-social-work/, accessed 4 April 2016.

International Labour Organization (ILO) (1999) *Convention182*. Geneva: ILO.

International Labour Organization (ILO) (2011) International Programme on the Elimination of Child Labour (IPEC), available at http://www.ilo.org/ipec/lang--en/index.htm, accessed 12 July 2017.

Jack, G. (2008) Place Matters: The Significance of Place Attachments for Children's Well-Being, *British Journal of Social Work*, 40 (3): 755–771.

James, A. and James, A.L. (2004) *Constructing Childhood: Theory, Policy and Practice*. Basingstoke: Palgrave Macmillan.

James, A. and Prout, A. (eds) (1997) *Constructing and Reconstructing Childhood*, 2nd edition. London: Falmer.

James, A. and Prout, A. (eds) (2015) *Constructing and Reconstructing Childhood*, Classic edition. London: Falmer.

Jay, A. (2014) *Independent Inquiry into Child Sexual Exploitation in Rotherham 1997–2013*. Rotherham: Rotherham Metropolitan Borough Council.

Jelicic, H., La Valle, I., Hart, D. and Holmes, L. (2014) *The Role of Independent Reviewing Officers (IROs) in England: Final Report*. London: NCB.

Jenks, C. (1982) *The Sociology of Childhood*. Aldershot: Batsford.

Jenks, C. (1996) *Childhood*. London: Routledge.

Jenks, C. (2004) Constructing Childhood Sociologically. In Kehily, M.J. (ed.), *An Introduction to Childhood Studies*. Maidenhead: Open University Press.

Jobe, A. and Gorin, S. (2013) 'If Kids Don't Feel Safe They Don't Do Anything': Young People's Views on Seeking and Receiving Help from Children's Social Care Services in England, *Child and Family Social Work*, 18 (4): 429–438.

Johnson, G. and Scholes, K. (2008) *Exploring Corporate Strategy*, 8th edition. Harlow: Financial Times/Prentice Hall.

Jones, C. (2001) Voices from the Front Line: State Social Work and New Labour, *British Journal of Social Work*, 31: 547–562.

Jones, G.A. (2005) Children and Development: Rights, Globalization and Poverty, *Progress in Development Studies*, 5 (4): 336–342.

Jones, R. (2014) *The Story of Baby P. Setting the Record Straight*. Bristol: Policy Press.

Jones, R. (2015) The End Game: The Marketisation and Privatisation of Children's Social Work and Child Protection, *Critical Social Policy*, 35 (4): 1–23.

Kadushin, A. and Kadushin, G. (2013) *The Social Work Interview*, 5th edition. New York: Columbia University Press.

Katz, C. (2013) Internet-Related Child Sexual Abuse: What Children Tell Us in Their Testimonies, *Children and Youth Services Review*, 35 (9): 1536–1542.

Katz, E. (2015) Domestic Violence, Children's Agency and Mother–Child Relationships: Towards a More Advanced Model, *Children & Society*, 29 (1): 69–79.

Kehily, M.J. (ed.) (2015) *An Introduction to Childhood Studies*, 3rd edition. Maidenhead: Open University Press.

Kendrick, A. (2012) What Research Tells Us about Residential Child Care. In Davies, M. (ed.), *Social Work with Children and Families*. Basingstoke: Palgrave Macmillan.

Kilbourne, S. (1998) The Wayward Americans – Why the USA has not Ratified the UN Convention on the Rights of the Child, *Child and Family Law Quarterly*, 10 (3): 243–256.

Kitson, A., Marshall, A., Bassett, K. and Zeitz, K. (2013) What are the Core Elements of Patient-Centred Care? A Narrative Review and Synthesis of the Literature from Health Policy, Medicine and Nursing, *Journal of Advanced Nursing*, 69 (1): 4–15.

Kjørholt, A. T. (2013) Childhood as Social Investment, Rights and the Valuing of Education, *Children and Society*, 27: 245–257.

Kondrat, D.C. (2014) Person-Centred Approach. In Teater, B. (ed.), *An Introduction to Applying Social Work Theories and Methods*. Maidenhead: Open University Press.

Kottman, T. (2014) *Play Therapy: Basics and Beyond*, 2nd edition. Alexandria, VA: John Wiley & Sons.

Kowalski, R.M., Limber, S.P. and Agatston, P.W. (2012) *Cyber Bullying: Bullying in the Digital Age*, 2nd edition. Chichester: Wiley-Blackwell.

Laming, H. (2003) *The Victoria Climbié Inquiry*. London: The Stationery Office.

Laming, H. (2009) The Protection of Children in England: A Progress Report. London: The Stationery Office.

Lansdown, G. (2001) 'Children's Welfare and Children's Rights'. In Foley, P., Roche, J. and Tucker, S. (eds), *Children in Society: Contemporary Theory, Policy and Practice*. Basingstoke: Palgrave Macmillan.

Lee, N. (2001) *Childhood and Society: Growing Up in an Age of Uncertainty*. Buckingham: Open University Press.

Lee, N. (2005) *Childhood and Human Value: Development, Separation and Separability*. Maidenhead: Open University Press.

Lee, S. (2007) *Making Decisions: The Independent Mental Capacity Advocacy Service*. London: Mental Capacity Implementation Programme.

Lefevre, M. (2010) *Communicating with Children and Young People: Making a Difference*. Bristol: Policy Press.

Lessing, D. (1974) *Memoirs of a Survivor*. London: Octagon Press.

Liebel, M. (2003) Working Children as Social Subjects: The Contribution of Working Children's Organizations to Social Transformation, *Childhood*, 14 (2): 279–284.

Lister, R. (2003) Investing in the Citizen-Workers of the Future, *Social Policy and Administration*, 37 (5): 427–443.

London Borough of Brent (1985) *A Child in Trust: The Report of the Panel of Inquiry into the Circumstances Surrounding the Death of Jasmine Beckford*. London: London Borough of Brent.

London Borough of Greenwich (1987) *A Child in Mind: The Report of the Commission of Inquiry into the Circumstances Surrounding the Death of Kimberley Carlile*. London: London Borough of Greenwich.

Lymbery, M. (2012) Critical Commentary: Social Work and Personalisation, *British Journal of Social Work*, 42 (4): 783–792.

Lyon, C.M. (2007) Interrogating the Concentration on the UNCRC Instead of the ECHR in the Development of Children's Rights in England?, *Children and Society*, 21 (2): 147–153.

MacIntyre, A. (1984) *After Virtue*. Notre Dame, IN: University of Notre Dame Press.

McLellan, D. (ed.) (1971) 'On the Jewish Question', *Karl Marx: Early Texts*. Oxford: Basil Blackwell.

McLeod, A. (2007) Whose Agenda? Issues of Power and Relationship When Listening to Looked After Children, *Child and Family Social Work*, 12: 278–286.

McLeod, A. (2008) *Listening to Children: A Practitioner's Guide*. London: Jessica Kingsley Publishers.

McLeod, A. (2010) A Friend and an Equal: Do Young People in Care Seek the Impossible from Their Social Workers?, *British Journal of Social Work*, 40 (3): 772–788.

McMurray, I., Connolly, H., Preston-Shoot, M. and Wigley, V. (2011) Shards of the Old Looking Glass: Restoring the Significance of Identity in Promoting Positive Outcomes for Looked-After Children, *Child and Family Social Work*, 16 (2): 210–218.

McPherson, L. and Macnamara, N. (2016) *Supervising Child Protection Practice: What Works? An Evidence Informed Approach*. Cham: Springer.

Martin, P.Y. and Jackson, S. (2002) Educational Success for Children in Public Care: Advice From a Group of High Achievers, *Child and Family Social Work*, 7 (2):121–130.

Matthews, A. (2011) *Landing in Kent: The Experience of Unaccompanied Children Arriving in the UK*. London: Office of the Children's Commissioner.

Mayall, B. (2002) *Towards a Sociology for Childhood: Thinking from Children's Lives*. Buckingham: Open University Press.

Mehrabian, A. (1972) *Nonverbal Communication*. Chicago, IL: Aldine.

Mekonen, Y. (2010) Measuring Government Performance in Realising Child Rights and Child Well-Being: The Approach and Indicators, *Child Indicators Research*, 3: 205–241.

Middleton, L. (1999) *Disabled Children: Challenging Social Exclusion*. Oxford: Blackwell.

Ministry of Health (1959) *The Welfare of Children in Hospital, Platt Report*. London: HMSO.

Ministry of Justice (2011) *Achieving Best Evidence in Criminal Proceedings: Guidance on Interviewing Victims and Witnesses, and Guidance on Using Special Measures*. London: Ministry of Justice.

Mitchell, M.B., Kuczynski, L., Tubbs, C.Y. and Ross, C. (2010) We Care about Care: Advice by Children in Care for Children in Care, Foster Parents and Child Welfare Workers about the Transition into Foster Care, *Child and Family Social Work*, 15 (2): 176–185.

Morgan, R. (2005) *Being Fostered: A National Survey of the Views of Foster Children, Foster Carers and Birth Parents about Foster Care*. Newcastle: Office of the Children's Rights Director.

Morgan, R. (2006) *About Adoption: A Children's Views Report*. Newcastle: Office of the Children's Rights Director.

Morgan, R. (2009) *Children's Care Monitor 2009: Children on the State of Social Care in England Reported by the Children's Rights Director for England*. London: Ofsted.

Morgan, R. (2010a) *Planning, Placement and Review: A Report by the Children's Rights Director for England*. Manchester: Ofsted.

Morgan, R. (2010b) *Children's Messages on Care 2010: A Report by the Children's Rights Director for England*. Manchester: Ofsted.

Morris, J. (1998) *Still Missing: Disabled Children and the Children Act*. London: Who Cares? Trust.

Morris, K. and Connolly, M. (2012) Family Decision Making in Child Welfare: Challenges in Developing a Knowledge Base for Practice, *Child Abuse Review*, 21 (1): 41–52.

Morrow, V. (1999) 'We are People too.' Children's and Young People's Perspectives on Children's Rights and Decision Making in England, *The International Journal of Children's Rights*, 7: 149–170.

Moss, B. (2015) *Communication Skills for Health and Social Care*, 3rd edition. London: Sage.

Moss, P., Clark, A. and Kjørholt, A. (2005) Introduction. In Clark, A., Kjørholt, A. and Moss, P. (eds), *Beyond Listening: Children's Perspectives on Early Childhood Services*. Bristol: Policy Press.

Mullender, A., Hague, G., Imam, U.F., Kelly, L., Malos, E. and Regan, L. (2002) *Children's Perspectives on Domestic Violence*. London: Sage.

Munro, E. (2001) Empowering Looked-After Children, *Child and Family Social Work*, 6: 129–137.

Munro, E. (2004) The Impact of Audit on Social Work Practice, *British Journal of Social Work*, 34 (8): 1075–1095.

Munro, E. (2011) *The Munro Review of Child Protection: Final Report: A Child-Centred Approach*. London: The Stationery Office.

Murphy, D., Duggan, M. and Joseph, S. (2013) Relationship-Based Social Work and its Compatibility with the Person-Centred Approach: Principled Versus Instrumental Perspectives, *British Journal of Social Work*, 43 (4): 703–719.

National Audit Office (2014) *The Impact of Funding Reductions on Local Authorities,* available at https://www.nao.org.uk/report/the-impact-funding-reductions-local-authorities/, accessed 17 February 2017.

National Crime Agency (2015) *Sexting Becoming the Norm for Teens,* available at http://www.nationalcrimeagency.gov.uk/news/news-listings/632-sexting-becoming-the-norm-for-teens, accessed 7 June 2017.

Nieuwenhuys, O. (2009) From Child Labour to Working Children's Movements. In Qvortrup, J., Corsaro, W.A. and Honig, M.-S. (eds), *The Palgrave Handbook of Childhood Studies*. Basingstoke: Palgrave Macmillan.

NTT DOCOMO (2014) *Children's Use of Mobile Phones*, available at https://www.gsma.com/publicpolicy/wp-content/uploads/2012/03/GSMA_Childrens_use_of_mobile_phones_2014.pdf, accessed 7 June 2017.

Ofsted (2010a) *The Voice of the Child: Learning Lessons from Serious Case Reviews. A Thematic Report of Ofsted's Evaluation of Serious Case Reviews from 1 April to 30 September,* available at https://www.gov.uk/government/uploads/system/uploads/attachment_data/file/526983/Summary_-_The_voice_of_the_child.pdf, accessed 17 January 2018.

Ofsted (2010b) *Children on Rights and Responsibilities: A Report of Children's Views by the Children's Rights Director for England*. Manchester: Ofsted.

Ofsted (2011) *Outstanding Children's Homes*. Manchester: Ofsted.

Ofsted (2013) *Independent Reviewing Officers: Taking Up the Challenge?* London: Ofsted.

O'Hagan, K. (2001) *Cultural Competence in the Caring Professions*. London: Jessica Kingsley Publishers.

Oliver, C. (2010) *Children's Views and Experiences of Their Contact with Social Workers: A Focused Review of the Evidence*. London: Children's Workforce Development Council.

Oliver, C. and Dalrymple, J. (eds) (2009) *Developing Advocacy for Children and Young People*. London: Jessica Kingsley Publishers.

Oliver, C., Knight, A. and Candappa, M. (2006) *Advocacy for Children and Young People: Achievements and Challenges: Briefing Paper*. London: Thomas Coram Research Unit/Institute of Education: University of London.

Oliver, M. (1990) *The Politics of Disablement*. Basingstoke: Palgrave Macmillan.

O'Reilly, L. and Dolan, P. (2016) The Voice of the Child in Social Work Assessments: Age-Appropriate Communication with Children, *British Journal of Social Work*, 46 (5): 1191–1207.

Parker, R. (1987) *A Forward Look at Research and the Child in Care*. Bristol: School of Applied Social Studies.

Parsons, T. (1956) The American Family: Its Relation to Personality and the Social Structure'. In Parsons, T. and Bales, R.F. (eds), *Family: Socialization and Interaction Process*. London: Routledge and Kegan Paul.

Parton, N. (1998) Risk, Advanced Liberalism and Child Welfare, *British Journal of Social Work*, 28: 5–27.

Parton, N. (2003) Rethinking Professional Practice: The Contributions of Social Constructionism and the Feminist 'Ethic of Care', *British Journal of Social Work*, 33: 1–16.

Parton, N. (2012) The Munro Review of Child Protection: An Appraisal, *Children and Society*, 26: 150–162.

Payne, R. (2012) 'Extraordinary Survivors' or 'Ordinary Lives'? Embracing 'Everyday Agency' in Social Interventions with Child-Headed Households in Zambia, *Children's Geographies*, 10 (4): 399–411.

Pearce, J.J. (2014) Moving on with Munro: Child Sexual Exploitation within a Child Protection Framework. In Blyth, M. (ed.), *Moving on from Munro: Improving Children's Services*. Bristol: Policy Press.

Penna, S. (2005) The Children Act 2004: Child Protection and Social Surveillance, *Journal of Welfare and Family Law*, 27 (2): 143–157.

Pert, H., Diaz, C. and Thomas, N. (2017) Children's Participation in LAC Reviews: A Study in One English Local Authority, *Child and Family Social Work*, 22 (S2): 1–10.

Petrie, P., Boddy, J., Cameron, C., Heptinstall, E., McQuail, S., Simon, A. and Wigfall, V. (2009) *Pedagogy: A Holistic, Personal Approach to Work with Children and Young People, Across Services*. London: Thomas Coram Research Unit/ Institute of Education: University of London.

Piaget, J. (1955) *The Child's Construction of Reality*. London: Routledge and Kegan Paul.

Pithouse, A. and Crowley, A. (2007) Adults Rule? Children, Advocacy and Complaints to Social Services, *Children and Society*, 21: 201–213.

Plowden Report (1967) *Children and Their Primary Schools*. London: HMSO.

Power, M. (1997) *The Audit Society*. Oxford: Oxford University Press.

Prout, A. (2005) *The Future of Childhood*. London: RoutledgeFalmer.

Prout, A. and James, A. (1997) A New Paradigm for the Sociology of Childhood? Provenance, Promise and Problems. In James, A. and Prout, A. (eds), *Constructing and Reconstructing Childhood*, 2nd edition. London: Falmer.

Quitak, N. (2004) Difficulties in Holding the Role of the Observer, *Journal of Social Work Practice*, 18 (2): 247–253.

Qvortrup, J. (1994) Introduction. In Qvortrup, J., Brady, M., Sgritta, G. and Wintersberger, H. (eds), *Childhood Matters: Social Theory, Practice and Politics*. Aldershot: Avebury.

Qvortrup, J. (1997) A Voice for Children in Statistical and Social Accounting: A Plea for Children's Right to be Heard. In James, A. and Prout, A. (eds), *Constructing and Reconstructing Childhood*, 2nd edition. London: Falmer.

Rasmusson, B., Hyvönen, U., Nygren, L. and Khoo, E. (2010) Child-Centred Social Work Practice –Three Unique Meanings in the Context of Looking after Children and the Assessment Framework in Australia, Canada and Sweden, *Children and Youth Services Review*, 32 (3): 452–459.

Reddy, N. (2007) Working with Working Children in India. In Hungerland, B., Liebel, M., Milne, B. and Wihstutz, A. (eds), *Working to be Someone: Child*

Focused Research and Practice with Working Children. London: Jessica Kingsley Publishers.

Robertson, J. (1952) *A Two-Year-Old Goes to Hospital.* Film in English and French, Concord Video and Film Council, New York University, Film Library.

Roche, J. (1999) Children: Rights, Participation and Citizenship, *Childhood,* 6: 473–493.

Rogers, C.R. (1951) *Client-Centred Therapy: Its Current Practice, Implications and Theory.* Boston: Houghton Mifflin.

Rogers, C.R. (1957) The Necessary and Sufficient Conditions of Therapeutic Personality Change, *Journal of Consulting Psychology,* 21: 95–103.

Rogers, J. (2016) 'Different' and 'Devalued': Managing the Stigma of Foster-Care with the Benefit of Peer Support, British Journal of Social Work. doi: 10.1093/bjsw/bcw063.

Rowe, D. (1989) Foreword. In Masson, J. (ed.), *Against Therapy.* London: Collins.

Rowe, J. and Lambert, L. (1973*) Children who Wait: A Study of Children Needing Substitute Families.* London: Association of British Adoption Agencies.

Ruch, G. (2010) Theoretical Frameworks Informing Relationship-Based Practice. In Ruch, G., Turney, D. and Ward, A. (eds), *Relationship-Based Social Work: Getting to the Heart of Practice.* London: Jessica Kingsley Publishers.

Ruch, G., Turney, D. and Ward, A. (eds) (2010) *Relationship-Based Social Work: Getting to the Heart of Practice.* London: Jessica Kingsley Publishers.

Ruch, G., Winter, K., Cree, V., Hallett, S., Morrison, F. and Hadfield, M. (2016) Making Meaningful Connections: Using Insights from Social Pedagogy in Statutory Child and Family Social Work Practice, *Child & Family Social Work,* doi:10.1111/cfs.12321.

Ryan, T. and Walker, R. (2007) *Life Story Work: A Practical Guide to Helping Children Understand Their Past.* London: BAAF.

Sandbaek, M. and Einarsson, J.H, *Children and Young People Report to the UN on Their Rights, NOVA Report. 2b/ 08.* Oslo: NOVA., available at http://www. nova.no/asset/3182/2/3182_2.pdf, accessed 10 December 2017.

Scottish Government (2012) *Getting it Right for Every Child* (GIRFEC), available at www.gov.scot/Publications/2012/11/7143/2, accessed 8 July 2017.

Secure Training Centre (STC) Rules (1998) *Secure Training Centres, England and Wales,* available at http://www.legislation.gov.uk/uksi/1998/472/made, accessed 10 December 2017.

Seden, J. (2001) Assessment of Children in Need and Their Families: A Literature Review. In Department of Health (ed.), *Studies informing the Framework for the Assessment of Children in Need and Their Families.* London: The Stationery Office.

Sevenhuijsen, S. (1998) *Citizenship and the Ethics of Care.* London: Routledge.

Shaw, C. (1998) *Remember my Messages....The Experiences of 2000 Children in the Public Care in the UK.* London: Who Cares? Trust.

Shayer, M., Ginsburg, D. and Coe, R. (2007) Thirty Years on – A Large Anti-Flynn Effect? The Piagetian Test Volume and Heaviness Norms 1975–2003, *British Journal of Educational Psychology,* 77 (1): 25–41.

Shepherd, J. (2009) New Children's Database Faces Criticism, *Guardian* 26 January, available at http://www.guardian.co.uk/society/2009/jan/26/childrens-database-contactpoint, accessed 17 February 2017.

Sheridan, M.D. (1997) *From Birth to Five Years. Children's Developmental Progress.* Revised and updated by M. Frost and A. Sharma. London: Routledge.

Sidebotham, P., Brandon, M., Bailey, S., Belderson, P., Dodsworth, J., Garstang, J., Harrison, E., Retzer, A. and Sorensen, P. (2016) *Pathways to Harm, Pathways to Protection: A Triennial Analysis of Serious Case Reviews 2011 to 2014 Final Report*. London: Department for Education.

Simcock, P. and Castle, R. (2016) *Social Work and Disability*. Cambridge: Polity Press.

Smart, C. (2007) *Personal Life*. Cambridge: Polity Press.

Smith, R. (2010) *A Universal Child?* Basingstoke: Palgrave Macmillan.

Social Services Inspectorate (1991) *Getting the Message Across: A Guide to Developing and Communicating Policies, Principles and Procedures on Assessment*. London: HMSO.

Solberg, A. (1997) Negotiating Childhood: Changing Constructions of Age for Norwegian Children. In James, A. and Prout, A. (eds), *Constructing and Reconstructing Childhood*. Basingstoke: Falmer.

Stalker, K. and Connors, C. (2003) Communicating with Disabled Children, *Adoption and Fostering*, 27 (1): 26–35.

Stein, M. (2005) *Resilience and Young People Leaving Care: Overcoming the Odds*. York: Joseph Rowntree Foundation.

Stein, M. (2012) *Young People Leaving Care: Supporting Pathways to Adulthood*. London: Jessica Kingsley Publishers.

Stewart-Brown, S. (2008) Improving Parenting: The Why and the How, *Archives of Disease in Childhood*, 93: 102–104.

Street, A. (1992) *Cultural Practices in Nursing*. Geelong: Deakin University.

Tait, A. and Wosu, H. (2013) *Direct Work with Vulnerable Children: Playful Activities and Strategies for Communication*. London: Jessica Kingsley Publishers.

Taylor, D. (1996) Citizenship and Social Power. In Taylor, D. (ed.), *Critical Social Policy*. London: Sage.

Taylor, K. (2007) The Participation of Children with Multi-sensory Impairment in Person-centred Planning, *British Journal of Special Education*, 34 (4): 204–211.

The College of Social Work (TCSW) (2012) *Professional Capabilities Framework*, available at https://www.basw.co.uk/pcf/, accessed 7 June 2017.

Thomas, N. (2000) *Children, Family and the State: Decision-making and Child Participation*. Macmillan: Bristol: Policy Press.

Thomas, N. (2005) *Social Work with Young People in Care: Looking After Children in Theory and Practice*. Basingstoke: Palgrave Macmillan.

Thomas, N. (2011) Care Planning and Review for Looked After Children: Fifteen Years of Slow Progress?, *British Journal of Social Work*, 41 (2): 387–398.

Thomas, N.P., Street, C., Ridley, J., Crowley, A., Moxon, D., Joshi, P., Amalathas, E., Rix, K. and Edwards, A. (2016) *Independent Advocacy: Impact and Outcomes for Children and Young People*. London: Office of the Children's Commissioner.

Thompson, K. (2016) *Strengthening Child Protection: Sharing Information in Multi-Agency Settings*. Bristol: Policy Press.

Thompson, N. (2016) *Anti- Discriminatory Practice*, 6th edition. Basingstoke: Palgrave Macmillan.

Thorne, B. and Sanders, P. (2013) *Carl Rogers*, 3rd edition. London: Sage.

Timms, J. and Thoburn, J. (2003) *Your Shout! A Survey of the Views of 706 Young People in Public Care*. London: NSPCC.

Trevithick, P. (2012) *Social Work Skills and Knowledge*, 3rd edition. Maidenhead: Open University Press.

Tronto, J. (1993) *Moral Boundaries: A Political Argument for an Ethic of Care*. London: Routledge.

Tsegaye, S. (2009) *Orphaned in Africa: Old Problems and New Faces*, African Child Poverty Forum.

Turnell, A. and Edwards, S. (1999) *Signs of Safety: A Solution and Safety Oriented Approach to Child Protection Casework*. New York: W. W. Norton.

Turner, C. (2003) *Are You Listening? What Disabled Children and Young People in Wales Think about the Services they Use*. Cardiff: Welsh Assembly.

United Nations (2000) *Millennial Development Goals*, available at http://www.un.org/millenniumgoals/, accessed 8 July 2017.

UNCRC (1989) *The Convention on the Rights of the Child*. United Nations.

Utting, W. (1997) *People Like Us: The Report of the Review of Safeguards for Children Living Away from Home*. London: HMSO/Department of Health/Welsh Office.

Van Bijleveld, G.G., Dedding, C.W.M. and Bunders-Aelen, J.F.G. (2013) Children and Young People's Participation Within Child Welfare and Child Protection Services: A State-of-the-Art Review, *Child and Family Social Work*, 20: 129–138.

Wade, J., Mitchell, F. and Baylis, G. (2005) *Unaccompanied Asylum Seeking Children: The Response of Social Work Services*. London: BAAF.

Wade, J., Sinclair, I.A.C., Stuttard, L. and Simmonds, J. (2014) *Investigating Special Guardianship: Experiences, Challenges and Outcomes*. London: Department for Education.

Walker, G. (2011) Safeguarding and Protection: What Does a Rights-Based Approach Mean Across Different Disciplines? In Jones, P. and Walker G. (eds), *Children's Rights in Practice*. London: Sage.

Walkerdine, V. (2004) Developmental Psychology and the Study of Childhood. In Kehily, M.J. (ed.), *An Introduction to Childhood Studies*. Maidenhead: Open University Press.

Wardle, L. (1996) The Use and Abuse of Rights Rhetoric: The Constitutional Rights of Children, *Loyola University Chicago Law Journal*, 27: 321–348.

Wastell, D. and White, S. (2012) Blinded by Neuroscience: Social Policy, the Family and the Infant Brain, *Families, Relationships and Societies*, 1 (3): 397–414.

Waterhouse, R. (2000) *Lost in Care: Report of the Tribunal of Inquiry into the Abuse of Children in Care in the Former County Council Areas of Gwynedd and Clywd since 1974*. London: HMSO.

Weaver, M. (2016) *Hate Crimes Soar After EU Referendum, Home Office Figures Confirm*. The Guardian, 13 October, available at https://www.theguardian.com/politics/2016/oct/13/hate-crimes-eu-referendum-home-office-figures-confirm, accessed 8 July 2017.

Weber, M. (1947) *The Theory of Social and Economic Organization*. Translated by A.M. Henderson and Talcott Parsons. London: Collier Macmillan Publishers.

Weld, N. (2008) The Three Houses Tool: Building Safety and Positive Change. In Calder, M. (ed.), *Safeguarding Children*. Lyme Regis: Russell House Publishing.

White, M. and Epston, D. (1990) *Narrative Means to Therapeutic Ends*. Adelaide: Dulwich Centre.

Wilks, T. (2012) *Advocacy and Social Work Practice*. Maidenhead: McGraw-Hill.

Williams, J. (2007) Incorporating Children's Rights: The Divergence in Law and Policy, *Legal Studies*, 27 (2): 261–287.

Willis, R. and Holland, S. (2009) Life Story Work: Reflections on the Experience by Looked After Children and Young People, *Adoption and Fostering*, 33 (4): 44–52.

Willow, C. (2009) Putting Children and Their Rights at the Heart of the Safeguarding Process. In Cleaver, H., Cawson, P., Gorin, S. and Walker, S. (eds), *Safeguarding Children: A Shared Responsibility*. Chichester: Wiley-Blackwell.

Winnicott, C. (1964) Communicating with Children, *Child Care Quarterly Review*, 18 (3): 85–93.

Winter, K. (2011) *Building Relationships and Communicating with Young Children: A Practical Guide for Social Workers*. Abingdon: Routledge.

Winter, K. (2014) Understanding and Supporting Young Children's Transitions into State Care: Schlossberg's Transition Framework and Child-Centred Practice, *British Journal of Social Work*, 44 (2): 401–417.

Winter, K., Cree, V., Hallett, S., Hadfield, M., Ruch, G., Morrison, F. and Holland, S. (2016) Exploring Communication between Social Workers, Children and Young People, *British Journal of Social Work*. doi:10.1093/bjsw/bcw083.

Woodhead, M. (2006) Changing Perspectives on Early Childhood: Theory, Research and Policy', Paper Commissioned for the EFA Global Monitoring Report 2007: *Strong Foundations: Early Childhood Care and Education*.

Wyness, M. (2006) *Childhood and Society. An Introduction to the Sociology of Childhood*. Basingstoke: Palgrave Macmillan.

Wyness, M. (2015) *Childhood*. Cambridge: Polity Press.

Index

A

activities with children, 82–83
adolescents, 35–36, 39
adoption, 34, 40, 159–160
Adoption and Children Act (2002),
    18, 156
advocacy
Advocacy Standards, 66, 102
    Assertiveness, 99
    and child-centred practice, 29
    children's views, 105
    definition, 96–97
    entitlement, 65–66
    local services, 64–65, 101
    negotiation, 99–100
    skills, 98–100
    in social work, 98–100
    types, 97–98
advocates, professional
    difficulties in working together,
        102–103
    issues dealt with, 101
    working with, 100–105
Africa and children's rights, 62–64
African Charter on the Rights and
    Welfare of the Child (ACRWC),
    62–63
after care (see leaving care)
age distinction, 41–42, 57
agency, children's, 42
Ainsworth, Mary, 40
alcohol abuse, 146–147
Amplify, 55
anti-discriminatory practice, 74,
    81–82, 161–166
Ariès, Phillipe, 32–34
assertiveness, 99
assessment, 16–17, 41, 75–76, 131,
    137, 139–141

asylum seekers, 165–166
attachment, 28, 39–40, 76
attitudes to children
    historical, 32–35
    as immature, 32–33
    as innocent/evil, 34–36
    liberationist, 54
    protectionist, 34–35, 53
    social workers', 115–116
austerity, 108, 134
authority, parents', 47–49
autonomy, 15–16, 19, 54, 57
Axline, Virginia, 25

B

Baby Peter (see Connelly, Peter)
barriers to child-centred practice
    attitudes to children and young
        people, 115–116
    culture, 118–119
    bureaucracy, 110–111, 119
    decisions/procedures, 113–115
    marketisation, 107–108
    organisational, 109–112
    overcoming, 117–122
    resources, 109–110
barriers to relationships, 116–117
Beck, Ulrich, 31
Beckford, Jasmine, 130
Become (formerly Who Cares? Trust),
    64
being/becoming, 43–44
best interests, 13, 53–54, 60, 102–103
biological theories of childhood,
    37–38, 40
Black and minority ethnic children,
    10, 80–81, 163–165
blame culture, 133–134
body language, 84, 86

Bowlby, John, 28, 39–40
Bronfenbrenner, Ulrich, 47
bullying, 136, 169–170
bureaucracy, 74, 110–111, 119
business culture, 108
Butler-Sloss, Baroness, 131, 145

C

CAFCASS, 134
capacity (see competence)
Care Act 2014, 22
care proceedings, 19, 134
Carlile, Kimberley, 4, 130
child-centred practice
    barriers, 109–117
    and child protection, 4–5, 129–133,
        135–136
    children's views, 7–10
    critiques, 23–24
    definition, 11–13
    in education, 26–27
    in health, 27–29
    law/policy, 13–19
    and looked after children, 6–9, 156
    Munro Review, 11, 18, 132–133
    origins, 21–23
    in play therapy, 24–25
    rationale, 4
    supervision, 119–121
child development (see developmental
    theories)
child-directed practice, 12, 24
child-headed households, 45–46
childhood theories
    Ariès, Phillipe, 32–34
    biological, 37–38, 40
    liberationist, 54
    protectionist, 38–41
    psychological, 38–41
    social constructionist, 41–43, 44
    sociological, 41–44
child labour, 35, 45, 63
child observation (see observation)
child protection
    assessments, 137, 139–141
    case conferences/core groups,
        141–144

categories of abuse, 145
    definition, 127
    focus on child, 4–5, 129–133,
        135–136
    initial enquiries, 137
    law/policy, 130–135
    Munro Review, 5, 132–133
    principles, 135–136
    processes, 135–143
    public inquiries, 4–5, 128–130
    sharing information, 114–115,
        128–129
    Working Together, 19, 135–136,
        139–140, 145
child sexual exploitation, 145,
    148–150
Children Act 1989
    child-centred principles, 14–16
    child protection, 131, 137
    children in need, 16–17, 18
    children looked after, 155
Children Act 2004, 18, 131, 156
Children and Families Act 2014, 19,
    134
Children and Social Work Act 2017,
    135
Children and Young Persons Act 2008,
    18, 156
Children (Leaving Care) Act 2000,
    175
Children (Northern Ireland) Order
    1995, 16, 130, 155
Children (Scotland) Act 1995, 16,
    130, 155
children in care/looked after (see
    looked after children)
Children's Commissioner, 55, 62,
    64
children's guardians, 14
children's hearings/panels, 16, 130
children's views
    adoption, 160
    adults' attitudes, 47–49
    advocacy, 105
    child-centred practice, 7–10
    child protection meetings, 143
    child protection procedures/
        assessments, 136, 140–141

children's views *(Continued)*
  disabled children's views, 9–10, 88, 93–95, 162–163
  foster care 157–158
  leaving care, 176
  professionals, 9–10
  residential care, 158–159
  rights, 66–68
  social workers, 6–10, 112, 114–115, 116
  telling about abuse, 137–139
citizenship rights, 53, 55
Cleveland, 131, 145
client-centred therapy, 23
Climbié, Victoria, 4, 35, 74, 129–130
cognitive development, 38–39
Colwell, Maria, 4, 129, 130
communicating
  cultural issues, 80–82
  with disabled children, 87–88
  language, 81–82
  listening, 86–87
  non-verbal, 84
  play/activity, 82–84
  with teenagers, 36
  with young children, 5–6, 79
competence, 15–16, 28–29, 57
complaints, 15, 65, 101–102, 104
conferences and core groups, 141–144
confidentiality, 78–79, 103–104, 114–115
Connelly, Peter, 4, 35, 127, 128, 132, 134
consultation, 96
contact with family, 167–168, 172
control, 35–36, 92
counselling, 23
culture, changing, 118–119
cyber-bullying, 151–152

D

decision making, young people's involvement, 15–16, 28–29, 57, 93–95, 113–116, 141–144, 172–174
developmental theories, 37–41

deviance, 36
disabled children, 9–10, 24, 87–88, 93–95, 157, 162–163
domestic violence, 145, 146
drawing, 79, 82–84

E

ecomaps, 83
education
  best interests, 53–54
  child-centred, 26–27
  cognitive development, 38–39
Education Acts, 26–27, 34
  ethnographic studies, 48
  in Global South, 45, 63
  and leaving care, 175, 177
  Kindergarten movement, 26
  emotional abuse, 145
emotional development, 39–40
empowerment, 74–75, 91–92, 96–97
Erikson, Erik, 39
ethics of care, 52–53
ethnic minorities (see minority ethnic)
European Convention (ECHR), 61
Every Child Matters, 18, 131

F

family, 46–47, 58–59
feminist theory, ethics of care, 52–53
foster care, 157–158, 167, 168, 169–170, 171–172, 173
Framework for Assessment, 11, 16–17, 41, 139
Fraser Guidelines, 16, 57
Freud, Sigmund, 39

G

Gillick principle, 15–16, 28, 57, 115
global child, 44–46
Global North, 44–45, 62
Global South, 44–46, 62–64, 145

H

Hart's ladder of participation, 55–56, 96
health, 27–29, 38

hospital visiting, 27–28
human rights, 51, 59, 61
Human Rights Act, 61, 67–68

I

Identity, 170–171
information sharing, 103–104,
    114–115, 128–129
Independent Reviewing Officers
    (IROs), 93, 156, 173–174
inquiries, public, 4–5, 128–130
International Association of Schools of
    Social Work (IASSW), 19, 91, 97
International Federation of Social
    workers (IFSW), 19, 91, 97
International Labour Organisation
    (ILO), 45
internet, 145, 150–151
internet abuse, 145, 150–152
interpreters, 81–82
intimidation, 4, 129
invisible child, 136

J

jargon, 82

K

Kindergarten movement, 26
kinship care, 161
Knowledge and Skills Statements,
    20–21, 91

L

labour, child, 35, 45, 63
Laming, Lord, 4, 128, 129–130,
    131, 132
language, 81–82
learning culture, 110
leaving care, 175–177
liberationist views, 54
life story work, 168
listening, 8–9, 86–87
Locke, John, 32
looked after children
    abuse, 169–170
    adoption, 34, 40, 159–160

Black and minority ethnic children,
    163–165
care plans, 173
contact with family, 167–168,
    171–172
disabled children, 157, 162–163
effects of poverty/class, 162
entering care, 167–169
forms of care, 157–161
foster care, 157–158, 167, 168,
    169–170, 171–172, 173
identity, 170–171
kinship care, 161
law/policy, 155–157
leaving care, 175–177
life story work, 168
moves in care, 171–172
processes, 166–174
refugees and asylum seekers,
    165–166
residential care, 158–159, 169
reviews/meetings, 93, 95, 118,
    172–174
special guardianship, 160–161
statistics, 157, 161–162
stigma and bullying, 169–170

M

managerialism, 74, 110–111
marketisation, 74, 107–108
meetings
    child friendly, 118, 174
    child protection, 141–144
    looked after reviews, 93, 95, 118,
        172–174
mental ill health, 146, 147
Millennial Development Goals,
    63–64
minority ethnic children, 10, 80–81,
    163–165
Munro Review
    child-centred system, 11, 18,
        132–133
    definition of child-centred practice,
        5, 11
    supervision, 120
    'three houses' tool, 83–84, 133

N

NSPCC, 35, 153
neglect, 141–142, 145–146
negotiating, 99–100
neuroscience, 40
Northern Ireland, law, 16, 64, 76,
    130, 155

O

observation, 17, 85–86
offices, social work, 118
organisation of social work, 107–111,
    119

P

Parsons, Talcott, 41
participation
    capacity/competence, 15–16, 28–29,
        57
    child protection, 141–144
    citizenship rights, 53, 55
    disabled children, 93–95
    group, 96
    Hart's ladder, 55–56
    involvement in decisions, 15–16,
        28–29, 57, 93–95, 141–144,
        172–174
    looked after children, 93, 95,
        172–174
    preparation, 95, 142
    principles in Children Act 1989,
        14–15
    principles in UNCRC, 13–14, 60
    social workers' views, 116
Pelka, Daniel, 129
personalisation, 22
person-centred, 21–22, 23–24
physical abuse, 145–146
physical development, 37–38
Piaget, Jean, 38–39
play, 82–84
play therapy, 24–25
poverty, 45, 145–146, 162
power dynamics, 52, 92
privatisation, 134–135
procedural, 113–114, 133
process of work, 79, 105

Professional Capabilities Framework,
    20–21
protectionist views, 34–35, 53, 115–116
psycho-analytical theory, 74–75
psychological theories, 38–41
Public Law Outline, 134, 161
Putting People First, 22

R

refugees, 165–166
relationship
    barriers, 116–117
    based social work, 74–75
    building, 73–75
    in child protection, 76, 144
    communication, 79–88
    listening, 86–87
    trust, 78–79
residential care, 158–159,
        169
resources, 109–110, 113, 134
reviews, looked after, 93, 95, 118,
        172–174
rights
    in Africa, 62–64
    children's knowledge of, 66–68
    citizenship, 53, 55
    development, 51–52
    in families, 58, 59
    feminist theories, 52
    human rights, 51, 59, 61
    law/policy, 59–62
    liberationist views, 54
    organisations, 64–65, 66
    participation, 13–14, 60
    power dynamics, 52
    in practice, 64
    protectionist views, 53
    social workers' views of, 116
    UNCRC, 13–14, 59–62
Rogers, Carl, 23
Rousseau, Jean-Jacques, 26, 34

S

safeguarding (see also child
    protection), 4–5, 127
Scandinavian research, 44

school studies (Corsaro), 48
Scotland law/policy, 16, 62, 64, 76, 130, 155, 175
separation of childhood/adulthood, 34–35, 42–43
serious case reviews, 4–5, 129, 132, 140
sexting, 151
sexual abuse, 131, 145, 148–151
sharing information, 103–104, 114–115, 128–129
Sheridan charts, 38
significant harm, 131, 137, 155
Signs of Safety, 142–143
social actors, children as, 42
social constructionist theories, 41–43, 44
social pedagogy, 27, 76–78
social work
 with adults, 21–22
 development of services, 107–108
 principles and standards, 19–21
 values, 19–21
sociological theories, 41–44
Special Guardianship, 160–161
Staying Put, 19, 175–176
substance misuse, 146–148
supervision, 119–121

T

Tavistock model of observation, 85–86
teenagers, 35–36
therapy, 23, 24–25
'third object', 77–78, 82
time, 109, 111, 116–117, 121–122
training, 116–117, 122
transference, 75
trust, 7–8, 78–79, 116–117

U

United Nations Convention on the Rights of the child (UNCRC)
 and African Charter, 62–63
 articles, 13–14, 60–61
 best interests, 13–14, 60
 as child-centred framework, 11, 132
 children's knowledge of, 66–68
 definition of child, 60
 discrimination, 60
 origins, 59–60
 participation, 13–14, 60
 principles, 11, 60
 protection and provision rights, 60
 progress in UK, 62
Utting Report, 64–65

V

values and ethics, 19–21
Valuing People, 21
views of children (see children's views)
voicing, 102–103

W

Wales, children's commissioner, 64
welfare checklist, 14
Winnicott, David, 77, 82
wishes and feelings, 14–15, 17, 98, 156
work in Global South, 45, 63
Working Together to Safeguard Children, 19, 135–137, 139–140, 145, 148

Y

young carers, 46, 147–148
youth offending, 35–36
youth parliament, 64